Mometrix
TEST PREPARATION

SST®

uman/Cultural eography

xam Secrets tudy Guide

Dear Future Exam Success Story

First of all, **THANK YOU** for purchasing Mometrix study materials!

Second, congratulations! You are one of the few determined test-takers who are committed to doing whatever it takes to excel on your exam. **You have come to the right place.** We developed these study materials with one goal in mind: to deliver you the information you need in a format that's concise and easy to use.

In addition to optimizing your guide for the content of the test, we've outlined our recommended steps for breaking down the preparation process into small, attainable goals so you can make sure you stay on track.

We've also analyzed the entire test-taking process, identifying the most common pitfalls and showing how you can overcome them and be ready for any curveball the test throws you.

Standardized testing is one of the biggest obstacles on your road to success, which only increases the importance of doing well in the high-pressure, high-stakes environment of test day. Your results on this test could have a significant impact on your future, and this guide provides the information and practical advice to help you achieve your full potential on test day.

Your success is our success

We would love to hear from you! If you would like to share the story of your exam success or if you have any questions or comments in regard to our products, please contact us at **800-673-8175** or **support@mometrix.com**.

Thanks again for your business and we wish you continued success!

Sincerely,
The Mometrix Test Preparation Team

Need more help? Check out our flashcards at:
http://MometrixFlashcards.com/DSST

Written and edited by the Mometrix Exam Secrets Test Prep Team
Printed in the United States of America

Table of Contents

Introduction

Thank you for purchasing this resource! You have made the choice to prepare yourself for a test that could have a huge impact on your future, and this guide is designed to help you be fully ready for test day. Obviously, it's important to have a solid understanding of the test material, but you also need to be prepared for the unique environment and stressors of the test, so that you can perform to the best of your abilities.

For this purpose, the first section that appears in this guide is the **Secret Keys**. We've devoted countless hours to meticulously researching what works and what doesn't, and we've boiled down our findings to the five most impactful steps you can take to improve your performance on the test. We start at the beginning with study planning and move through the preparation process, all the way to the testing strategies that will help you get the most out of what you know when you're finally sitting in front of the test.

We recommend that you start preparing for your test as far in advance as possible. However, if you've bought this guide as a last-minute study resource and only have a few days before your test, we recommend that you skip over the first two Secret Keys since they address a long-term study plan.

If you struggle with **test anxiety**, we strongly encourage you to check out our recommendations for how you can overcome it. Test anxiety is a formidable foe, but it can be beaten, and we want to make sure you have the tools you need to defeat it.

Secret Key #1 – Plan Big, Study Small

There's a lot riding on your performance. If you want to ace this test, you're going to need to keep your skills sharp and the material fresh in your mind. You need a plan that lets you review everything you need to know while still fitting in your schedule. We'll break this strategy down into three categories.

Information Organization

Start with the information you already have: the official test outline. From this, you can make a complete list of all the concepts you need to cover before the test. Organize these concepts into groups that can be studied together, and create a list of any related vocabulary you need to learn so you can brush up on any difficult terms. You'll want to keep this vocabulary list handy once you actually start studying since you may need to add to it along the way.

Time Management

Once you have your set of study concepts, decide how to spread them out over the time you have left before the test. Break your study plan into small, clear goals so you have a manageable task for each day and know exactly what you're doing. Then just focus on one small step at a time. When you manage your time this way, you don't need to spend hours at a time studying. Studying a small block of content for a short period each day helps you retain information better and avoid stressing over how much you have left to do. You can relax knowing that you have a plan to cover everything in time. In order for this strategy to be effective though, you have to start studying early and stick to your schedule. Avoid the exhaustion and futility that comes from last-minute cramming!

Study Environment

The environment you study in has a big impact on your learning. Studying in a coffee shop, while probably more enjoyable, is not likely to be as fruitful as studying in a quiet room. It's important to keep distractions to a minimum. You're only planning to study for a short block of time, so make the most of it. Don't pause to check your phone or get up to find a snack. It's also important to **avoid multitasking**. Research has consistently shown that multitasking will make your studying dramatically less effective. Your study area should also be comfortable and well-lit so you don't have the distraction of straining your eyes or sitting on an uncomfortable chair.

The time of day you study is also important. You want to be rested and alert. Don't wait until just before bedtime. Study when you'll be most likely to comprehend and remember. Even better, if you know what time of day your test will be, set that time aside for study. That way your brain will be used to working on that subject at that specific time and you'll have a better chance of recalling information.

Finally, it can be helpful to team up with others who are studying for the same test. Your actual studying should be done in as isolated an environment as possible, but the work of organizing the information and setting up the study plan can be divided up. In between study sessions, you can discuss with your teammates the concepts that you're all studying and quiz each other on the details. Just be sure that your teammates are as serious about the test as you are. If you find that your study time is being replaced with social time, you might need to find a new team.

Secret Key #2 – Make Your Studying Count

You're devoting a lot of time and effort to preparing for this test, so you want to be absolutely certain it will pay off. This means doing more than just reading the content and hoping you can remember it on test day. It's important to make every minute of study count. There are two main areas you can focus on to make your studying count.

Retention

It doesn't matter how much time you study if you can't remember the material. You need to make sure you are retaining the concepts. To check your retention of the information you're learning, try recalling it at later times with minimal prompting. Try carrying around flashcards and glance at one or two from time to time or ask a friend who's also studying for the test to quiz you.

To enhance your retention, look for ways to put the information into practice so that you can apply it rather than simply recalling it. If you're using the information in practical ways, it will be much easier to remember. Similarly, it helps to solidify a concept in your mind if you're not only reading it to yourself but also explaining it to someone else. Ask a friend to let you teach them about a concept you're a little shaky on (or speak aloud to an imaginary audience if necessary). As you try to summarize, define, give examples, and answer your friend's questions, you'll understand the concepts better and they will stay with you longer. Finally, step back for a big picture view and ask yourself how each piece of information fits with the whole subject. When you link the different concepts together and see them working together as a whole, it's easier to remember the individual components.

Finally, practice showing your work on any multi-step problems, even if you're just studying. Writing out each step you take to solve a problem will help solidify the process in your mind, and you'll be more likely to remember it during the test.

Modality

Modality simply refers to the means or method by which you study. Choosing a study modality that fits your own individual learning style is crucial. No two people learn best in exactly the same way, so it's important to know your strengths and use them to your advantage.

For example, if you learn best by visualization, focus on visualizing a concept in your mind and draw an image or a diagram. Try color-coding your notes, illustrating them, or creating symbols that will trigger your mind to recall a learned concept. If you learn best by hearing or discussing information, find a study partner who learns the same way or read aloud to yourself. Think about how to put the information in your own words. Imagine that you are giving a lecture on the topic and record yourself so you can listen to it later.

For any learning style, flashcards can be helpful. Organize the information so you can take advantage of spare moments to review. Underline key words or phrases. Use different colors for different categories. Mnemonic devices (such as creating a short list in which every item starts with the same letter) can also help with retention. Find what works best for you and use it to store the information in your mind most effectively and easily.

Secret Key #3 – Practice the Right Way

Your success on test day depends not only on how many hours you put into preparing, but also on whether you prepared the right way. It's good to check along the way to see if your studying is paying off. One of the most effective ways to do this is by taking practice tests to evaluate your progress. Practice tests are useful because they show exactly where you need to improve. Every time you take a practice test, pay special attention to these three groups of questions:

- The questions you got wrong
- The questions you had to guess on, even if you guessed right
- The questions you found difficult or slow to work through

This will show you exactly what your weak areas are, and where you need to devote more study time. Ask yourself why each of these questions gave you trouble. Was it because you didn't understand the material? Was it because you didn't remember the vocabulary? Do you need more repetitions on this type of question to build speed and confidence? Dig into those questions and figure out how you can strengthen your weak areas as you go back to review the material.

Additionally, many practice tests have a section explaining the answer choices. It can be tempting to read the explanation and think that you now have a good understanding of the concept. However, an explanation likely only covers part of the question's broader context. Even if the explanation makes perfect sense, **go back and investigate** every concept related to the question until you're positive you have a thorough understanding.

As you go along, keep in mind that the practice test is just that: practice. Memorizing these questions and answers will not be very helpful on the actual test because it is unlikely to have any of the same exact questions. If you only know the right answers to the sample questions, you won't be prepared for the real thing. **Study the concepts** until you understand them fully, and then you'll be able to answer any question that shows up on the test.

It's important to wait on the practice tests until you're ready. If you take a test on your first day of study, you may be overwhelmed by the amount of material covered and how much you need to learn. Work up to it gradually.

On test day, you'll need to be prepared for answering questions, managing your time, and using the test-taking strategies you've learned. It's a lot to balance, like a mental marathon that will have a big impact on your future. Like training for a marathon, you'll need to start slowly and work your way up. When test day arrives, you'll be ready.

Start with the strategies you've read in the first two Secret Keys—plan your course and study in the way that works best for you. If you have time, consider using multiple study resources to get different approaches to the same concepts. It can be helpful to see difficult concepts from more than one angle. Then find a good source for practice tests. Many times, the test website will suggest potential study resources or provide sample tests.

Practice Test Strategy

If you're able to find at least three practice tests, we recommend this strategy:

Untimed and Open-Book Practice

Take the first test with no time constraints and with your notes and study guide handy. Take your time and focus on applying the strategies you've learned.

Timed and Open-Book Practice

Take the second practice test open-book as well, but set a timer and practice pacing yourself to finish in time.

Timed and Closed-Book Practice

Take any other practice tests as if it were test day. Set a timer and put away your study materials. Sit at a table or desk in a quiet room, imagine yourself at the testing center, and answer questions as quickly and accurately as possible.

Keep repeating timed and closed-book tests on a regular basis until you run out of practice tests or it's time for the actual test. Your mind will be ready for the schedule and stress of test day, and you'll be able to focus on recalling the material you've learned.

Secret Key #4 – Pace Yourself

Once you're fully prepared for the material on the test, your biggest challenge on test day will be managing your time. Just knowing that the clock is ticking can make you panic even if you have plenty of time left. Work on pacing yourself so you can build confidence against the time constraints of the exam. Pacing is a difficult skill to master, especially in a high-pressure environment, so **practice is vital**.

Set time expectations for your pace based on how much time is available. For example, if a section has 60 questions and the time limit is 30 minutes, you know you have to average 30 seconds or less per question in order to answer them all. Although 30 seconds is the hard limit, set 25 seconds per question as your goal, so you reserve extra time to spend on harder questions. When you budget extra time for the harder questions, you no longer have any reason to stress when those questions take longer to answer.

Don't let this time expectation distract you from working through the test at a calm, steady pace, but keep it in mind so you don't spend too much time on any one question. Recognize that taking extra time on one question you don't understand may keep you from answering two that you do understand later in the test. If your time limit for a question is up and you're still not sure of the answer, mark it and move on, and come back to it later if the time and the test format allow. If the testing format doesn't allow you to return to earlier questions, just make an educated guess; then put it out of your mind and move on.

On the easier questions, be careful not to rush. It may seem wise to hurry through them so you have more time for the challenging ones, but it's not worth missing one if you know the concept and just didn't take the time to read the question fully. Work efficiently but make sure you understand the question and have looked at all of the answer choices, since more than one may seem right at first.

Even if you're paying attention to the time, you may find yourself a little behind at some point. You should speed up to get back on track, but do so wisely. Don't panic; just take a few seconds less on each question until you're caught up. Don't guess without thinking, but do look through the answer choices and eliminate any you know are wrong. If you can get down to two choices, it is often worthwhile to guess from those. Once you've chosen an answer, move on and don't dwell on any that you skipped or had to hurry through. If a question was taking too long, chances are it was one of the harder ones, so you weren't as likely to get it right anyway.

On the other hand, if you find yourself getting ahead of schedule, it may be beneficial to slow down a little. The more quickly you work, the more likely you are to make a careless mistake that will affect your score. You've budgeted time for each question, so don't be afraid to spend that time. Practice an efficient but careful pace to get the most out of the time you have.

Secret Key #5 – Have a Plan for Guessing

When you're taking the test, you may find yourself stuck on a question. Some of the answer choices seem better than others, but you don't see the one answer choice that is obviously correct. What do you do?

The scenario described above is very common, yet most test takers have not effectively prepared for it. Developing and practicing a plan for guessing may be one of the single most effective uses of your time as you get ready for the exam.

In developing your plan for guessing, there are three questions to address:

- When should you start the guessing process?
- How should you narrow down the choices?
- Which answer should you choose?

When to Start the Guessing Process

Unless your plan for guessing is to select C every time (which, despite its merits, is not what we recommend), you need to leave yourself enough time to apply your answer elimination strategies. Since you have a limited amount of time for each question, that means that if you're going to give yourself the best shot at guessing correctly, you have to decide quickly whether or not you will guess.

Of course, the best-case scenario is that you don't have to guess at all, so first, see if you can answer the question based on your knowledge of the subject and basic reasoning skills. Focus on the key words in the question and try to jog your memory of related topics. Give yourself a chance to bring the knowledge to mind, but once you realize that you don't have (or you can't access) the knowledge you need to answer the question, it's time to start the guessing process.

It's almost always better to start the guessing process too early than too late. It only takes a few seconds to remember something and answer the question from knowledge. Carefully eliminating wrong answer choices takes longer. Plus, going through the process of eliminating answer choices can actually help jog your memory.

Summary: Start the guessing process as soon as you decide that you can't answer the question based on your knowledge.

How to Narrow Down the Choices

The next chapter in this book (**Test-Taking Strategies**) includes a wide range of strategies for how to approach questions and how to look for answer choices to eliminate. You will definitely want to read those carefully, practice them, and figure out which ones work best for you. Here though, we're going to address a mindset rather than a particular strategy.

Your odds of guessing an answer correctly depend on how many options you are choosing from.

Number of options left	5	4	3	2	1
Odds of guessing correctly	20%	25%	33%	50%	100%

You can see from this chart just how valuable it is to be able to eliminate incorrect answers and make an educated guess, but there are two things that many test takers do that cause them to miss out on the benefits of guessing:

- Accidentally eliminating the correct answer
- Selecting an answer based on an impression

We'll look at the first one here, and the second one in the next section.

To avoid accidentally eliminating the correct answer, we recommend a thought exercise called **the $5 challenge**. In this challenge, you only eliminate an answer choice from contention if you are willing to bet $5 on it being wrong. Why $5? Five dollars is a small but not insignificant amount of money. It's an amount you could afford to lose but wouldn't want to throw away. And while losing $5 once might not hurt too much, doing it twenty times will set you back $100. In the same way, each small decision you make—eliminating a choice here, guessing on a question there—won't by itself impact your score very much, but when you put them all together, they can make a big difference. By holding each answer choice elimination decision to a higher standard, you can reduce the risk of accidentally eliminating the correct answer.

The $5 challenge can also be applied in a positive sense: If you are willing to bet $5 that an answer choice *is* correct, go ahead and mark it as correct.

Summary: Only eliminate an answer choice if you are willing to bet $5 that it is wrong.

Which Answer to Choose

You're taking the test. You've run into a hard question and decided you'll have to guess. You've eliminated all the answer choices you're willing to bet $5 on. Now you have to pick an answer. Why do we even need to talk about this? Why can't you just pick whichever one you feel like when the time comes?

The answer to these questions is that if you don't come into the test with a plan, you'll rely on your impression to select an answer choice, and if you do that, you risk falling into a trap. The test writers know that everyone who takes their test will be guessing on some of the questions, so they intentionally write wrong answer choices to seem plausible. You still have to pick an answer though, and if the wrong answer choices are designed to look right, how can you ever be sure that you're not falling for their trap? The best solution we've found to this dilemma is to take the decision out of your hands entirely. Here is the process we recommend:

Once you've eliminated any choices that you are confident (willing to bet $5) are wrong, select the first remaining choice as your answer.

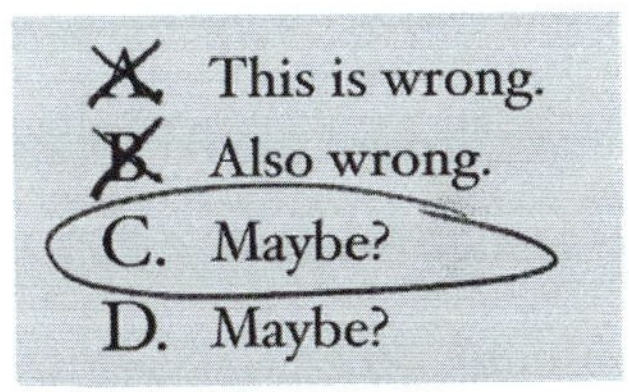

Whether you choose to select the first remaining choice, the second, or the last, the important thing is that you use some preselected standard. Using this approach guarantees that you will not be enticed into selecting an answer choice that looks right, because you are not basing your decision on how the answer choices look.

This is not meant to make you question your knowledge. Instead, it is to help you recognize the difference between your knowledge and your impressions. There's a huge difference between thinking an answer is right because of what you know, and thinking an answer is right because it looks or sounds like it should be right.

Summary: To ensure that your selection is appropriately random, make a predetermined selection from among all answer choices you have not eliminated.

Test-Taking Strategies

This section contains a list of test-taking strategies that you may find helpful as you work through the test. By taking what you know and applying logical thought, you can maximize your chances of answering any question correctly!

It is very important to realize that every question is different and every person is different: no single strategy will work on every question, and no single strategy will work for every person. That's why we've included all of them here, so you can try them out and determine which ones work best for different types of questions and which ones work best for you.

Question Strategies

☑ Read Carefully

Read the question and the answer choices carefully. Don't miss the question because you misread the terms. You have plenty of time to read each question thoroughly and make sure you understand what is being asked. Yet a happy medium must be attained, so don't waste too much time. You must read carefully and efficiently.

☑ Contextual Clues

Look for contextual clues. If the question includes a word you are not familiar with, look at the immediate context for some indication of what the word might mean. Contextual clues can often give you all the information you need to decipher the meaning of an unfamiliar word. Even if you can't determine the meaning, you may be able to narrow down the possibilities enough to make a solid guess at the answer to the question.

☑ Prefixes

If you're having trouble with a word in the question or answer choices, try dissecting it. Take advantage of every clue that the word might include. Prefixes can be a huge help. Usually, they allow you to determine a basic meaning. *Pre-* means before, *post-* means after, *pro-* is positive, *de-* is negative. From prefixes, you can get an idea of the general meaning of the word and try to put it into context.

☑ Hedge Words

Watch out for critical hedge words, such as *likely, may, can, often, almost, mostly, usually, generally, rarely,* and *sometimes.* Question writers insert these hedge phrases to cover every possibility. Often an answer choice will be wrong simply because it leaves no room for exception. Be on guard for answer choices that have definitive words such as *exactly* and *always.*

☑ Switchback Words

Stay alert for *switchbacks.* These are the words and phrases frequently used to alert you to shifts in thought. The most common switchback words are *but, although,* and *however.* Others include *nevertheless, on the other hand, even though, while, in spite of, despite,* and *regardless of.* Switchback words are important to catch because they can change the direction of the question or an answer choice.

⊘ Face Value

When in doubt, use common sense. Accept the situation in the problem at face value. Don't read too much into it. These problems will not require you to make wild assumptions. If you have to go beyond creativity and warp time or space in order to have an answer choice fit the question, then you should move on and consider the other answer choices. These are normal problems rooted in reality. The applicable relationship or explanation may not be readily apparent, but it is there for you to figure out. Use your common sense to interpret anything that isn't clear.

Answer Choice Strategies

⊘ Answer Selection

The most thorough way to pick an answer choice is to identify and eliminate wrong answers until only one is left, then confirm it is the correct answer. Sometimes an answer choice may immediately seem right, but be careful. The test writers will usually put more than one reasonable answer choice on each question, so take a second to read all of them and make sure that the other choices are not equally obvious. As long as you have time left, it is better to read every answer choice than to pick the first one that looks right without checking the others.

⊘ Answer Choice Families

An answer choice family consists of two (in rare cases, three) answer choices that are very similar in construction and cannot all be true at the same time. If you see two answer choices that are direct opposites or parallels, one of them is usually the correct answer. For instance, if one answer choice says that quantity x increases and another either says that quantity x decreases (opposite) or says that quantity y increases (parallel), then those answer choices would fall into the same family. An answer choice that doesn't match the construction of the answer choice family is more likely to be incorrect. Most questions will not have answer choice families, but when they do appear, you should be prepared to recognize them.

⊘ Eliminate Answers

Eliminate answer choices as soon as you realize they are wrong, but make sure you consider all possibilities. If you are eliminating answer choices and realize that the last one you are left with is also wrong, don't panic. Start over and consider each choice again. There may be something you missed the first time that you will realize on the second pass.

⊘ Avoid Fact Traps

Don't be distracted by an answer choice that is factually true but doesn't answer the question. You are looking for the choice that answers the question. Stay focused on what the question is asking for so you don't accidentally pick an answer that is true but incorrect. Always go back to the question and make sure the answer choice you've selected actually answers the question and is not merely a true statement.

⊘ Extreme Statements

In general, you should avoid answers that put forth extreme actions as standard practice or proclaim controversial ideas as established fact. An answer choice that states the "process should be used in certain situations, if…" is much more likely to be correct than one that states the "process should be discontinued completely." The first is a calm rational statement and doesn't even make a definitive, uncompromising stance, using a hedge word *if* to provide wiggle room, whereas the second choice is far more extreme.

✓ Benchmark

As you read through the answer choices and you come across one that seems to answer the question well, mentally select that answer choice. This is not your final answer, but it's the one that will help you evaluate the other answer choices. The one that you selected is your benchmark or standard for judging each of the other answer choices. Every other answer choice must be compared to your benchmark. That choice is correct until proven otherwise by another answer choice beating it. If you find a better answer, then that one becomes your new benchmark. Once you've decided that no other choice answers the question as well as your benchmark, you have your final answer.

✓ Predict the Answer

Before you even start looking at the answer choices, it is often best to try to predict the answer. When you come up with the answer on your own, it is easier to avoid distractions and traps because you will know exactly what to look for. The right answer choice is unlikely to be word-for-word what you came up with, but it should be a close match. Even if you are confident that you have the right answer, you should still take the time to read each option before moving on.

General Strategies

✓ Tough Questions

If you are stumped on a problem or it appears too hard or too difficult, don't waste time. Move on! Remember though, if you can quickly check for obviously incorrect answer choices, your chances of guessing correctly are greatly improved. Before you completely give up, at least try to knock out a couple of possible answers. Eliminate what you can and then guess at the remaining answer choices before moving on.

✓ Check Your Work

Since you will probably not know every term listed and the answer to every question, it is important that you get credit for the ones that you do know. Don't miss any questions through careless mistakes. If at all possible, try to take a second to look back over your answer selection and make sure you've selected the correct answer choice and haven't made a costly careless mistake (such as marking an answer choice that you didn't mean to mark). This quick double check should more than pay for itself in caught mistakes for the time it costs.

✓ Pace Yourself

It's easy to be overwhelmed when you're looking at a page full of questions; your mind is confused and full of random thoughts, and the clock is ticking down faster than you would like. Calm down and maintain the pace that you have set for yourself. Especially as you get down to the last few minutes of the test, don't let the small numbers on the clock make you panic. As long as you are on track by monitoring your pace, you are guaranteed to have time for each question.

✓ Don't Rush

It is very easy to make errors when you are in a hurry. Maintaining a fast pace in answering questions is pointless if it makes you miss questions that you would have gotten right otherwise. Test writers like to include distracting information and wrong answers that seem right. Taking a little extra time to avoid careless mistakes can make all the difference in your test score. Find a pace that allows you to be confident in the answers that you select.

⊘ KEEP MOVING

Panicking will not help you pass the test, so do your best to stay calm and keep moving. Taking deep breaths and going through the answer elimination steps you practiced can help to break through a stress barrier and keep your pace.

Final Notes

The combination of a solid foundation of content knowledge and the confidence that comes from practicing your plan for applying that knowledge is the key to maximizing your performance on test day. As your foundation of content knowledge is built up and strengthened, you'll find that the strategies included in this chapter become more and more effective in helping you quickly sift through the distractions and traps of the test to isolate the correct answer.

Now that you're preparing to move forward into the test content chapters of this book, be sure to keep your goal in mind. As you read, think about how you will be able to apply this information on the test. If you've already seen sample questions for the test and you have an idea of the question format and style, try to come up with questions of your own that you can answer based on what you're reading. This will give you valuable practice applying your knowledge in the same ways you can expect to on test day.

Good luck and good studying!

Mapping the Earth

Maps and Globes

A **map** is a diagrammatic representation of all or part of the three-dimensional world on a two-dimensional (flat) surface. A given map conveys data about certain characteristics of a region, such as human settlement patterns, climate variations, or geologic quality, which is difficult to observe otherwise. Maps can also display spatial relationships between locations and natural or human-made formations. The science of mapmaking is called cartography. General cartography entails the creation of maps for a general audience; thematic cartography involves the creation of maps with specific geographic themes. Because Earth is a spherical object, flat maps cannot accurately convey all shapes, distances, and directions. A **globe** is a representation of Earth drawn to scale, which means that shapes, distances, and directions are accurately denoted. Globes are round objects mounted upon rotational axes. They are most often used to display topographical (surface) features of the planet; however, they have also been employed as representations of the ocean floor or celestial objects other than Earth.

Review Video: Elements of a Map
Visit mometrix.com/academy and enter code: 437727

Latitude and Longitude

Latitude is an angular measurement expressing the angle (in degrees, minutes, and seconds) between any point and the equator (where latitude equals zero). Lines of **latitude** are the east-west lines circling the globe. All east-west lines are equidistant from each other. This means that they are all parallel to the equator and to each other. Every point on a given east-west line, therefore, is the same distance from the equator, the same distance from the North Pole, and the same distance from the South Pole. For this reason, east-west lines, or lines of latitude, are called parallels. **Longitude** is an angular measurement expressing the angle between any point and the prime meridian (where longitude equals zero). On the globe, lines of constant longitude ("meridians") extend from pole to pole, like the segment boundaries on a peeled orange. These north-south lines are of the same length, unlike the parallels of latitude, that are all parallel to the equator and whose perimeter decreases as the distance from the equator increases.

Circles of Latitude

Circle of latitude is simply another term for any of the parallels in the graticule. Certain of these parallels are distinguished due to their relationships with the Sun. The five main **circles of latitude** are the following:

- The **equator** (0 degrees latitude) is characterized by the fact that the Sun passes directly over this parallel twice each year, during the vernal and autumnal equinoxes.
- The **Tropic of Cancer** (23 degrees, 26 minutes, and 22 seconds North latitude) represents the northernmost area of the globe, at which the Sun may be seen directly overhead during midsummer.
- The **Tropic of Capricorn** (23 degrees, 26 minutes, and 22 seconds South latitude)represents the southernmost area of the globe, at which the Sun may be seen directly overhead during midwinter.

- The **Arctic Circle** (66 degrees, 33 minutes, and 38 seconds North latitude)represents the northernmost location that may experience days without sunrises.
- The **Antarctic Circle** (66 degrees, 33 minutes, and 38 seconds South latitude) represents the southernmost location that may experience days without sunrises.

MAP INTERPRETATION SCALES

In order to provide relatively accurate representations of Earth's surface, cartographers use specific scales in map creation. The term *map scale* refers to the size of the representation of an element on a map as compared to its actual size on Earth's surface. The smaller the area represented on a map, the larger the scale; a larger scale provides more detail about a region. Map scale is usually expressed proportionally, as a ratio of the distance on a map to that actual distance on Earth's surface. This ratio is often expressed as inches to miles. For example, 1:63,360 indicates that one inch on the map equals one mile on the surface. Knowledge of a map's scale can provide information about the intended use of that map. For instance, large-scale maps typically convey information about small, specific areas, such as planned housing developments. Smaller-scale maps, such as world land use maps, represent larger areas of the surface in less detail.

SCALES OF MEASUREMENT

NOMINAL AND ORDINAL SCALES

A nominal scale, one of four different types of numerical scales, or levels, used in scientific measurement, is a list of categories to which objects can be classified. At the **nominal** level, also referred to as the classificatory level, variable attributes are identified through the use of numbers or symbols. For example, a land use map may use green shading to identify woodland areas. Different symbols are seen as equivalent; they involve no hierarchical ordering of attributes.

An **ordinal scale**, one of four different types of numerical scales, or levels, used in scientific measurement, is one in which the numbers assigned to objects or events represent the rank order (1st, 2nd, 3rd, etc.) of the entities assessed. At the ordinal level, numbers and symbols serve both to identify objects and to express their relations to other objects. For instance, a cartographer might use dots of different sizes to convey the relative sizes of individual human settlements.

INTERVAL AND RATIO SCALES

An interval scale, one of four different types of numerical scales, or levels, used in scientific measurement, is one that represents quantity and has equal units, but for which zero represents simply an additional point of measurement. The Fahrenheit scale is a clear example of the interval scale of measurement. In **interval** measurement, the distance between objects is relevant. Variable categories are actual numbers (rather than convenient labels); the intervals between adjacent categories anywhere on the scale are equal. The ratio between any two points depends upon the unit of measurement.

A **ratio scale,** one of four different types of numerical scales, or levels, used in scientific measurement, is similar to the interval scale in that it also represents quantity and has equality of units. However, this scale also has an absolute zero (no numbers exist below zero). Very often, physical measures will represent ratio data (for example, height and weight). If one is measuring the length of a piece of wood in centimeters, there is quantity and equal units, and that measure cannot go below zero centimeters. A negative length is not possible.

SYMBOLS AND LEGENDS

Symbols are used to represent the features shown on maps. They are a vital part of any graphic representation of Earth's surface. **Symbols** may be used in cartography to signify features existing at certain points, such as buildings or dams. Generally, dots of different sizes are used to convey the relative sizes of cities and towns (larger dots for larger, more populous settlements). Linear symbols identify features like roadways and rivers on maps. For instance, major highways are typically represented by double lines. Area symbols, created through the use of patterns, color, or shading, represent land conditions, land use, or land cover. A map **legend** is a key that lists and describes the symbols used on the map.

Compass Rose, Hemisphere, and the International Date Line

A **compass rose** is a symbol on a map or navigational chart that conveys the orientation of the four cardinal directions (north, south, east, and west) and often the intermediate directions (northeast, northwest, southeast, and southwest) as well. Modern compass roses are comprised of a large circle displaying the true (geographic) cardinal directions and a smaller inner circle displaying the magnetic (geomagnetic) cardinal directions.

The term **hemisphere** literally means half sphere. The graticule divides Earth's surface into four hemispheres. The equator separates the Northern Hemisphere from the Southern Hemisphere. The prime meridian is most widely (though not universally) accepted as the dividing line between the Eastern and Western Hemispheres.

The **International Date Line** (IDL) is the meridian opposite the prime meridian; it follows the line at 180 degrees longitude. This imaginary line serves as a time zone boundary—the date to the east of the International Date Line is one day earlier than the date to the west.

Map Creation Process

In order to create a useful map, a cartographer must determine the map's target audience and make appropriate decisions about style, content, and scale. The foundation of mapmaking is observation. Cartographers make use of several different observation techniques, including aerial surveys, land surveys, and satellite imagery. **Aerial survey**, the practice of collecting information about Earth from an aircraft, supplies valuable information to mapmakers. This information is conveyed through detailed photos developed from large-format film; aerial survey is a form of remote sensing (the collection of information about an object or region from a distance). **Conventional land surveys** describe the locations and measurements of boundaries and landforms (artificial or natural). **Satellite imagery** consists of photographs of Earth taken from space. Once all relevant data has been collected, the mapmaker then plots the location of many points on a grid, which corresponds to that which will be used in the final product. Color-coded versions of the map are printed on plastic and layered to create a complete representation.

GIS

The GIS, or **Geographic Information System**, is basically a system of computers and software that collects, records, analyzes, and displays (potentially) limitless amounts of geographic information about Earth. This data is usually based on aerial surveys, existing maps and surveys, and remote sensing. Once the data is entered into the GIS, users request specific information about certain regions, and then the system analyzes the relevant data and responds. The GIS is an interactive mapping system rather than a static representation of certain aspects of the world. This technology has recently become available in certain automobiles.

Using Maps to Process Information from a Spatial Perspective

Maps are useful as **abstract representations** of physical and human aspects of Earth's surface that cannot be observed from any single point on that surface. Each human observes the world from one location at a time. Graphic depictions of large portions of the surface enable the identification of the patterns and **spatial organizations** of physical and human surface features and may be used to report information about a region's subsurface characteristics (natural or artificial). Maps illustrate how natural landmarks such as rivers and mountains are oriented in relation to one another, they show how oil resources are distributed across the surface, and they convey the arrangement of human settlements. The information provided by maps facilitates the formation of mental maps and an understanding of the layout of the world in many different respects. Depending on the intended use of a particular map, different physical and cultural characteristics of Earth's surface are reported and emphasized.

Patterns of Spatial Organization

Patterns of spatial organization are the points, lines, areas, and volumes that describe the spatial properties of objects in a geographic study. For example, a city courthouse may be considered a **point**. Points are connected by lines, usually roadways or other transportation routes. The roads around which a courthouse is situated serve to connect it to other points and areas (such as neighborhoods or parks), whereas a nearby lake can be thought of as **volume**. After identification of the components of a pattern, one may examine concepts such as location, density, direction, and arrangement to discover the relationship between elements of the pattern. It is then possible to analyze the revealed **pattern**, using concepts such as diffusion, linkage, accessibility, and movement. This analysis provides reasons for the patterns and functions of phenomena on Earth's surface.

Quantitative and Qualitative Methods of Geographic Analysis

Quantitative analysis involves the use of mathematics and statistics to explain and make predictions about geographic data. This method of study entails the synthesis of factual geographic information, such as population data. Maps, charts, and graphs are helpful in this type of analysis. The use of **quantitative** techniques allows geographers to objectively process large quantities of data and many variables. Often, geographers use quantitative inquiry to formulate hypotheses about spatial trends and patterns; they then test these theories through qualitative methods.

Qualitative analysis involves the first-hand examination of geographic phenomena in their original or natural place or site. In human geography, for example, one conducting qualitative research might interview inhabitants of an area for their perspective on a certain trend or issue. In the social sciences, qualitative analysis generally involves extensive fieldwork.

Mental Maps

A mental map is a person's internalized representation of all or part of Earth's surface in a spatial context. **Mental maps** exist on a variety of scales. They may depict regions as small as a person's kitchen or as large as the entire surface of our planet. Because they are formed through the fusion of objective knowledge (such as facts about mountain elevation, the locations of cities, and the areas of countries) and subjective knowledge (such as priorities placed on knowledge of certain areas and impressions of places), each person's mental map is unique. Mental maps are vital in understanding the world. People use their mental maps during travel or when selecting a new place to live. These individual representations of the world are constantly growing and changing with the acquisition of new information, which may be gained through personal experience or secondhand from any source. As details are added to a person's mental map, he or she becomes more knowledgeable about and comfortable in the surrounding world.

Factors Affecting Accuracy of a Person's Mental Map

Just as some people possess "natural" aptitudes for algebra or drawing, some people are more able than others to envision human activity spatially. Geographic scholars refer to this capacity as

spatial cognition. The quality of a person's **mental map** is also affected by the geographic education he or she has received. For example, when asked to sketch a map of the world, many people across the globe would orient their maps with the North Pole at the top, the South Pole at the bottom, and Europe in the center. This is so because of educational conventions held over from the colonial period in America. A person's exposure to and study of certain areas may also affect his or her mental map. Naturally, the more one knows about, for example, a state, the larger that state will seem on one's mental map. Logically, the quality and accuracy of one's mental map may be improved through geographic study.

Location and Place

The location of a point is its precise spatial situation on Earth's surface. **Locations** are often identified through the use of maps and globe. The absolute location of a point is its definitive location on Earth's surface in a specific coordinate system. At the global level, it is usually expressed using the graticule. For example, Baltimore, Maryland, is at 39.3 degrees N, 76.6 degrees W. Locally, absolute location may be expressed as a specific street address. For example, the Texas State Capitol building is located at 1100 Congress Avenue. The relative location of a point is its location in relation to something else, such as a well-known landmark. For example, in giving a friend directions, you might say that your house is "two blocks north of the market." On a global scale, one might say that Chile is west of Argentina. The term **place** refers to the human and physical qualities of a location. A place's combined array of natural and manmade characteristics distinguishes it from any other place.

Site and Situation

A location's site is defined as the physical characteristics of the place it occupies. These qualities include topography, elevation, climate, soil, and resources, as well as spatial organization. **Site** refers to a location's internal locational attributes. A place's **situation** is its relative location or regional position with regard to surrounding places; it refers to the location's external locational attributes. These include its location relative to outside areas of productive capacity, other political entities or settlements, transportation routes, and barriers to access and movement. Site and situation are especially important to geographers studying the evolution of urban areas. For example, the original site of the city of Paris was an island in a highly-trafficked area of the Seine River; eventually, the island became too densely populated, and the city grew along the river's banks. Paris's situation was conducive to growth, for the city was surrounded by fertile areas of agricultural production and many land and water routes for transportation and trade.

Map Projections

A map projection is a method of portraying all or part of the round Earth on a flat surface. Any representation of the spherical globe on a flat map entails a degree of **distortion**. However, maps are more practically useful than globes—maps are smaller and easier to transport. A given map can only accurately represent selected globular features at the expense of others. This is generally accomplished through the creation of a projection surface, which is then flattened. To create such a surface, cartographers conceptually "touch" one or more areas of the surface to the globe; the regions touched by the projection surface exhibit the least distortion in map form.

Classifying Map Projections Based on Orientations and Metric Property

The orientation of a map projection surface can be **normal** (such that the surface's axis of symmetry coincides with Earth's axis), **transverse** (at right angles to Earth's axis), or **oblique** (any angle in between).

Map projections can be classified by the metric property each preserves, as follows:

- **Conformal** map projections preserve the angles between points.
- **Equal-area** map projections preserve area.
- **Equidistant** map projections preserve distance from some standard point or line.
  Gnomonic map projections display great circles as straight lines; this type of projection is the oldest.
- **Retroazimuthal** map projections preserve direction in the transfer from a spherical to a flat surface.

Cartographic Manipulation

Cartographic manipulation is the process by which the actual sizes and shapes of areas or countries are **distorted** on maps. This manipulation may be accidental or intended. A certain degree of manipulation is inherent in the creation of map projections—Earth's surface cannot be accurately represented on a flat piece of paper. Also, unintended distortion may occur due to a lack of cartographic knowledge or poor map design; maps used by media often suffer from this type of distortion. **Intentional cartographic manipulation** may be employed to convey a certain side of an issue. For example, if a community group wishes to protest the erection of a nuclear power plant near their neighborhood, they may create a map that shortens the distance between the potential plant and surrounding homes. **Cartographic aggression** is the use of map distortion by a nation to lay claim to territory over which they have no legal authority. For instance, prior to Operation Desert Storm, Iraq's officially-sanctioned maps portrayed Kuwait as a province of Iraq.

Review Video: Map Projections
Visit mometrix.com/academy and enter code: 327303

Standard Line, Bearing, Loxodrome, Geodesics

A **standard line** is a line on a map that corresponds in scale and distance to a line on Earth; such lines are rarely straight. A map that displays a well-defined set of standard lines may be referred to as equidistant.

A **bearing**, or course, is a standard direction.

A **loxodrome** (or rhumb line) is a line of constant bearing that represents the easiest route between two points. Loxodromes are often distorted in map projections.

A **geodesic** line is the shortest line between two points on any mathematically defined surface. The shortest route between two points on a spherical surface such as a globe is part of a **geodesic** line (also called a great circle path, orthodrome, or geodetic). These lines run through the two given points and are centered on the sphere. The equator is an example of a great circle.

Cylindrical Map Projections

On a cylindrical map projection, lines of latitude are parallel to one another, equally spaced, and perpendicular to lines of longitude. Lines of travel are consistent on such a projection, while size and shape distortions increase with distance from the equator (the coordinate origin of cylindrical projections). Therefore, **cylindrical map projections** are rectangular; if such a map was rolled up, it would form a cylinder without end caps. The most famous cylindrical projection is the **Mercator projection**.

Conic Map Projections

A conic map projection is created as though the surface of a globe was wrapped around a cone with the point oriented at the **North Pole** (the coordinate origin of this type of map). On **conic map projections**, longitudinal lines (meridians) are straight and equidistant; they may or may not converge at a pole. Latitudinal lines (parallels) distorted into concentric circles. Conic projections may be equal-area (areal relationships are maintained) or conformal (local angles and scale are preserved). The **Lambert conformal projection** is a type of conic projection which is often used in the creation of aeronautical charts.

Variations of Cylindrical Map Projections

Cylindrical projections treat Earth as a cylinder on which parallels are horizontal lines and meridians appear as vertical lines. There are many variations of cylindrical projections, including the following:

- The **transverse Mercator** projection, in which the cylinder is tangent to Earth not along the Equator but along a chosen meridian, a treatment that has advantages in drawing maps that are long in the north–south direction.
- The **Robinson projection**, which is neither completely conformal nor completely equal-area; instead, it occupies a space between the two extremes.
- The **Winkel tripel projection**, which is a modified azimuthal projection that is neither conformal nor equal-area. the central meridian and equator are straight lines; other parallels and meridians are curved. The projection is obtained by averaging the coordinates of the equidistant cylindrical and Aitoff (not Hammer-Aitoff) projections. The poles map into straight lines 0.4 times the length of the equator.

Azimuthal Map Projections

Azimuthal (or planar) map projections use the **azimuth** as a reference point and often have **polar** orientations. The azimuth of a surface is the angle a person at a reference point (A) and looking at one point (B) must turn to face another point (C). On a sphere, lines AB and AC are geodesic lines. **Azimuthal projections** accurately represent direction (but not necessarily distance) from the azimuth to any other point. On any azimuthal projection (regardless of its orientation), all straight lines touching the central point are geodesics; distortion varies with distance from the center. **Azimuthal orthographic projections** portray Earth as viewed from space (at any distance); orthographic projections exhibit severe distortion around their edges. **Azimuthal stereographic projections** are conformal and preserve circles. They are most useful in the examination of one hemisphere. **Azimuthal gnomic projections** are similar to stereographic maps; however, every geodesic is mapped as a straight line, resulting in pronounced distance distortion and some direction distortion.

Pseudoconic Projections

Pseudoconic projections normally display parallels as circular arcs with common central points. Unlike "true" conic projections, **pseudoconic projections** do not represent meridians as straight lines. There are several types of pseudoconic projections, including the following:

- **Cordiform projections**, which are also called Stabius-Werner projections, produce heart-shaped maps.
- In the **normal aspect**, cordiform maps exhibit similarities. First, the prime meridian is a straight standard line; second, all other meridians are curved lines; and third, parallels are drawn in equal liner scale as circular arcs centered at a pole (usually the North Pole). All cordiform maps are equal-area and convey Earth's spherical quality.

- **Bonne projections** include parallels that are equally spaced concentric circular arcs and are all standard lines. Each Bonne map has one parallel as its center, making all such maps different. This type of map has virtually no areal distortion but does have slight shape distortion (except far from the center). Once very popular for large-scale topographic maps, the "Bonne" pseudoconic projection has generally fallen in disuse.

Tissot's Indicatrix

Tissot's indicatrix is a tool used in cartography to assess the **distortion** inherent in all flat maps. First, many small circles are drawn onto the original sphere. Then, the same circles are mapped onto the flat projection. After undergoing this process, a given circle may change in size or shape. A comparison of the circles on each surface thus reveals the distortion patterns of shape, size, and angle on the projected map. For example, the examination of indicatrices on the Mercator projection, in which the **Tissot circles** retain their shapes and parallels remain parallel to one another and perpendicular to the straight meridians, proves that this type of projection is conformal, preserving shape, angle, and scale. The sizes of the circles change when they are mapped from the sphere to the Mercator projection (on the Mercator map, the circles increase in size with distance from the equator), indicating that areas are distorted.

Projections Created to Counteract Distortion

While all map projections have some type of distortion or deformation, the following are some types that attempt to **reduce distortion**:

- An **oblique map** is one in which neither the equator nor the prime meridian is centered on or aligned with the map axes. Oblique maps generally preserve area and shape but distort properties relating to the graticule orientation of the original sphere. They are usually created to move a large area of interest from an area of high distortion to a region of lower distortion.
- An **interrupted map** is one that is "cut" at certain (arbitrary) lines. The resultant sections (called lobes or gores) then project separately from the map. Interrupted maps are used in attempts to overcome shape, area, or distance distortion on "normal" projections. Goode's interrupted projection is a notable equal-area map; it accurately portrays size and shape but distorts distance.
- A **polyhedral map** is created by projecting separate regions of the globe onto different faces of a polyhedron. The polyhedron may then be cut and disassembled into a flat map (a net or fold-out).

Classifying Maps

A map is classified primarily by its **purpose** and **content** (i.e., topographic map, weather map, road map). Maps may also be classified by **scale** or **derivation** (the source of the data represented). A **topographic or reference map** conveys general information about a geographic area, including ground elevation, natural formations (such as lakes and mountains), and structures erected by men (such as roadways and dams). **Thematic or illustrative maps** are those that represent a specific geographic theme, such as demography, geology, or land use. Such maps are created for a specific purpose. For example, land condition maps delineate surface areas that are especially susceptible to flooding, mass movements, or earthquakes; these maps are used by engineers for city planning or related activities. Land use maps, tourist maps, road maps, and mineral maps are other kinds of thematic maps. An **analytical map** represents a geographer's hypothesis about the relationship between two or more elements of Earth's surface; the ideas suggested in analytical maps are tested using mathematics.

Proportional Symbol Maps

In the creation of a proportional symbol map, a cartographer selects a particular symbol form to represent a particular **variable**. Proportionally sized symbols are oriented in specific areas to convey the relative quantity of the variable in those areas. This method of mapping may be used when data occur at points (or can be aggregated at points) and when data can be measured as absolute values. The symbol most commonly used in the creation of **proportional symbol maps** is the **circle**, because circles are easy to construct to scale. Circles are also visually stable, aiding map readers in their interpretations. Variables such as population density are often represented on this type of map. A map reader forms an image of the spatial distribution of, for example, population density through observation of the pattern created by the differently sized symbols.

Choropleth Maps

In the creation of a choropleth map, a cartographer selects a unique color, shading technique, or pattern to identify a certain variable characteristic. This symbol is then applied to the appropriate **chorogram**. A chorogram is a discrete statistical area, such as a voting district, or administrative district, such as a state or township. This method of mapping may be used when data occur in or may be attributed to a distinct spatial unit. Also, the data to be conveyed should be derived rather than "raw." For instance, a **choropleth map** may display population density but not population distribution. In other words, ratio-level data should be used. Cartographers typically use **idiographic data classification**, which involves the delimitation of intervals between variable classes based on the array of data (i.e., natural breaks, equal intervals, etc.). A map reader analyzes the use of color or shading to determine the symbol class to which a particular chorogram belongs.

Cartograms

A cartogram is a map in which some **thematic mapping variable**, such as travel time, is substituted for land area. The geometry or space of the map is distorted in order to convey the information of this alternate variable. There are two main types of cartograms: area and distance cartograms. An **area cartogram**, which is also referred to as a value-by-area map, is similar to a proportional symbol map, in that the cartographer adjusts the sizes of artificial collection units (chorograms) to convey the relative data value for each; chorograms are thus proportionally sized. This type of map is useful when there is no data generalization (as occurs in choropleth maps). Also, the data (which may be absolute or derived, and of the interval or ratio measurement level) must be aggregated in chorograms. Area cartograms are most effective when data values correlate negatively with the areas or sizes of the chorograms (when large chorograms have small values and small chorograms have large values). This method of visual representation aids in the display of spatial idiosyncrasies that could be obscured in conventional maps (due to wide variations in the sizes of the collection units). A **distance cartogram**, which may also be called a central-point cartogram, is typically used to show relative travel times and directions from vertices in a network.

Geologic Map

A geologic map describes the rocks and soils at the surface, provides information about what rocks lie at depth, describes the ages of rocks and soils, and shows where features such as earthquake faults and landslides lie. **Geologic maps** are made by studying the rocks and materials exposed at the surface and depicting information about those rocks on a map. Unlike a topography map, which represents landforms on Earth's surface, a **thematic geologic map** represents rock or mineral ore formations that exist underneath the surface. On a geologic map, common rock types (such as limestone, shale, and granite) are represented by graphic patterns or colors. Lines are used to delineate contact planes (planes separating two rock formations). Cartographers use certain symbols to indicate the presence of horizontal beds, vertical beds, axes in folded rocks, etc. These maps are extremely useful in the location and recovery of mineral resources and fossil fuels. These formations are identified through the analysis of field research data and aerial photography.

Review Video: Geographical Features
Visit mometrix.com/academy and enter code: 773539

Relief

The term *relief* refers to the variations in elevation across a portion of Earth's surface. The most obvious way to depict **relief** is to imitate it at scale, as in molded or sculpted solid terrain models and molded-plastic raised-relief maps. On flat paper maps, terrain can be depicted in a variety of ways, including **contour lines** showing equal elevation, which is the most common way of numerically showing elevation; **hypsometric tints**, which are a variant on contour lines that depict ranges of elevation as bands of color, usually in a graduated scheme; **shaded relief**, or hill-shading, which simulates the cast shadow thrown upon a raised relief map; and physiographic illustration, which uses generalized texture to imitate landform shapes over a large area.

Geographic Instability

The term *geographic instability* refers to the transitory nature of **boundaries and place names** in certain areas of the globe. Periods of geographic change often follow events such as the colonization of a new area or the fall of an empire. For example, upon the disintegration of the former Soviet Union, cartographers faced a deluge of changes. New boundaries were created, forming new countries and provinces, and certain cities were renamed. Similarly, when China switched from its old spelling system to the new Pinyin system, all maps displaying the former spellings of place names became obsolete. Because we do not live on a static Earth, boundaries and place names will continue to change. This simply means that cartographers must continue to update existing maps to keep pace with **geographic instability**.

Nautical and Aviation Charts

A nautical chart, which may also be called a **hydrographic chart**, is a thematic map intended for use by sea-faring sailors in navigation. This type of map includes a latitude-longitude grid that aids marine navigators in the identification of potential hazards to a ship, such as massive coral reefs. In addition, a **nautical chart** conveys the locations of lighthouses and other artificial landforms, the relief and constituent materials of the seafloor, and the shapes of topographic features such as shorelines or islets.

An **aviation chart** (also called an aeronautical chart) is another kind of thematic map. It resembles a nautical chart but for its emphasis on airways, land topography, the heights of potential obstructions in an aircraft's path, and radio beacons.

Features of Graphs and Charts

A graph is a visual representation that exhibits a relationship, often functional, between two sets of numbers as a set of points having coordinates determined by the relationship. The term **chart** may be used as a synonym for graph, or it may refer to a specialized kind of map, such as a nautical chart. There are many different methods of displaying data in graphs and charts; most include the plotting of data in **two dimensions**. Many of these diagrams include several basic features. First of all, a title indicates the purpose and content of a graph or chart. Most diagrams have a **horizontal axis** (the x-axis) and a **vertical axis** (the y-axis); the intersection of these axes, where the value of each variable equals zero, is referred to as the **origin**. These axes are labeled to identify the variable being plotted and/or the range of values of that variable. Generally, independent variables (such as time) are represented on the x-axis, and dependent variables (such as temperature) are represented on the y-axis.

PIE CHARTS AND 100 PERCENT BAR CHARTS

A pie chart, also referred to as a circle graph, is a method of data representation that does not use the axes common in other kinds of graphs, and therefore does not involve the plotting of data in two dimensions. **Pie charts** are based on percentages of a total quantity; a full circle represents one hundred percent. This type of chart is useful when this quantity is known and the chart's creator wishes to convey the relative sizes of the "pieces" which add up to that total. For example, if a geographer knows the total number of people worldwide who identify themselves as having religious beliefs, he or she might create a pie chart to show what percentage of that total describes themselves as Muslims, Christians, Jews, etc. Percentages are converted to numbers of degrees and represented as sections of the circle. A **100 percent bar chart** uses represents percentages as proportional sections of a bar.

LINE GRAPHS

A line graph is a type of chart that is useful in representing relationships between sets of data. **Line graphs** are often used to show changes in a variable over time. For instance, in a graph of sale trends for a major company, a time scale (such as years or months) is laid out along the x-axis and an amount scale is oriented along the y-axis. Then, the respective sales figures corresponding to each time unit are plotted on the graph; these data points are connected with a line whose curvature conveys general tendencies about changes in sales over time. This feature of line graphs enables viewers to make educated predictions about future trends as well. In economics, a line graph may be used to show the relationship between quantity (on the x-axis) and price (on the y-axis). By connecting plotted points with lines, economists can identify changes in price as they relate to changes in the available quantities of goods.

BAR GRAPHS

A bar graph is a type of chart that is useful in **comparing quantities**. This type of chart is similar to a line graph in that each involves the placement of variables along two axes. Instead of displaying values as points on the grid, however, a **bar chart** uses rectangular bars extending from an axis and leveling off at the appropriate points. In other words, the length of a bar representing a particular variable conveys the value of that variable. Bar graphs may be vertical (in which independent variables are oriented along the x-axis and the rectangles extend vertically) or horizontal (in which independent variables are laid out along the y-axis and the rectangles extend horizontally). This type of graph aids in the observation of differences among similar things. For example, a bar chart may display the variations in population among several major cities. In a pictograph, small icons or figures relating are used in lieu of rectangles to represent values. This type of graph is eye-catching and instantly conveys the purpose of the graph.

SCATTER PLOTS

A scatter plot is a type of display that shows the values for two variables for a set of data. Like bar and line graphs, **scatter plots** use x- and y-axes to plot data points. However, their specific purpose is to display how one variable affects another. This relationship is referred to as **correlation**. Correlation between variables is identified through the examination of a large quantity of data, represented on the graph as points. The closer the points come to forming a straight line, the stronger the relationship (and the higher the correlation) between the variables. If the line formed by the points extends from a high point on the y-axis to a high value on the x-axis, the correlation is negative. Conversely, if the line extends from the origin to high x- and y-values, the correlation between the two variables is positive. One might use a scatter plot to examine the relationship between education and income by aligning education level along the x-axis of a graph and yearly income along the y-axis, and then plotting data points for a group of individuals.

Chapter Quiz

Ready to see how well you retained what you just read? Scan the QR code to go directly to the chapter quiz interface for this study guide. If you're using a computer, simply visit the online resources page at **mometrix.com/resources719/dssthumculgeog** and click the Chapter Quizzes link.

Culture and Environment

Environment and Society

Environmental Effects of Burning Fossil Fuels

Burning fossil fuels (naturally-occurring hydrocarbon compounds that may be used by humans for fuel), especially coal, releases harmful elements into the atmosphere. The chemical reaction of coal combustion produces, for example, large amounts of carbon dioxide. When these gases reach the atmosphere, they inhibit the release of infrared photons into space, as carbon dioxide molecules absorb the photons and may reflect them inward, back toward Earth. This phenomenon is called the **greenhouse effect**. While the greenhouse effect is desirable, to a certain degree, to maintain a comfortable climate on the planet, increased levels of carbon dioxide can change the balance of energy in the atmosphere. This is termed **global warming**. Coal burning can also cause acid rain. Sulfur dioxide, a byproduct of burning coal, rises to the atmosphere and combines with water molecules to form sulfuric acid. This **acid rain** falls back to Earth, where it can cause harm to plants, animals, water bodies, and exposed structures. Burning gasoline can also contribute to the formation of acid rain.

Ozone Depletion

Ozone depletion occurs when the balance between creation and destruction of ozone particles in the stratosphere is tipped toward destruction. **Chlorofluorocarbons** (or CFCs) are chemicals created by humans for use in, for example, refrigeration, aerosol cans, and cleaners. When these chemicals interact with sunlight in the atmosphere, chlorine atoms are released; these free atoms participate in processes that destroy ozone particles. **Ozone holes** (areas of severe ozone depletion) have been identified over Antarctica and various other areas, where spring sunlight contributes to the chlorine-ozone reactions that destroy the latter molecule. There are numerous reports that show that these ozone holes are able to repair themselves given the correct weather and atmospheric conditions.

Environmental Regulations and the Factor of Uncertainty

Environmental regulation frequently encounters the unknown. In many cases, it is not scientifically proven whether environmental damage exists or will occur, and if so, whether certain human activities have caused or will cause it. For example, in the past, it took much time to clarify whether sulfur dioxide emissions caused acid rain damage to forests. Currently, regarding global warming induced by greenhouse gas emissions, it is not clear whether counter-effects such as increased carbon dioxide emissions, which cause increased growth of vegetation, which in turn produces cooling effects, can reverse that global warming or not. In today's world, many nations adhere to the **precaution principle**. This principle demands that even in situations with no certainty of damage but with a risk of damage, preventative safeguards are used. It is easier thus to change or reverse decisions to allow risky endeavors if new information reveals hitherto unknown dangers.

Interactions Between Scientists, the Public, and Politics

The environmental issues of climate change and the loss of biodiversity are of great concern among both scientists and the public. Scientists have only recently begun to realize the weight of their potential influence on policymaking. They are thus learning how to communicate their research findings and theories to make impressions on the public. A side effect of this interaction is that scientists are becoming increasingly used for political purposes. Previously, a media network would use a scientist to further clarify or explain a technical or scientific phenomenon, however it is often the case now that a scientist is intentionally interviewed when they reject the seemingly more mainstream interpretation of data. Whether this is done specifically by the media to generate controversy, and thus, publicity, or is instead the concentrated effort of parties or businesses that stand to gain or suffer monetarily by bolstering or diminishing such data interpretations remains to be determined. Perhaps the only certain outcome of such controversies is that this type of opposition delays action in terms of policymaking.

Human-Induced Global Climate Change and Further Climate Change

Today, the climate change debate mostly focuses on whether it is specifically **human activities** that have wrought **changes in our world climate**; in other words, is mankind directly responsible for causing the change in global temperature and thus directly responsible for implementing choices to counteract the impact of its actions. For example, the United Nations Intergovernmental Panel on Climate Change, a multinational group of the world's leading environmental scientists, has documented increases in the average tidal levels, increasing temperatures at ground level, concentrations of greenhouse gases in the atmosphere, glaciers whose ice is melting, explorations of the Arctic ice core, and so forth. Based on this data, this panel has made predictions of variations in patterns of weather and temperatures in the near future. They believe these variations to be directly caused by emissions from human use of fossil fuels. These foremost scientists state that the climate likely will change dramatically within 50-100 years, almost completely due to human actions and their impact on the natural environment.

Example of Human Activity Destroying a Place where a Society of People Lives

A common argument presented by climate change advocates is melting **polar ice**, resulting in "sea-rise." This means that the sea level is becoming higher as the melted ice adds to the total volume of water in the oceans. A concrete example of the effects of sea-rise is that some **atolls** and/or islands in the tropical Pacific which are low-lying are threatened by the rising sea level. The encroaching salt water is destroying the people's crops and killing the trees that they use to build their homes. The tribal society of people living on these atolls will have to relocate to another island that has higher ground before their own land actually sinks beneath the ocean. While some people deny the reality or import of climate change, such concrete evidence—that an entire population's native habitat can simply vanish in short order—confirms that the environment is, at least, changing in ways previously unseen, and it is important for mankind to determine how it will respond to these changes as they come.

Recent Environmental Disasters

In 2010, the BP Oil company's Deepwater Horizon oil rig exploded, causing a massive **oil spill** that spread for miles and had far-reaching effects of environmental devastation that evidence suggests are still causing ramifications to this day. Fish, seals, and all forms of marine life were destroyed, fishermen's livelihoods were ruined, people lost their homes, and there were many more grave consequences. Despite public outcry, oil companies continue to pressure the government to allow unsafe drilling. On the one-year anniversary of the devastating explosion, another incident occurred. A gas-well used for **fracking**—the popular name for hydraulic fracturing to release natural gas underground—in Pennsylvania blew out, spilling toxic chemicals. (Fracking fluid contains 596 such chemicals.) These contaminated a local stream and farmland and required home evacuations. While the amount of oil spills and fracking related incidents does seem to be on a downward trend in recent years, there are still numerous occurrences each year that have devastating effects.

Managing Natural Resources for Our Benefit

Human enterprises, such as diverting water to provide farming irrigation and domestic water supplies, can be important for human well-being yet environmentally undesirable. For example, an irrigation company proposed to rebuild its dam inside a protected wilderness to meet federal safety standards. Environmental groups argued that the company should find alternatives using "traditional skills" including non-motorized, non-mechanized methods instead of the helicopters and heavy machinery it proposed to use, which would significantly damage the character of the wilderness. The groups pointed out that the dam was built without machines, and updated safety standards would not prohibit non-mechanized methods. They called for an **Environmental Assessment** and an **Environmental Impact Statement**, including minimum safety requirements, addressing the law regarding water storage capacity, clarifying the dam's hazard rating, etc. The environmental organizations have also offered help to the owner company in finding and applying alternatives.

Conflicting Efforts to Preserve Environmental Systems

One way to supply renewable energy is to use **wind power** rather than only fossil fuels. However, when large, powerful wind turbines are proposed to be built too close to wilderness, their noise, vibrations, and appearance directly interfere with objectives for preserving and maintaining natural areas, threatening public and wildlife health. For example, in 2012, a large-scale wind turbine project proposed in a national forest was protested by an environmental group because it would affect a protected wilderness area and set a negative precedent. The group supported its protest by showing that information given by the US Forest Service was outdated and not based on complete, objective information, because the preparer was not independent as regulations mandate and had a conflict of interest. They also found the project would not meet Forest Service regulations' goals and would not comply with federal and state regulations for water quality standards and dam safety or the national forest's land management plan.

Enacting Legislation to Protect and Restore Environmental and Public Health

While the US federal government has passed laws **regulating** our treatment of the environment and setting standards, our individual states can also do much to regulate activities affecting the environment. This not only helps the natural environment and public health within each state, but also influences the whole country to follow suit. For example, the state of California recently passed a new law that will require utility companies to derive 100% of their energy from clean and renewable sources, like sun and wind, by the year 2045. This requirement will reduce harmful emissions, slow the progression of climate change, make the air cleaner, and create new jobs to help workers and the economy. The law constitutes one of the most aggressive renewable energy requirements in the country. It establishes a precedent for other states and the federal government to follow.

Environmentalist Groups' Opposition of Coal Technology for Energy

Environmental groups are opposed to the use of **coal technology** because it releases many toxins into our air and water, including mercury. Environmental protection agencies find that thousands of babies are born annually with elevated mercury levels, which have been correlated with increased incidences of developmental disabilities in children. Many energy utility companies are currently interested in updating existing coal plants and/or building new ones. However, environmental organizations find through research that the millions of dollars this would cost are not a worthwhile expenditure, due to the long-term financial commitment and costs to our environment, our public health, and our economy caused by this outdated technology. Their analyses find that by increasing **energy efficiency** and using more **renewable sources** such as solar and wind energy, nearly all coal plants could be replaced within twenty years. This would save lives, slow down climate change, and decrease consumers' energy costs.

US Power Plant Emissions

Power plants in America source half of their energy from **coal**. The emissions from coal-fired power plants include arsenic, lead, mercury, and many other poisonous air pollutants. Death, respiratory illnesses like asthma, and developmental disabilities in children are all attributed to this **air pollution**. Historically, there have not been any legal regulations in the US to control power plants' emissions. However, the **EPA** has developed such regulation with laws such as the Disposal of Coal Combustion Residuals (CCR) that is continually updated and amended. The EPA holds public hearings in key cities, allowing people to voice their concerns. Environmental organizations enlist members' support by informing them of and encouraging their attendance at these hearings, where they can testify and submit comments supporting the EPA's proposal.

Using Factual Data to Fight Industrial Destruction of the Environment

Environmental organizations can not only cite predicted environmental damage by an industrial project, but moreover can conduct **research** demonstrating whether such activity is even justified. For example, when environmental authorities approved plans for a giant hydroelectric facility on two of the wildest rivers in Chile, an environmental organization reported this project would flood thousands of acres of wilderness, endangering many complex ecosystems, and that its power line would cut through national parks, protected areas, and more than a thousand private communities. They moreover conducted a technical study proving that projects already approved would supply more than enough energy for future needs. The majority of the public opposed and has protested voting for such construction. By exposing shortcomings in the project's environmental review, activists delayed the vote for years before it was finally rejected in 2014.

Effect of Federal Legislation and Mining Activities on Drinking Water Quality

The growing **mining industry** in America had caused so much water pollution in the past that by the 1970s, many lakes and rivers were closed to swimming, fishing, and drinking. In response, Congress passed the **Clean Water Act** in 1972 by an overwhelming majority, prohibiting mining and other industries from dumping waste directly into bodies of water. In 2002, lawmakers invented a different definition of "fill material," allowing coal miners to dump waste from blowing up mountaintops into streams. In 2004, they enlarged this loophole, later referred to as the Halliburton loophole, to include dumping toxic wastewater (from chemically extracting metals from ores) into streams, lakes, and wetlands. Recent high prices for gold and other metals have stimulated a mining boom, exacerbating the problem. Environmental groups are campaigning for stronger mining regulations to protect the world's fresh water. Legislation has been and continues to be proposed and ratified to attempt to further regulate toxic waste disposal, with the FRAC Act being one of the most recent.

Green Revolution

The Green Revolution began in 1945 with the development of **agricultural technologies** that aimed to improve the agricultural output of Mexico; these techniques were eventually diffused to regions all over the globe. The technologies that spawned the **Green Revolution** involved the breeding of new plant varieties and the application of modern farming practices, which included the heavy use of pesticides and fertilizers, irrigation methods, and machines to increase crop output. The techniques introduced during the Green Revolution did produce higher yields and decrease dependence on human labor in agriculture. However, the disadvantages of these techniques include decreased biodiversity (as fewer varieties of crops are produced), decreased crop quality (including health value), and the detrimental health effects of agricultural chemicals on plant, animal, and human life.

Influence of Topography on Climate

The **physical features** of a landmass have a significant influence on the climate. For instance, there are distinct climate patterns on the alternate sides of a mountain range. The windward side of a mountain, which in the United States is typically the western side, will have more precipitation. The leeward side, on the other hand, is arid and less cloudy. The dry valleys that extend out from the eastern side of mountain ranges in the United States are often said to have a rain shadow. The formation of clouds is affected by mountains as well. As air is forced up by mountains, it cools and forms clouds. This is why the tops of mountain ranges are frequently misty or cloudy. Bodies of water also affect climate. Water heats and cools more slowly than land, so places where air arrives from over a body of water will also have less-extreme variations in temperature.

Effect of Human Behavior on the Climate

Leaving aside the debate over whether climate change is a direct result of fossil-fuel combustion, there are numerous other ways in which **human behavior influences the climate**. Urban areas are warmer and drier than nearby areas, because the asphalt absorbs heat. Also, sewer and storm water drainage systems remove standing water from the terrain, so heat that otherwise would be evaporating water instead is absorbed by the land. Industrial facilities and large numbers of automobiles also affect the climate. Smokestacks and exhaust pipes emit tiny particulates and water vapor, which encourage the development of clouds downwind. This phenomenon is assisted by the natural heat of cities. It is typical for the area immediately downwind from a large city to have more cloud coverage and precipitation than would otherwise be expected.

Natural Resources

A **resource** is something valued by humans for its role in survival. A **natural resource** is a naturally occurring material (such as water, soil, minerals, or animals) that humans use to maintain their existences. Such resources are unevenly distributed across the globe; their monetary values vary with scarcity, technology, and specific human needs. For example, petroleum became much more valuable after the invention of automobiles, which require the substance to operate. Some natural resources are renewable, meaning that they are constantly being replenished in nature. Energy from the Sun, water, and soil are all renewable resources. **Nonrenewable resources** are those of which Earth has a limited supply. Fossil fuels such as coal and oil take millions of years to form in Earth's crust; therefore, once humans exhaust the current supply of these resources, no more will be naturally available in our lifetimes. Most natural resources (renewable or nonrenewable) are used to provide energy to fuel modern industry.

Distribution of Resources

Resources are not evenly distributed across the globe. Fossil fuels, for example, form over millions of years (under specific natural conditions) from the remains of fossilized plants and animals. Even renewable resources such as water are not equally distributed. Certain global regions experience droughts while others withstand deluges of rain. The **uneven distribution of natural resources** affects the locations and sizes of human settlements, the quality of life in those settlements, and the economic activities in which certain people can participate. A lack of resources in an area may lead to mass migration to an area with a larger supply or to the formation of trade networks with countries possessing higher quantities of a particular resource.

Earth's Physical Systems and Human Involvement in Those Systems

Each of the people who live on Earth has several basic needs, including food, water, and shelter. The planet's **physical systems** provide many natural resources (those that may be used by humans to meet a need), such as timber for building shelter, rainwater to drink, and plants and animals that may be consumed by humans. However, **human involvement** in these systems may be detrimental to their function. For example, high levels of human activity (including logging and the clearing of land for agricultural purposes, such as crop cultivation and animal grazing) are threatening rainforest ecosystems in low-latitude areas. When humans eliminate portions of a rainforest for their own purposes, the delicate balance between native plants and animals is damaged, sometimes irreparably. With increasing awareness of the threat to Earth's natural resources, some nations have created restrictions on their acceptable use. If the harvesting of natural resources for human use is practiced in small amounts with minimal use of dangerous chemicals, a balance may be achieved between Earth's physical and human systems.

Neolithic Revolution

The Neolithic Revolution, one of two eras of change that altered human life and its relationship with the environment, began approximately 10,000 years ago. Prior to this time, humans subsisted by hunting animals and gathering native plants for food. With the onset of the **Neolithic Revolution** (which probably began in the Middle East), people began to domesticate plants and animals. They started practicing agriculture (cultivating and storing certain plants for food) and herding (taming and raising animals specifically for human use). These developments allowed groups of people to settle in one area, rather than roaming the land in search of their basic needs. They irrigated lands and built stable, permanent shelters of wood. With stable sources of food, shelter, and clothing, populations began to expand. People had more time to practice other activities, which often bred technological advancements. Individual members of societies began to specialize in, for example, pottery creation or leatherwork. Increasing specialization eventually produced vast civilizations, which influenced the world as humans know it today.

Altering Average Surface Temperatures Through Human Activity

Humans change Earth's surface for reasons other than those which are agriculturally motivated. For example, the building of cities involves the elimination of native vegetation as well as the pavement of large sections of land (which effectively covers natural, usually moist soils). This, in turn, prevents naturally occurring plants from practicing transpiration. It also concentrates solar heat at the surface, since there are no leafy trees to intercept and diffuse the energy. Materials such as concrete and stone repel rainwater and absorb and trap heat. Thus, the net effect of city building is the production of an **urban heat island**. Air temperatures in a city are often several degrees higher than the temperatures of surrounding suburban or rural areas. The absence of heat-mediating plants and soils, taken with the high instance of heat-absorbing materials, creates an area in which air temperatures do not drop immediately with the sunset; heat collected during the day remains in the region after nightfall.

Water, Fisheries, and Forests

The United States contains abundant **water resources**. There are massive freshwater lakes, rivers and streams, and underground water tables to supply all the water needed for industry, agriculture, and consumption. Americans use about 450 billion gallons of water every day. The majority of this water is used for irrigation or steam power plants. There are also plentiful supplies of fish in the nation's waterways, though these supplies are being threatened by overfishing. The species most commonly drawn from the Pacific are cod, halibut, tuna, and salmon. The Atlantic Ocean supplies abundant cod, flounder, herring, lobsters, and other shellfish. The Gulf of Mexico is known for its abundant supplies of oysters and shrimp.

Mining

The United States ranks only behind Saudi Arabia and Russia in the production of **petroleum**, and only behind China in the extraction of **coal**. The largest deposits of petroleum are in Alaska, California, Louisiana, New Mexico, Oklahoma, and Texas. The most productive coal mines are in the Appalachian Mountains, particularly in Pennsylvania, Kentucky, and West Virginia. Some of the other products that are lucratively mined in the United States are copper, gold, cement, clay, granite, iron ore, zinc, salt, and sand. There are mining operations in virtually every state, though mountainous regions remain the most heavily mined.

Agriculture

Massive improvements in **agricultural technology** have reduced the energy and manpower required for American agriculture, even while increasing the overall yields. American farms grow enough to feed every American with some left over for the rest of the world. Indeed, about a quarter of American farm income comes from exports. The most lucrative product of American farms is beef cattle. These profitable animals are primarily raised on massive ranches in the West. Dairy cattle operations are more likely to be found in the northern states, primarily in a strip extending from New York to Minnesota. The other major crops and livestock in the United States are milk, chickens, eggs, corn, soybeans, wheat, hogs, and cotton.

Mineral Resources and Soil

The rise of the United States to global prominence was due in large part to the abundance of natural resources. With regard to **minerals**, the United States has significant deposits of coal, iron ore, natural gas, and petroleum. However, the enormous energy needs of the nation require it to import still more petroleum and iron. There are also large mining operations based on the extraction of gold, lead, sulfur, zinc, and silver. The **soil** of the United States is for the most part exceptionally fertile, particularly in the Midwest and South. There is a nutrient-rich, thin soil called **loess** that makes farming possible in Washington State. The Mississippi River brings a rich soil known as **alluvium** to the region around the Gulf of Mexico.

Modes of Transportation in the United States

The United States has one of the highest per-capita rates of **automobile ownership** in the world, as well as a vast network of roads and highways to accommodate all those drivers. For every four Americans, there are three automobiles. There are also approximately 50,000 miles of federal interstate highway, many of them built during the Eisenhower administration. A little more than a quarter of all commercial freight moves in trucks. The leading freight carrier, however, remains the **rail system**. Though only about 1% of passenger traffic takes place on the rails, close to 40% of commercial shipping is done on railroads. Another 15% of freight moves over **water**, whether across Great Lakes or along rivers like the Mississippi, Arkansas, and Ohio. Boats can reach the inner parts of the United States from the Atlantic Ocean by means of the Saint Lawrence Seaway. The busiest ports in the United States are New Orleans, Houston, and New York.

Environmental Ethics vs. Frontier Ethics

In contrast to the frontier ethic, which assumes unlimited resources for unlimited growth potential, an **environmental ethic** is becoming more popular. It assumes that Earth's resources are limited, and that rather than being managers of their natural environment, humans are a part of it. Thus, human activities such as uncontrolled use of natural resources can harm the natural world, and such activities are restricted under the environmental ethic. A **sustainable ethic** is a type of environmental ethic. It proposes that humans need to utilize and conserve our planet's natural resources to enable their future ongoing use. Also, the sustainable ethic maintains that if a natural ecosystem is harmed, human beings will in turn suffer from harm, because they are viewed as being a part of the natural environment.

Anthropocentric and Biocentric Approaches to Sustainable Environment

Anthropocentric approaches are human-centered and consider only human needs. **Biocentric approaches** are life-centered and consider ecological needs. Since sustainable ethics consider human populations part of their ecosystems, practices causing ecological damage must also cause damage to the humans inhabiting them. Sustainable ethics may be anthropocentric or biocentric. For example, relative to an oil shortage, an anthropocentric sustainable ethic would regard oil as human property and focus on the conservation and wise use of oil to further its availability to posterity. Conversely, a biocentric sustainable ethic would be more likely to seek alternative, renewable energy sources, such as solar energy, wind energy, water energy, and biomass energy instead of depleting the limited oil. A main difference is that anthropocentric sustainable ethics concentrate on extending the future access to a limited natural resource, while biocentric sustainable ethics concentrate on controlling the use of limited natural resources to prevent environmental damage and hence, human damage.

Varying Ethical Codes Affecting the Environment

Ethical codes are based on standards of conduct that differentiate between right and wrong behaviors. However, these vary across people and situations; there is no universally agreed upon code of ethics. For example, an impoverished small farmer might be considered justified by some in clearing a portion of rainforest land for planting crops to support his family; others more concerned with the effects of deforestation on climate change and soil erosion would consider his action unjustified. A society's ethics are typically based on the ethics of the majority of the society's individuals. The **frontier ethic** is anthropocentric, considering only human needs, assuming resources are unlimited and/or depleted resources can be replaced or substituted. Historically, European settlers exhausted natural resources in eastern America and then expanded westward to fresh resources. Currently, proponents of the frontier ethic believe outer space is the next frontier. Opponents find this unrealistic, as terrestrial population growth would exceed extraterrestrial colonization rates. However, additional resources could be obtained from space.

Principles of a Sustainable Environmental Ethics

Sustainable ethics espouse principles including the following: The planet Earth's natural resources are limited in their amounts. Human beings must conserve our finite natural resources. Humans also have to share Earth's natural resources with the planet's other living things. Human beings are a part of nature. Human beings are also subject to natural laws. Growth is a process that is not sustainable. Moreover, a key guiding principle of the sustainable environmental ethic is that human beings and their endeavors are the most successful when they cooperate with nature, work in harmony with nature, and protect and preserve the integrity of natural environmental processes.

Land Ethic

The land ethic is an environmental ethic that is sustainable and **biocentric** (life-centered) rather than **anthropocentric** (human-centered). Human beings are seen as one part of an ethical framework. Including the land in this ethical framework constitutes the land ethic. This was originated by **Aldo Leopold**, the American philosopher and wildlife natural historian. Leopold proposed that humans have always viewed land as property, comparable to the ancient Greeks viewing slaves as property. Leopold found mistreating the land, like mistreating slaves, economically and morally irrational. He wrote: "The land ethic simply enlarges the boundary of the community to include soils, waters, plants, and animals; or collectively, the land. In short, a land ethic changes the role of Homo sapiens from conqueror of the land-community to plain member and citizen of it. It implies respect for his fellow members, and also respect for the community as such." (Aldo Leopold, *A Sand County Almanac*, 1949)

Types of Conservationists

According to Aldo Leopold, who first proposed the land ethic, conservationists of one type see the soil as a **commodity**, while the other type sees the soil as **biota** with diverse functions. For example, in forestry terms, conservationists, seeing soil as a commodity, would plant as many trees as possible; conservationists, seeing soil as biota, would work instead to preserve the natural ecosystem as much as possible. In the **land ethic**, all components of the natural environment are respected regardless of utility/lack thereof. Many species with no human economic worth are vital parts of working ecosystems. Removing them would unbalance and could destroy ecosystems. Leopold insisted that economic necessity was an insufficient basis for the conservation movement. Land-ethic-based decisions promote **biological stability**. As Leopold wrote, "Anything is right when it tends to preserve the integrity, stability, and beauty of the biotic community. It is wrong when it tends to do otherwise." (*A Sand County Almanac*, 1949)

Utilitarian Conservation vs. Preservation

Utilitarian conservationists believe in conserving natural resources for the public good, while **preservationists** believe in saving the wilderness for its own value. For example, California's Yosemite is a protected National Park. However, after the 1906 San Francisco earthquakes caused fires destroying much of the city, many residents were in favor of damming the Hetch Hetchy Valley in Yosemite to create a dependable water supply. President Teddy Roosevelt and his Chief Forester, Gifford Pinchot, advocated the dam. John Muir, founder of the Sierra Club, opposed it. Though the preservationists lost the conflict when Congress voted in 1913 to dam the valley, they nevertheless influenced America to rethink its traditional values: by 1916, Congress had passed the National Park System Organic Act, decreeing that our public parks must be preserved undamaged for posterity.

Shared Beliefs in the Early 20th Century

Conservationists in general believed in conserving our natural resources, regarding them as finite. As such, both utilitarian and preservationist conservationists rejected the first belief of the frontier ethic, that our natural resources and our growth potential were unlimited. However, **utilitarian conservationists** accepted other principles of frontier ethics, including using natural resources for human purposes without regard for consequences. **Preservationists** rejected these; since humans were part of the ecology, ecological harm would cause human harm. Each view is reflected in two quotations: "The fundamental principle of the whole conservation policy is that of use, to take every part of the land and its resources and put it to that use in which it will serve the most people," (US Chief Forester Gifford Pinchot, 1913) and "These temple destroyers, devotees of ravaging commercialism, seem to have a perfect contempt for Nature, and instead of lifting their eyes to the God of the Mountains, lift them to the Almighty Dollar," (John Muir, Sierra Club founder, 1912).

Regulatory Instruments and Economic Instruments

Regulatory instruments for environmental protection include specific standards, such as emissions limits, quality standards for products, and goals for environmental quality; regulatory powers to order measures for adjustment; license requirements; and obligations of the administration and the industry to monitor environmental outcomes. Many economists find **regulatory instruments** inefficient for not taking into account the varying costs of reducing pollution to various entities, costing more for all without commensurate protective results. They propose using **economic**

instruments instead, such as pollution charges and tradable pollution rights. They find these more efficient by allowing businesses the choice of polluting and paying for it, or investing in abating pollution and not paying. However, research finds that administrative agencies are flexible regarding their investment requirements. Research also finds that enforcement agencies have a bargaining advantage through stringent and uniform standards. Additionally, research shows that both regulatory and economic instruments require close monitoring to be effective.

Difficulties in Enforcing Legal Protection Against Environmental Risks

While there are civil and public laws to protect against environmental risk, one problem inherent in litigating environmental risk is that when a third party is affected by environmental damage, such damage may extend **beyond** the individual. For example, damage could be caused on land that is someone's property, but also involves destroying a biotope that could lead to a whole species' extinction. Another difficulty is when a third party is affected only **indirectly** or **morally**. For example, an area could be deforested and the third parties affected are birdwatchers losing this field. Or pesticide use could contaminate groundwater, and the affected third parties are those who would have used it as a source of drinking water. Legal systems can address these challenges by extending arguments in scope to encompass group issues, and/or permitting groups as well as individuals to defend collective interests. US law requires plaintiffs to be affected in a factual interest and that said interest is protected or regulated by the pertinent law.

Environmental Education

Educational theorists frequently describe **Environmental Education (EE)** with three divisions: in, for, and about the environment. Many subjects in higher education, such as environmental engineering (e.g., dam construction or forestry), recycling education, and environmental politics and management, relate to the study of EE for the environment. Studied separately, this is informative, but it may not influence student beliefs or values or be relevant to real-life issues. EE about the environment is common in secondary schools, exemplified by subjects like geology, biology, physics, etc. While this content is relevant, and its application could forge great connections among students, it is typically taught in isolation. Considering EE's ultimate purpose as developing politically informed, involved persons, all three categories must be taught together. Students must be given environmental knowledge, critical thinking skills, democratic skills, and experience with environmental politics in its daily and long-term processes. Scholars believe teaching the interdisciplinary concept of the "earth system" gives a perspective of humanity within our environment, removing walls between nature and society.

Environmental Issues Becoming Political Issues

Such matters as toxic emissions, global climate change, and the availability of clean water may be considered the concerns of individuals when their effects are limited. However, as their impacts increase to encompass common regional and global spheres, the concern extends to governments and becomes **political**. **Public education** is in a singularly powerful position to teach awareness of environmental impact issues and our capacity as citizens to effect democratic changes to address those issues. Teaching students critical thinking skills is essential generally and will gain specific importance relative to the environment as its problems increase, and both our government and our culture will need to make serious interventions to perpetuate the quality of all life on our planet. Education thus must address not only content knowledge, but the skills of logic and argumentation that allow citizens to make adaptive responses to political demands.

Japanese Events Illustrating Interaction with Unexpected Natural Events

Japan suffered its biggest earthquake ever recorded in 2011, triggering an equally devastating tsunami. Although Japan leads the world in earthquake preparedness and management, the scope of these disasters was so great that it damaged the country's **infrastructure**, compromising **nuclear reactors** at the Fukushima Daiichi nuclear power plant. While scientists were aware of the dangers inherent in nuclear power plants during their construction, the current situation was not likely anticipated. Environmental groups condemned the energy company for not controlling massive radiation emissions and for keeping information secret from authorities and the public for weeks. Some groups also asked the US government to help. The energy company admitted dumping hundreds of tons of radioactive wastewater into the ocean. A Japanese senior nuclear advisor resigned when the Japanese government allowed local elementary school children to be exposed to high radiation levels, for which it also received much public criticism.

New Developments Presenting Additional Threats to the Environment

One of the most common methods of obtaining natural gas from the earth, **hydraulic fracturing**—more commonly known as **fracking**—involves injecting millions of gallons of fracking fluids made up of water, sand, and chemicals into gas wells. The pressure cracks open underground rocks to release natural gas. This procedure is highly controversial for its dangers, including explosions, radioactive wastewater, and contamination of drinking water. Natural gas providers have found a legal loophole to avoid disclosing the numerous fracking chemicals they use. Environmentalist groups, such as Save Our Environment's Food and Water Watch, have asked the public to urge Congress to pass the **FRAC Act**, a law that would close the loophole and enforce compliance with the **Clean Water Act**, which includes requiring energy companies to disclose the chemicals they are pumping into the ground.

Conflicts of Commercial Industrial Activities and the Environmental Damage

In addition to causing explosions, purposefully or accidentally contaminating the supply of drinking water, and generating radioactive wastewater, the process of fracking also appears to be associated with increased **earthquake activity**. Seismologists have been studying the effects of injection wells and the process of fracking in respect to the generation of earthquakes. Studies suggest that not only are earthquakes becoming more frequent as fracking processes increase, but the earthquakes themselves are growing more potent as well. Whereas it was traditionally believed that wastewater injections seemed to be the major culprit in terms of generated seismic activity, studies from various scientists in geologically diverse areas have shown much more direct correlations between earthquakes and the fracking process. Shale gas firms in the Sichuan province of Rongxian, China were instructed to temporarily suspend their operations in response to three earthquakes striking the region in 2019, which killed two people and injured twelve. Despite these incidences, it is unlikely that major reductions of operations are likely to occur.

Example of a Non-Sustainable Energy Damaging the Environment

In May 2011, the Dakota Access **pipeline** spilled thousands of gallons of oil in southeastern North Dakota and had to be shut down. The ruptured pipeline created a gusher of oil six stories high at a pumping station. The oil spray contaminated a neighboring field's soil and water before the gusher could be contained. In only its first year of operation, the pipeline sustained twelve oil spills. Despite this dismal accident rate, an even larger pipeline to move tar sands oil across the US was founded by the same company. The Keystone XL pipeline would transport close to a million barrels of oil a day from Canada to Texas. It would cross several major rivers, a great deal of farmland, and the Ogallala, the country's biggest aquifer. It has been a major point of contention throughout three presidential terms over the course of a decade—having been vetoed twice and reinstated once with about 8% total completion to date.

General Measures Protecting the Environment and Citizens

New offshore oil drilling and development is an activity that demands new **safety requirements** in order to meet the demands of a growing but dangerous industry. Members of the oil industry are known to fight against safety inspections, which are obviously necessary considering the dangerous nature of the operations and the industry's accident records. The Bureau of Safety and Environmental Enforcement issued rules in 2016 that firmly regulated offshore drilling, but were revised in 2019 in order to,"...[correct] errors and [reduce] certain unnecessary regulatory burdens imposed under the existing regulations." When lawmakers try to enable royalties to give public taxpayers fair value in return for the oil industry's use of public lands, industry forces block such endeavors.

Political Conflicts in the USA Over Commercial Oil Interests

One of the frequently recurring battles within legislation is how **subsidies**—financial aid provided to industries by US tax dollars in the form of cash payments or tax incentives or reductions—are to be implemented or restricted when the oil sector is involved. The oil industry accounts for nearly a tenth of the overall Gross Domestic Product of the US. Because of how lucrative and influential these companies are, the idea of how much the government should be involved in helping them maintain such a dominant position in the economic sector is highly contested. Many claim that the government hands out money to "big oil" well beyond anything necessary or fair to keep commodities and services at reasonable rates. Major proponents and lobbyists for the industry claim they pay more than their fair share of the taxes, and that to continually force them to pay more and more will pressure these industries to leave for other countries that would be glad to receive their lucrative industry.

Legislative Proposal to End America's Subsidy of Corn Ethanol

Corn ethanol was introduced as a potential alternative to fossil fuels. However, ethanol production not only causes pollution, it also diverts corn from the food supply, increases food prices, and seems to create more problems than it solves. The Environmental Working Group found ethanol cultivation adds chemicals, depletes soil, contaminates water, and was ineffective at lessening our oil dependence because blends of gasoline with too much ethanol are wholly inefficient. This was all compounded by the fact that our government subsidized ethanol, at taxpayer expense, including a mandate, an import tariff, and refundable tax credits for blending ethanol into gasoline. Congress allowed the subsidies given to the ethanol industry to officially expire in 2012, but the remaining initiatives of the Renewable Fuel Standard (RFS) still remain in effect. Ethanol is still required to be blended with gasoline in order to meet EPA guidelines and the RFS, but the hope is that these policy changes have helped address hunger in a growing world population as well as promote continual research into renewable and clean energy.

Federal Laws Protecting the Natural Quiet in National Parks

When we think of protected national parks, we usually think of protecting concrete features like land, vegetation, water, and wildlife. However, **noise** is also considered a type of pollution that destroys **natural quiet**—an integral part of the national park experience. In 2000, Congress passed the **National Parks Air Tour Management Act** that is still in effect to this day. While commercial air tours allow aerial views of national parks, aircraft noise ruins enjoyment below for visitors in the parks. This law requires tour planes to use quiet-aircraft technology as well as requires the FAA and NPS to maintain and develop Air Tour Management Plans (ATMPs) in order to effectively mitigate adverse effects of commercial air tour operations. The related **1987 Overflight Act** regulates flight of other/non-tour airplanes over national parks. The Grand Canyon, Hawai'i Volcanoes, and Mount Rainier National Parks prepare **environmental impact statements (EIS)** for managing air tours. The National Park Service has an EIS with flight rules for the area around Grand Canyon National Park, and works with the FAA to enforce the Overflight Act and reduce air tours.

Environmental Groups Addressing the Need for Protection of Wildlife

There are some instances where the Fish, Wildlife, and Parks (FWP) Departments want permission from the US Fish and Wildlife Service (FWS) to hunt **endangered animal species** in an area of federally protected public land. Montana is one such state, where the balance between the population of wolves and elk is continuously being shifted because of human action. Conservationists find the elk population is being reduced more by human hunters than natural predation. However, Montana's FWP has continually raised its maximum elk population goals and even implemented wolf bounties to stimulate even more wolf hunting. Its wolf-killing project is regarded as motivated by state hostility against wolves and not in line with objective data by many professional wildlife biologists and former employees of the FWP. These members of the Montana Wildlife Federation have joined together to oppose various policies they believe will ultimately tarnish the image of hunters and hunting in Montana, as well as disturb and damage the **ecosystem**.

Backfiring of Human Conservation Efforts Protecting Wildlife

Sometimes human efforts are well-intentioned, such as conserving a critically endangered wildlife species. Yet these efforts may not foresee the possible unintended **negative environmental impacts** in the methods they use to accomplish their goal. For example, the monarch butterfly population has been steadily decreasing over the past few decades. In an attempt to try and help the population rebound, well-meaning butterfly lovers began planting milkweed—a weed butterflies eat and rely on to breed that has been increasingly eradicated by farmers. What these people did not know, was that the type of milkweed they were planting was actually a non-native species that significantly increased the likelihood that the monarch butterflies would become infected with a deadly parasite. This type of tropical milkweed does not die as easily in the winter as the traditional native species, which means that this milkweed lasts long enough for multiple generations of monarchs to be born on the same plants. This ultimately results in an increase of parasitic spores on the milkweed leaves which then get transferred to caterpillars.

Opinions, Beliefs, or Attitudes on Decisions Affecting the Environment

It is no secret that the **leadership** within a business has the greatest impact on overall business enterprises. When the leaders change, so can the directions of their businesses. Consequently, when major business leaders begin producing more efficient and environmentally conscious products, the industry as a whole can be impacted as well. For example, Tesla, Inc. produced and promoted its solar roof panel technology to mixed reactions from the greater community. However, it continues to innovate and upgrade its technology with great success in a variety of areas. When a major company and its leaders begin establishing a presence of commitment to futurizing energy production or meeting some particular niche, many other companies begin to start advancing and developing products and research to stay relevant and competitive.

Nature Outings

One of the largest environmental organizations in the United States, the **Sierra Club**, is known for originating the idea of "eco-travel" or nature outings. Such outings range from longer trips farther away to local day hikes. Outings are led by trained volunteers. These trips not only afford participants the enjoyment and exploration of nature, and educate them about natural history, wildlife, and conservation; they give them experiences that make them better environmentalists and/or create new environmentalists. For example, the experience of witnessing a giant leatherback sea turtle dig a nest to lay her eggs on a beach in the moonlight creates real motivation to take action against commercial developers who would build on such coastal land, destroying the habitat of endangered species. Actually experiencing nature that could be lost is a more powerful motivator than only learning facts and figures or hearing/reading reports.

Importance of National Forests

America's **public lands** constitute an area the size of Texas (193 million acres). These areas are keeping 20% of federally protected threatened and endangered species alive. Our country's **national forests** include rivers, streams, and lakes that supply clean drinking water to over 20% of American citizens. They also support a great diversity of ecosystems, plants, and wildlife. Many groups, such as the Wilderness Society and Save Our Environment, find the Forest Service's current plan inadequate to protect these resources. They call for strengthening it by the following: expanding wildlife safeguards; maintaining healthy, sustainable fish and wildlife populations; removing discretion from individual forest managers to abandon the protection of endangered species without public accountability; setting enforceable clean water and healthy watershed standards in national forests; making forest plans congruent with the best science; and maintaining public accountability by keeping the existing 90-day standard for public review and appeal of forest plans.

Importance of Biodiversity

The majority of scientists concur that **biodiversity** is important in terms of several specific aspects. Many recreational activities and tourism industries heavily rely on unique biodiversity. It is important in terms of niche complementarity; the greater the variety of species living in an ecosystem, the more efficiently each of them occupies a niche, job, or function in the system, with fewer or no vacancies. Biodiversity is important in production of crop biomass because greater variety avoids depleting soil of nutrients and provides a more varied diet to consumers, promoting public health. Despite their consensus on the value of these aspects, scientists find it difficult to identify which one is most important in biological management.

Types of Value Attributed to Biodiversity

Biodiversity affords a functional value to natural ecosystems because it sustains **biological, geological, and chemical cycles** (and/or cycles combining all three elements) and keeps these systems stable, protecting them from invasions. It confers a utilitarian value in crop production by making the most efficient use of the resources of land and time. It has a serendipitous value in conferring unexpected salutary benefits, such as the discoveries of medicinal properties in rare plant species as one example. **Biodiversity** also has an intrinsic value in that many traditional cultures regard it as necessary and valuable. Biological and land management are valued by both politicians and public citizens. Public lands offer many physical, psychological, and social benefits to human beings. Additionally, because public lands are publicly managed, they represent a significant investment of taxpayers' dollars. Environmental educators find that because the different values of biodiversity can conflict, managers must strive to achieve a balance among all of them.

Degree of Political Participation in American Society

Public comments and testimony are allowed during open periods between the proposal and the voting on many proposed government bills affecting the environment. Environmental organizations also encourage their members to engage in such **participation**. However, even while members of these groups have influenced legislation with their responses, in general the American public is not that invested in participating in their government, as evidenced by eligible voter percentages in election years. The principles that underlie citizen democracy and "citizen science" are actually quite similar in many respects. Both processes are social, based on some kind of consensus; both demand strong evidence to back them up; both employ models that appear universal, but really are bound by local contexts; and both call for critical thinking skills, especially those related to persuasion and argumentation. Therefore, teaching either citizen democracy or citizen science can significantly inform the other and vice versa.

Rare Earth Elements

For environmentally responsible or green economies to succeed in the United States and globally, we need more access to **rare earth elements (REEs)**. These are minerals used in many of today's technologies, including cell phones, laptop PCs, and military weapons systems and radar, the world's most powerful magnets; and in "green" alternative energy sources, such as wind turbines and electric cars. The USA has been mining and processing only a small fraction of these minerals, while the vast majority of this industry is in China. To supply its own national revolution in "green" technology, **China** is stockpiling its REEs. This allows the Chinese greater control of international prices for these elements, which have risen dramatically over the years. China's monopoly on REEs is a competitive disadvantage to America in the areas of clean energy and defense. American leaders find it also threatens the USA's national security by causing strategic vulnerability.

Responding to Trends and Supporting Environmental Literacy

Too much natural biodiversity has already been lost through the destruction and extinction of plant and animal species. Trends in our societal practices can lead to losing our connections to nature; losing the experiences of addressing natural challenges, which have evolved qualities of leadership and cooperation; and our children losing comprehension of natural cycles of growth and death so we cannot teach them about the origins of their foods. More wilderness and nature will always be needed in our classrooms. Meanwhile, educators can teach students to become engaged with and excited about our environment, teach them information about and care for it, and encourage passion for its cause. Constructing **environmental literacy** builds communities and creates learning opportunities.

Physical Geography

El Niño

El Niño refers to the unusual **warming** of surface waters near the equatorial coast of South America. This phenomenon occurs during the winter approximately every two to seven years, lasting from a few weeks to a few months. **El Niño** can cause torrential rains, violent winds, drought, and dangerously high temperatures in surrounding areas. El Niño is caused by a reversal of the atmospheric pressures on the eastern and western sides of the Pacific (normally, pressure is high on the eastern side near South America and lower on the western side near the Indonesian coast). This reversal causes a wave of warm water to flow eastward and sea levels to fall on the western side. The changes in air pressure and ocean temperature cause moisture levels in the western Pacific to rise drastically, while the region east of the Pacific experiences drought. The air pressure changes also weaken the region's trade winds, which normally serve to distribute heat and moisture.

Ecosystems

An ecosystem (an abbreviated term for ecological system) is a system in the biosphere that consists of a biotic community (a regional group of living organisms) and the surrounding environment, called a biotope. Some characteristics include:

- Ecosystems may be studied at different **scales**. For example, an ecosystem may be as small as an area within a pond or as large as the entire planet.
- Ecosystems exist in **dynamic equilibrium**, a relatively steady state maintained by various symbiotic (interactive) processes such as predation (wherein one organism, a predator, overwhelms and consumes another, the prey) and mutualism (interspecies relationships which benefit both parties).
- Ecosystems receive **energy inputs** (mainly from the Sun); this energy is transformed through the process of photosynthesis and transferred among constituents via the food web.
- Ecosystems also produce **natural resources** used by human beings, including structural materials, food, and fuel.
- Ecosystems are broadly described as **terrestrial** (those which include land animals and exist atop continents) or **aquatic** (those dominated by water and marine or freshwater life).

Ecological Succession

Ecological succession is the process that occurs after a significant disturbance or disaster has simplified an ecosystem. **Primary succession** follows a disaster that eliminates all living organisms in a region (such as a volcanic eruption). **Secondary succession** refers to the process that succeeds a disturbance in which some life survives (such as deforestation). **Ecological succession** is the change of a biotic community from a simpler state to one that is more diverse and complex. Through this process, members of an ecosystem mature and develop more intricate relationships. Though ecologists in earlier times envisioned a climax stage that represented the end point of ecosystem development, this idea is largely absent in current ecological discourse. Rather, modern ecologists believe that ecosystems are always changing and reacting to various degrees and frequencies of disturbances, making a climax community unreachable.

Review Video: Ecological Succession
Visit mometrix.com/academy and enter code: 466994

Food Web

The food web, or **food network**, is a model used to describe the transfer of energy (in the form of sustenance) between organisms in an ecosystem. Organisms feed on one another to stay alive; this process also helps to regulate the populations of species within an ecosystem. Organisms in a **food web** are generally organized into **trophic levels** that reflect their relative positions in this system. **Primary producers**, usually photosynthetic plants and algae, exist at the base of a food web. These organisms produce vital **biochemical molecules** (including carbohydrates) from light energy derived from the Sun's energy. The primary producers are consumed by **small primary consumers**, such as insects and fish. These organisms are in turn eaten and digested by **secondary consumers**, which are later preyed upon by larger organisms, and so on. **Decomposers** are soil-dwelling microorganisms that rely on detritus (decaying organic materials) for sustenance. Because energy is lost in transfer throughout the food web (due to respiration), the number of organisms and their sizes decline up the chain.

Review Video: Food Webs
Visit mometrix.com/academy and enter code: 853254

Respiration

Respiration is the process whereby energy is burned by an organism to keep it alive. It is basically the opposite of photosynthesis. This chemical process involves the decomposition of carbohydrates, which then combine with oxygen, releasing water, carbon dioxide, and heat energy into the atmosphere. Organisms' cells store the **chemical energy** produced through respiration; this energy is later used to create vital **biochemical molecules**. Respiration is thus a counterpart of photosynthesis in the cycling of elements through an ecosystem. Due to the energy loss inherent to the process of respiration, only 10-50% of the energy stored in organic matter at one level of the food web moves up to the next level.

Process of Transpiration

Transpiration is the mechanism by which water evaporates into the atmosphere from the leaves or stems of plants. Plants absorb water into their roots through osmosis. Then, as explained by **cohesion-tension theory**, water moves upward from the roots of a plant to its leaves. Some transpiration occurs directly through surface cells on the stem of a plant. More often, however, water escapes through pores in its leaves called **stomates**. Water droplets on the exterior surface of the leaves (usually on the bottom of the leaves) are consequently subjected to the process of evaporation. The process of transpiration enables **photosynthesis**, which in turn releases vital oxygen into Earth's atmosphere. Transpiration also has a cooling effect on the surface and air around the plant.

Biogeochemical Cycle

The term *biogeochemical cycle* refers to one of several chemical processes in which chemical elements are (re)cycled among **biotic** (living) and **abiotic** (nonliving) constituents of an ecosystem. The theory of relativity necessitates the presence of such cycles in nature by virtue of its supposition that energy and matter are not created or destroyed in a closed system such as Earth's ecosystem. Generally, a **biogeochemical cycle** operates as follows: Inorganic compounds are converted from water, air, and soil to organic molecules by organisms called **autotrophs**. **Heterotrophs** (organisms that cannot independently produce their own food) consume the autotrophs; some of the newly formed organic molecules are transferred. Finally, the organic molecules are broken down and processed once again into inorganic compounds by secondary and tertiary consumers and replaced within water, air, and soil. Carbon, nitrogen, and phosphorus provide examples of nutrients that are recycled in Earth's ecosystem.

Biome

A biome is the broadest general subdivision of terrestrial ecosystems. This term is used to describe a region that exhibits the distinctive plant and animal life best adapted to an area's particular soil type and climate. This concept is associated with the interrelationships between organisms and their environment. Since vegetation is more abundant than any other species in the biosphere, **biomes** are often classified according to **climax vegetation type** (the type of vegetation that exists in mature or old-growth ecosystems). The global distribution of biomes is closely related to climate and soil variations at different latitudes. The subdivision of a biome may be further differentiated into formation classes, based upon the structural and dimensional characteristics of regional vegetation.

Forest Biomes

The forest biome is typified by an abundance of soil and moisture, as well as warm temperatures for at least a portion of the year. Trees are the dominant vegetation type in this biome.

Savanna Biome

The savanna biome exists between forest and grassland on the spectrum of biomes. It is often situated near the boundary of an equatorial rainforest. This type of biome is commonly found in regions that experience a wet-dry tropical climate. The lack of moisture in the soil during the dry season causes trees in the savanna biome to grow in spacious patterns. This enables the growth of a dense lower layer of grasses and other plants. The trees of the **savanna biome** are similar in height and shape to those found in a monsoon forest. Though fire is a fairly common occurrence in savannas during the dry season, the vegetation in these regions tends to be quite fire-resistant. In fact, many geographers believe that such fires prevent rainforest vegetation from overrunning the savanna biome.

Grassland Biome

The grassland biome is commonly subdivided into two types: tall-grass prairie and steppe. The **tall-grass prairie subdivision** is characterized by an absence of trees and a high occurrence of tall grasses and broad-leaved herbs called forbs. This kind of biome usually forms in regions with distinct summer and winter seasons, in subtropical or midlatitude climates. The **steppe, or short-grass prairie, subdivision** is typified by sparse clumps of short grasses, existing alongside the occasional shrub or small tree. Many grass species and forbs populate this kind of region. Steppes are usually found in midlatitude areas with dry continental climates; vegetation grows in wet spring months and becomes dormant during dry summer months.

Desert Biome

The desert biome may be subdivided into two types: semidesert and dry desert. The **semidesert subdivision** is found at a wide range of latitudes. It is characterized by thinly-spaced xerophytic shrubs (those adapted to survival in arid climates). Steppe regions may be converted to semidesert through, for example, high levels of cattle moving through the area, treading upon and consuming regional vegetation. The thorntree semidesert is found in the tropical zone, which experiences a long, dry hot season and a short, severe rainy season. Thorny vegetation (such as cacti), called thornbush or thornwoods, populate the thorntree semidesert.

The **dry desert subdivision** is even barer than the semidesert. Only tough xerophytes, such as cacti and hard grasses, can survive under dry desert conditions. Many dry desert areas display no plant life at all, due to the unfertile sand that covers the ground.

Tundra Biome

The tundra biome may be subdivided into two types: arctic or alpine. The **arctic tundra** exists at very high latitudes near the poles. During the brief summer season in these areas, low vegetation such as herbs, mosses, and grasses are able to grow because above-freezing air temperatures enable melting of the surface layer. The type and occurrence of plant species depend upon the moisture levels in the (usually frozen) ground during the warm season. In the cold season, frost action snaps roots in the ground. Freezing wind and snow kill plants above the ground. **Alpine tundra** is located at high elevations, above the tree line and below bare mountain tops. Physically, the alpine tundra is quite similar to the arctic tundra.

Various Forets and Formation Classes

Characteristics of the Low-Latitude Rainforests

The low-latitude rainforest formation class exists in equatorial and tropical climate zones. This class is characterized by many different species of tall, densely spaced trees, normally with broad leaves. The canopy created by this vegetation casts shade on the ground below, inhibiting the growth of flora on the bottom layer.

Monsoon Forests

Monsoon forests may also be found in tropical latitude zones; however, this formation class exists in regions that experience a wet season and a dry season, during which the many tree species lose their leaves. This enables the growth of vegetation on the lower layer of the forest.

Subtropical Evergreen Forest Formation Classes

The subtropical evergreen forest may be broadleaf or needleleaf (found only in the southeastern United States). This formation class consists of fewer, shorter tree species than the low-latitude rainforest. It also includes a lush lower layer of vegetation.

Midlatitude Deciduous Forest

The midlatitude deciduous forest formation class is common in regions of the northern hemisphere with distinct seasons. During the warm summer season, the tall broadleaf trees in this type of forest form a nearly closed canopy. In the winter season, these trees lose their leaves. The lower level vegetation also varies with the season, growing in the spring and dying out with the summertime formation of a dense upper canopy.

Needleleaf Forest

A needleleaf forest is made up largely of conifers (cone-shaped trees with short branches, straight trunks, and small, thin leaves reminiscent of needles). Many trees in this type of forest (usually found at higher latitudes or regions where orogenies and/or plateaus are found) are evergreen, meaning that they shed their leaves once every several years. The spacing of the trees in this formation class may be dense, preventing the growth of vegetation on the ground.

Sclerophyll Forest

The sclerophyll forest contains widely spaced trees that are able to survive dry, hot seasons (short, with low branches; tough, thick bark; and short, thick leaves).

Earth's Rotation

Earth rotates **eastward** (from the equator) about its **rotational axis** (an imaginary line running north to south through the center of the planet). This motion exposes each section of Earth to direct sunlight for a limited period of time, thus creating the sensations of day and night. Due to minute variations in the sidereal day, which is defined as the exact amount of time it takes for a reference star to cross an imaginary north-south line above an observer (a meridian), we use the **mean sidereal day** (a period of exactly 24 hours) in timekeeping. Earth's rotation creates **diurnal** (daily) variations in air humidity, air temperature, and air motion. These patterns affect plant and animal life on the planet and also influence the **hydrosphere**, causing tidal movement and the Coriolis effect.

Earth's Revolution

Earth revolves around the Sun in an **orbit**. This process takes just over 365 days (our calendar year). The consequence of the elliptical shape of Earth's orbit is that the distance between the planet and the Sun varies over time. At **perihelion**, the minimum heliocentric distance, Earth is 147 million kilometers from the Sun. At **aphelion**, the maximum heliocentric distance, Earth is 152 million kilometers from the Sun. Earth's revolution about the Sun and the tilt of the planet's rotational axis (approximately 23.5 degrees from its orbital plane) produce the **seasons** we experience on Earth; certain areas of the surface receive different amounts of sunlight throughout the year. For example, during the portion of Earth's orbit when the Northern Hemisphere tilts toward the Sun, it is exposed to higher amounts of nearly direct sunlight than any other time of year (because days are longer and the direction of the Sun's rays striking the surface is nearly perpendicular). This time period is summer in the Northern Hemisphere and winter in the Southern Hemisphere.

Global Energy Flow System

The global energy flow system is comprised of the pathways through which energy travels between the Sun and Earth, including its storage as well as its losses in the atmosphere. A main tenet of physics is that energy, like matter, cannot be created or destroyed in a **closed system** such as Earth. This fact necessitates the **recycling of energy** from the Sun to Earth and back again. Earth receives energy from the Sun in the form of light and heat. It moves through the atmosphere as short-wave radiation and is converted to different forms, fueling nearly all of the natural physical phenomena that occur on the planet in one way or another (either directly or indirectly). **Solar energy** is also "lost" due to scattering and absorption in the atmosphere. The rate of this incoming energy, which is nearly constant, is referred to as the **solar constant**. Long-wave radiation is emitted from Earth into space, often through the release of gases such as carbon dioxide and water vapor.

Weather

Weather is the result of transfers of kinetic (heat) energy due to differences in temperature between objects as well as transfers of moisture in Earth's atmosphere. Most of the activity that produces the **weather** we experience on Earth takes place in the **troposphere**, the lowest level of the atmosphere (0-15 kilometers above Earth's surface). Atmospheric pressure, temperature, humidity, elevation, wind speed, and cloud cover are all factors in the formation of weather. A **weather system** is an organized atmospheric state, associated with a particular weather pattern such as cyclones or tornadoes. **Meteorology**, the study of weather, entails the observation of natural phenomena such as rain, fog, snow, and wind. The processes that occur at different stages in the **hydrologic cycle** form the basis of meteorological events.

Cycles of Air Temperature

The two main cycles of air temperature are **insolation** and **net radiation**. Due to Earth's rotation, **insolation** (interception of solar energy by an exposed surface) varies from location to location with the angle at which solar rays hit Earth and the length of time a particular location is exposed to direct sunlight. **Net radiation** is the difference between incoming and outgoing radiation. This quality is positive when more energy is flowing in than out, and vice versa. During daylight hours, a surface location experiences positive net radiation, causing it to gain heat; at night, the location loses heat. This pattern is the daily air temperature cycle. The annual air temperature cycle results from Earth's revolution. When a region of Earth experiences summer, the region's net radiation is positive. In wintertime, net radiation is low. Air temperature is also affected by altitude (temperature generally decreases as altitude increases), location (continental or oceanic—air temperature in maritime areas is less variable), and surface features (which may absorb or reflect heat waves). Isotherms are lines on a map connecting points with equivalent air temperatures.

Hydrologic Cycle

The hydrologic cycle, also known as the **water cycle**, is the circulation of water i Earth's hydrosphere (below the surface, on the surface, and above Earth's surface). This continuous process involves five physical actions:

- **Evaporation** entails the change of water molecules from a liquid to a gaseous state.
- **Condensation** occurs when liquid water on Earth's surface (often contained in a large body of water) becomes water vapor and enters the atmosphere when its component molecules gain enough kinetic (heat) energy to escape the liquid form. As the vapor rises, it cools and therefore loses its ability to maintain the gaseous form. It begins to condense (return to a liquid or solid state) and forms clouds.
- **Precipitation** occurs when the clouds become sufficiently dense and the water falls back to Earth.
- Water is then either trapped in **vegetation** (interception) or **infiltration** (absorption of water into the surface).
- **Runoff**, caused by gravity, physically moves water downward into oceans or other water bodies.

Review Video: Bodies of Water
Visit mometrix.com/academy and enter code: 463122

Review Video: Hydrologic Cycle
Visit mometrix.com/academy and enter code: 426578

Precipitation

Precipitation is water that falls back to Earth's surface from the atmosphere. This water may be in the form of **rain**, which is water in liquid form. Raindrops are formed in clouds due to the process of **condensation**. When the drops become too heavy to remain in the cloud (due to a decrease in their kinetic energy), gravity causes them to fall down toward Earth's surface. Extremely small raindrops are called **drizzle**. If the temperature of a layer of air through which rain passes on its way down is below the freezing point, the rain may take the form of **sleet** (partially frozen water). Precipitation may also fall in the form of **snow**, or water molecules sublimated into ice crystals. When clumps of snowflakes melt and refreeze, **hail** is formed. Hail may also be formed when liquid water accumulates on the surface of a snowflake and subsequently freezes.

Types of Clouds

The four main types of clouds are cirrus, cumulus, nimbus, and stratus.

- A **cirrus cloud** forms high in a stable atmosphere, generally at altitudes of 6,000 meters or higher. Temperatures at these altitudes (in the troposphere) decrease with increased altitude; therefore, the precipitation in a cirrus cloud adopts the form of ice crystals. These usually thin traces of clouds may indicate an approaching weather depression.
- A **cumulus cloud** is a stereotypical white, fluffy ball. Cumulus clouds are indicators of a stable atmosphere and also of the vertical extent of convection in the atmosphere; condensation and cloud formation begin at the flat base of a cumulous cloud. The more humid the air, the lower a cumulus cloud will form.
- A **nimbus cloud** is, generally speaking, a rain cloud. Nimbus clouds are usually low, dark, and formless, sometimes spanning the entire visible sky.

- A **stratus cloud** is basically a cloud of fog that forms at a distance above Earth's surface. This type of cloud forms when weak convective currents bring moisture just high enough to initiate condensation (if the temperature is below the dew point).

Review Video: Types of Clouds
Visit mometrix.com/academy and enter code: 803166

Cloud Subtypes

The four cloud subtypes are cumulonimbus, cirrostratus, altocumulus, and stratocumulus.

- A **cumulonimbus cloud** is produced by rapid convection in unstable air. This type of cloud (which is often dark) is formed as a large, tall "tower." Collections of these towers (squall lines) often signal a coming cold front. Thunderstorms often involve cumulonimbus clouds.
- A **cirrostratus cloud** is an ultrathin formation with a white tint and a transparent quality.
- An **altocumulus cloud** forms at an altitude from 1,980 to 6,100 meters. Clouds of this type, which appear to be flattened spheres, often form in clumps, waves, or lines.
- A **stratocumulus cloud** forms as a globular mass or flake. Stratocumulus clouds usually come together in layers or clumps.

Atmospheric Pressure

Atmospheric pressure is the pressure exerted by air in the atmosphere on the surface beneath it. This pressure subsists because the air's mass is continuously being drawn toward Earth's surface by the force of gravity. The amount of **atmospheric pressure** increases with proximity to the surface because there is more mass above the lower layers. Pressure causes air mass to compress; therefore, the layer of air nearest Earth's exterior is denser than air at higher altitudes. Atmospheric pressure is measured as force per unit area. This may be the **pascal** (Pa), which is one newton per square meter, or the **millibar** (mb); one millibar equals 100 Pa. These measurements are taken with a **barometer**. An **isobar** is a line on a map that connects all points with equal levels of atmospheric pressure.

Prevailing Winds and Wind Belts

Wind (the horizontal movement of air with respect to Earth's surface) forms due to pressure gradients (differences) in the atmosphere. Air tends to move from areas of high pressure,such as the poles to areas of low pressure, such as the tropics. **Prevailing winds**, or trade winds, are the winds (named in meteorology for the direction they come from) that blow most frequently in a particular region. For instance, the prevailing winds most common in the region from 90 to 60 degrees north latitude blow from the northeast and are generally called the Polar Easterlies. **Wind belts** are created in areas where prevailing winds converge with other prevailing winds or air masses. The Intertropical Convergence Zone (ITCZ), where air coming from tropical areas north and south of the equator come together, is an example of a wind belt.

Air Mass

An air mass is a sizeable region of air that displays consistent levels of moisture and uniform temperature throughout. The characteristics of a particular **air mass** develop in a source region, where air remains stable for a period of time long enough for said air to adopt the moisture and temperature qualities of the surface below. Air masses move due to atmospheric pressure gradients or the influence of winds. Corresponding changes in the surface environment may cause an air mass to take on new properties. These pockets of air are named for the qualities of the surface environment (**maritime** or **continental**), which determine the humidity of the mass, as well as the latitudinal position at which they form, which, in turn, determines the temperature of the mass. For example, an air mass that forms over a continent at a high latitudinal location is called a continental polar air mass (denoted as cP).

Air Stability in the Atmosphere

Air stability is the tendency for air to rise or fall through the atmosphere under its own power. Heated air rises because it is less dense than the surrounding air. As a pocket of air rises, however, it will expand and become cooler with changes in atmospheric pressure. If the ambient air into which rising air ascends does not cool as quickly with altitude as the rising air does, that air will rapidly become cooler (and heavier) than the surrounding air and descend back to its original position. The air in this situation is said to be stable. However, if the air into which the warm pocket rises becomes colder with increased altitude, the warm air will continue its ascent. In this case, the air is unstable. Unstable air conditions (such as those that exist in depressions) lead to the formation of large clouds of precipitation.

Cyclones and Anticyclones

Both cyclones and anticyclones are weather systems in which air masses move in spirals. Most such systems move across Earth's surface, affecting weather as they travel. A **cyclone** occurs when low pressure in the interior of an air mass draws air inward and upward. The risen air often forms clouds, which, in turn, produce cyclonic precipitation. A cyclone that involves large pressure disparities produces intense weather referred to as a cyclonic storm. In **anticyclones**, the movement of air is opposite to that in cyclones; air pressure in the center of an air mass is higher than the surrounding air, forcing air outward and downward. Because descending warm air does not produce precipitous clouds, anticyclones are often referred to as fair weather systems.

Weather Fronts

A front is the distinct boundary that usually forms between an air mass and the surrounding air. This boundary may be sloped or nearly vertical in orientation, depending on the relative movement of abutting air masses. There are four types of fronts:

- A **cold front** occurs when a cold air mass moves into an area inhabited by a mass of warm air. In this situation, the colder, denser air mass remains near the surface, pushing the warmer mass upward. When the ascending air is unstable, this movement may create severe weather, such as thunderstorms.
- A **warm front** is formed when a warm air mass enters an area of colder air. Again, the warmer air ascends, creating precipitation.
- An **occluded front** occurs when a cold air mass (which generally moves more quickly than a warmer mass of air due to its higher density) overtakes a moving mass of warm air near Earth's surface. As in other front systems, the coldest air remains near the ground, forcing the warmer air to rise.
- A **stationary front** forms when warm and cold air meet and neither air mass has the force to move the other. They remain stationary.

Wave Cyclones

A wave cyclone is a type of cyclone that forms at mid- to high-latitudinal regions. This kind of weather system forms at the boundary between dry polar air masses and humid tropical air masses, called a **polar front**. The cyclone forms, intensifies, and ebbs repeatedly in a low-pressure trough between the converging masses. Cyclonic motion begins with the initial contact between the two air masses; the motion of both air bodies intensifies. Then, when the colder mass overtakes and elevates the warmer one, an occluded front forms in the middle of the weather system. The polar front is then reestablished, and the process begins anew. **Wave cyclones** affect wind, temperature, cloud formation, and precipitation in the surface regions over which they occur.

TORNADOS

A tornado is a particularly intense cyclone, which may exhibit wind speeds of up to 400 miles per hour. **Tornadoes** often form alongside mid-latitude thunderstorms over continental North America; they are also commonly observed inside of tropical hurricanes. In fact, tornadoes are most often formed at a cold front where maritime polar air forces warm, moist tropical air upward. This type of cyclone is bred from **cumulonimbus clouds** moving ahead of a **cold front**. A dark funnel-shaped cloud extends downward from a dense cumulonimbus cloud. The funnel's base appears especially dense, due to the accumulating moisture, dust, and debris being swept up by the formation. When the base of a tornado makes landfall, it can be completely devastating.

Review Video: Tornadoes
Visit mometrix.com/academy and enter code: 540439

TROPICAL CYCLONES

A tropical cyclone is potentially the most destructive and dangerous type of cyclone. Such a formation is referred to as a **hurricane** when it occurs over the Atlantic Ocean or as a **typhoon** when it occurs over the Pacific or Indian Oceans. **Tropical cyclones** develop at low latitudes (specifically, between 8 and 15 degrees North or South latitude) when the surface waters below reach temperatures of 81 degrees Fahrenheit or above. From their zone of origination, tropical cyclones often travel westward through the trade-wind belt; westerly winds may push the storm northward as well. This type of cyclone is associated with high wind speeds and high levels of rainfall. A tropical cyclone also displays extremely low pressure in its center, or eye, where weather conditions are fair (in contrast to the rest of the storm). These weather systems occur seasonally: in the Northern Hemisphere, cyclonic activity is highest from May to November; in the Southern Hemisphere, the cyclone season is roughly the opposite.

TROPICAL AND EQUATORIAL WEATHER SYSTEM TERMS

An **easterly wave** is formed in the belt of tropical trades. This formation is a trough of low pressure, which travels slowly through the belt. Easterly waves occur above oceans at latitudes of 5 to 30 degrees North or South. The influence of surface winds forces the air in an easterly wave upward, causing light rainfall and occasional thunderstorms. A **weak equatorial low** is a disturbance that occurs near the center of an equatorial trough (area of low pressure). Moist air masses meet at this point, creating precipitation. A **polar outbreak** occurs when a small region of frigid polar air reaches low latitudes near the equator. This type of air mass enters a low-latitude region as a cold front, which is followed by clear but cold weather and strong winds. While polar outbreaks are not inherently dangerous, the low temperatures involved can damage crops in low-latitude regions.

FORMATION OF LIGHTNING

Lightning is a natural electrostatic discharge that produces light and releases electromagnetic radiation. It is believed that the separation of positive and negative charge carriers within a cloud is achieved by the **polarization mechanism**. The first step of this mechanism occurs when falling precipitation particles become electrically polarized after they move through Earth's magnetic field. The second step of the polarization mechanism involves **electrostatic induction**, the process whereby electrically charged particles create charges in other particles without direct contact. Ice particles are charged through this method, and then energy-storing electric fields are formed between the charged particles. The positively charged ice crystals tend to rise to the top of the cloud, effectively polarizing the cloud with positive charges on top and negative charges at the middle and bottom. When charged clouds conglomerate, an electric discharge (a **lightning bolt**) is produced, either between clouds or between a cloud and Earth's surface.

THUNDERSTORMS

A thunderstorm is a weather phenomenon that includes lightning, thunder, and usually large amounts of precipitation and strong winds. **Thunder** is the noise made by the rapid expansion and contraction of air due to the heat energy produced by lightning bolts. A **thunderstorm** develops when heating on Earth's surface causes large amounts of air to rise into an unstable atmosphere. This results in large clouds of rain and ice crystals. The associated condensation releases high levels of heat, which, in turn, power the **growth cycle** of the cloud. The clouds created during thunderstorms are immense, sometimes reaching widths of several miles and extending to heights of 10,000 meters or more. The precipitation in such clouds eventually becomes heavy enough to fall against the updraft of unstable air; the consequent downpour is often short but intense. The differential speeds at which light and sound travel through the atmosphere enable one to estimate the distance between oneself and the storm by observing the interval between a lightning bolt and a thunderclap.

CLIMATES

Climate is usually defined as the "average weather" in a particular area on Earth. The timespan over which **climate** is measured is variable, but it is generally accepted that the climate of an area does not vary during a human life span (though climate is extremely various in geologic time). This may change, however, due to the increasing greenhouse effect. Meteorologists measure climate by averaging certain quantifiable elements such as rainfall or temperature. Climate may be studied on several different scales:

- **Local climate** refers to the climate of small geographic areas (generally up to tens of miles wide). The local climate of an area is affected by things such as its location relative to an ocean and the presence of mountains near the location.
- A **regional climate** is the climate of a larger geographic area, such as a country. A regional climate may also be delineated due to climate features that are distinctive from the surrounding climate.
- **Global climate** refers to the average weather experienced across Earth.

CLIMATE ZONES

Climate zones are areas of regional climate. These zones are created by the general circulation of the air in Earth's atmosphere. Generally, the warmest air moves from the equator (where the greatest amount of solar energy is received) toward the higher latitudes at the poles. The **latitudinal temperature gradient** produces atmospheric pressure. At the equator, solar energy heats air near the surface, causing it to rise and decreasing air pressure. The risen air is transported by winds to cooler areas at higher latitudes, where the air then descends (because cool air is heavier than warmer air), creating an area of high pressure. The descended air is then moved by surface winds, either back to the equator or up to higher latitudes, where it encounters colder air. The air then rises again in an area of low pressure. The air in polar regions is very cold, which causes it to sink, creating high pressure. Winds are thus generated to move air from warmer regions to colder ones.

The **tropical** (low-latitude) **climate zone** covers the area around the equator. This area receives a large portion of the Sun's solar energy, making average temperatures in this zone fairly high. The consistent levels of hot air in the region indicate that air is often moving upward. This convective process, in turn, produces large levels of precipitation in the area, resulting in a humid climate. Seasons in the tropical zone are delineated by the amount of rainfall, instead of by changes in temperatures. **Subtropical** (mid-latitude) **climate zones** are found about thirty degrees north and south of the equator. These zones generally consist of dry descending air, clear skies, and high atmospheric pressure. Desert climates (extreme heat during the day, cold temperatures at night, and lack of precipitation) are common in these zones. **Polar** (high-latitude) **climate zones** are found at the north and south poles. They are characterized by high air pressure (due to descending air), low temperatures (rarely above freezing), and lack of precipitation (because air cannot evaporate from frozen water).

Review Video: Climates
Visit mometrix.com/academy and enter code: 991320

Maritime, Continental, and Temperate Climates

Maritime climates are greatly affected by airflow from nearby oceans. This influence prevents extreme temperatures in such regions, which normally experience cool summers and mild winters. Also, **maritime climates** are usually quite humid, with large amounts of precipitation. **Continental climates**, unlike maritime climates, experience variations in temperature with changes in seasons (i.e., cold winters and hot summers). This is so because rock and soil have lower heat capacities than water, which serves to moderate ambient temperatures. Continental climates are usually relatively dry. A **temperate climate** is one with low variation in average temperature. Temperate climates may be maritime or continental.

Influence of Mountains on Climate

At the level of local climate, the presence of **mountains** forces air to rise in order to travel above them; this contributes to increased formation of clouds and consequently increases in levels of precipitation. **Mountain chains** can affect regional and even global climates by deflecting airflow. The **Coriolis force** causes most of Earth's atmospheric airflow to move east and west. Therefore, the presence of north-south-oriented mountain chains can forcibly alter general circulation patterns. For example, the Rocky Mountains in western North America force air to move northward; the air cools near the North Pole before blowing back down. This causes winter temperatures in Canada and parts of the United States to be very cold.

Effect of Atmosphere and Hydrosphere Interactions on Climate

The **hydrosphere** (all the water on Earth), specifically the oceans, stores much higher quantities of heat energy than the **atmosphere** is able to hold. Energy in the oceans, like energy in the atmosphere, is transferred around the globe, redistributing heat from areas of low latitudes to areas of high latitudes. Water on the surface of the ocean is driven by atmospheric wind patterns. Energy transfers between the oceans and the atmosphere effect temperatures and precipitation in regions across the globe. For example, the Gulf Stream is an ocean current that exerts an important influence on the climates of the United Kingdom and northwest Europe. This surface current originates in the Gulf of Mexico and carries warm water (about 25 degrees Celsius) northeast across the Atlantic at speeds of three miles per hour. When the ocean cools down at night, it releases warm air, regulating the temperatures of the regions mentioned above. Without the activity of the Gulf Stream, those regions would be as cold as Canada (which is at roughly the same latitude).

Earth's Ozone Layer

Earth's ozone layer is the region of the stratosphere with a high concentration of ozone (a form of oxygen) particles. These molecules are formed through the process of **photolysis**, which occurs when ultraviolet light from the Sun collides with oxygen molecules (O2) in the atmosphere. The ultraviolet radiation splits the oxygen atoms apart; when a free oxygen atom strikes an oxygen molecule, it combines with the molecule to create an ozone particle (O3). Ozone molecules may be broken down by interaction with nitrogen-, chlorine-, and hydrogen-containing compounds, or by thermal energy from the Sun. Under normal conditions, these creative and destructive processes balance the levels of ozone in the stratosphere. The concentration of ozone molecules in the atmosphere absorbs **ultraviolet radiation**, thus preventing this harmful energy from reaching Earth's surface. Ozone particles form in the region of the atmosphere over the equator, which receives the most direct sunlight. Atmospheric winds then disperse the particles throughout the rest of the stratosphere.

Divergent Plate Boundary

A divergent, or constructive, plate boundary exists when two adjacent plates move away from one another. Observation of activity at **diverging boundaries** has provided unquestionable proof of the seafloor-spreading hypothesis. At this type of plate boundary, kinetic energy generated by asthenospheric convection cells cracks the lithosphere and pushes molten magma through the space left by separating **tectonic plates**. This magma cools and hardens, creating a new piece of Earth's crust. In the oceanic lithosphere, diverging plate boundaries form a series of rifts known as the **oceanic ridge system**. The Mid-Atlantic Ridge is a consequence of undersea diverging boundaries. At divergent boundaries on the continental lithosphere, plate movement results in **rift valleys**, typified by the East African Rift Valley.

Transform Plate Boundary

A transform (conservative) plate boundary exists when two tectonic plates slide past each other laterally and in opposite directions. Due to the rocky composition of lithospheric plates, this motion causes the plates to grind against each other. **Friction** causes stress to build when the plates stick; this potential energy is finally released when the built-up pressure exceeds the slipping point of the rocks on the two plates. This sudden release of energy causes **earthquakes**. This type of plate boundary is also referred to as a **strike-slip fault**. The San Andreas fault in California is the most famous example of such a boundary.

Review Video: Plate Tectonic Theory
Visit mometrix.com/academy and enter code: 535013

Types of Geologic Faults

A geologic fault is a fracture in Earth's surface created by movement of the crust. The majority of faults are found along **tectonic plate boundaries**; however, smaller faults have been identified at locations far from these boundaries. There are three types of geologic faults, which are named for the original direction of movement along the active fault line. The landforms on either side of a fault are called the **footwall** and the **hanging wall**, respectively. In a **normal fault**, the hanging wall moves downward relative to the footwall. A **reverse fault** is the opposite of a normal fault; the hanging wall moves upward relative to the footwall. The dip of a reverse fault is usually quite steep; when the dip is less than 45 degrees, the fault is called a thrust fault. In the third type of geologic fault, the **strike-slip fault**, the dip is virtually nonexistent, and the rocks on either side move horizontally left (sinistral) or right (dextral). A transform plate boundary is a specific instance of a strike-slip fault.

Humidity and Cloud Cover

Humidity is a measure of the amount of water vapor in the air. **Specific humidity** is the expression of humidity as a ratio of aqueous vapor to dry air; it is expressed as a ratio of mass of water vapor per unit mass of natural (dry) air. **Absolute humidity** measures the mass of water vapor in a given volume of moist air or gas; it is expressed in grams per cubic foot or per cubic meter. The equilibrium (or saturated) vapor pressure of a gas is the vapor pressure (created by the movement of molecules) of water vapor when air is saturated with water vapor. **Relative humidity**, usually expressed as a percentage, is the ratio of the vapor pressure of water in air (or another gas) to the equilibrium vapor pressure. In other words, it is a ratio of the mass of water per volume of gas and the mass per volume of a saturated gas. **Cloud cover** refers to the amount of sky blocked by clouds at a given location.

Subdiscipline of Physical Geography

Physical geography is the scientific study of life environments. These environments exist in the life layer, the space where the four realms—the **atmosphere** (the layer of gases that surrounds Earth), the **hydrosphere** (the water on Earth), the **lithosphere** (the solid part of Earth), and the **biosphere** (life on Earth)—interact. The life layer encompasses the lower atmosphere and the upper lithosphere, where land and water bodies meet. The science of physical geography examines systems and cycles within the life layer; these continuous processes cause modifications in the life layer (in different areas and on different time scales), thereby creating Earth's diverse physical environments.

Systems in Physical Geography

In physical geography, the term *system* is used to refer to the processes that operate to modify and diversify various physical environments. **Physical systems** are usually natural flow systems, in which something (such as energy, water, or a chemical element) moves along one or more pathways from one place to another due to a natural power source. A system may be **open**, in which case matter enters and exits the system. All **energy systems** are open. A system may also be **closed**. Closed systems are referred to as cycles; in these systems, no matter is inputted or outputted from the system. The hydrologic (water) cycle is an example of a closed system. Feedback is the mechanism by which the flow in one pathway influences the flow in another pathway. Positive feedback speeds up a process, while negative feedback retards a process. **Equilibrium** is the state of a system in which the flow rates on all the system's pathways are constant and nearly the same.

Earth's Layers

Earth consists of several layers. The three main layers are the core, the mantle, and the crust. The **crust** is the outermost layer of the planet Earth. It is located 0-35 kilometers below the surface. Earth's crust is composed mainly of basalt and granite. The crust is less dense, cooler, and more rigid than the planet's internal layers. This layer floats on top of the mantle. The **mantle** is located 35-2,890 kilometers below Earth's surface. It is separated from the crust by the Mohorovicic discontinuity, or Moho (which occurs at 30-70 kilometers below the continental crust and at 6-8 kilometers beneath the oceanic crust). The mantle is made up of rocks such as peridotite and eclogite; its temperature varies from 100 to 3,500 degrees Celsius. Material in the mantle cycles due to convection. The **core** is the innermost layer of Earth, which consists of two layers (a liquid outer layer and a solid inner layer). It is located 2,890-6,378 kilometers below the surface. The core is thought to be composed of iron and nickel and is the densest layer of Earth.

Earth's Sublayers

Earth also consists of several sublayers, including the lithosphere, the asthenosphere, and the mesosphere.

- The **lithosphere** consists of the crust and the uppermost portion of Earth's mantle. It is located 0-60 kilometers below the surface. The lithosphere is the cooling layer of the planet's convection cycle and thickens over time. This solid shell is fragmented into pieces called tectonic plates. The oceanic lithosphere is made up of mafic basaltic rocks and is thinner and generally denser than the continental lithosphere (composed of granite and sedimentary rock); the lithosphere floats atop Earth's mantle.
- The **asthenosphere** is the "soft," topmost layer of the mantle. It is located 100-700 kilometers below the surface. A combination of heat and pressure keeps the asthenosphere's composite material "plastic."
- The **mesosphere** is located 900-2,800 kilometers below the surface and therefore spans from the lower part of the mantle to the mantle-core boundary. The liquid outer core exists at 2,890-5,100 kilometers below surface level, and the solid inner core exists at depths of 5,100-6,378 kilometers.

Sources of Tectonic Plate Motion

The two main sources of tectonic plate motion are **gravity** and **friction**. The energy driving tectonic plate motion comes from the dissipation of heat from the mantle in the relatively weak asthenosphere. This energy is converted into gravity or friction to incite the motion of plates. Gravity is subdivided by geologists into ridge-push and slab-pull. In the phenomenon of **ridge-push**, the motion of plates is instigated by the energy that causes low-density material from the mantle to rise at an oceanic ridge. This leads to the situation of certain plates at higher elevations; gravity causes material to slide downhill. In **slab-pull**, plate motion is thought to be caused by cold, heavy plates at oceanic trenches sinking back into the mantle, providing fuel for future convection. Friction is subdivided into mantle drag and trench suction. **Mantle drag** suggests that plates move due to the friction between the lithosphere and the asthenosphere. **Trench suction** involves a downward frictional pull on oceanic plates in subduction zones due to convection currents.

Convergent Plate Boundaries

A convergent (destructive) plate boundary occurs when adjacent plates move toward one another. Earth's diameter remains constant over time. Therefore, the formation of new plate material at diverging plate boundaries necessitates the destruction of plate material elsewhere. This process occurs at **convergent** (destructive) **plate boundaries**. One plate slips underneath the other at a subduction zone. The results of converging plates vary, depending on the nature of the lithosphere in said plates. When two oceanic plates converge, they form a deep underwater trench. If each of the converging plates at a destructive boundary carries a continent, the light materials of the continental lithosphere enable both plates to float above the subduction area. They crumple and compress, creating a **mid-continent mountain range**. When a continental plate converges with an oceanic plate, the denser oceanic lithosphere slides beneath the continental lithosphere. The result of such convergence is an **oceanic trench** on one side and a **mountain range** on the other.

Fault Mechanics

Slip is a measurement of the net relative displacement of structural surfaces along a fault. **Dip** is the angle that a rock body or structural rock surface makes with the horizontal surface plane. True dip is quantified through downward measurement of the angle in the direction of greatest inclination; apparent dip is the measurement of dip in any direction. Dip is equal to zero in the direction of strike and has its maximum measurement in the direction of true dip. **Strike** is the direction of a line of intersection drawn between the horizontal surface plane and the surface of an uptilted rock structure.

Geologic Folding

A geologic fold is a region of curved or deformed stratified rocks. Folding is one process by which Earth's crust is deformed. **Rock strata** are normally formed horizontally; however, geologists have identified areas where these strata arc upward or downward. **Anticlines** are upfolded areas of rock; downfolds are called **synclines**. In anticlines, the rocks are oldest along the axis (a horizontal line drawn through the point of the fold's maximum curvature), and in synclines, the youngest rocks are at the axis. **Monoclines**, or flexures, are rock structures that slope in one direction only, and often pass into geologic fault lines. The process of folding usually occurs underneath Earth's surface, but surface erosion eventually exposes these formations. Folding is generally thought to be caused by the horizontal compression of Earth's surface, which is related to the movement of tectonic plates and fault activity.

Orogenesis

Orogenesis refers to mountain-building processes, specifically as they relate to the movement of tectonic plates. An individual **orogeny** can take millions of years. Generally, mountains are created when compressional forces push surface rock upward, resulting in a landform that is higher than the land around it. There are four broad categories of mountains (which are not mutually exclusive); these categories are based on the mountain's formative origin. **Folded mountains**, formed from the long-term deformation and metamorphosis of sedimentary and igneous rocks, usually occur in chains. This type of mountain often forms at convergent plate boundaries. **Fault-block mountains** occur at normal or reverse faults with high dips. Portions of Earth's crust are vertically displaced along the faults. **Oceanic ridges** are formed at divergent boundaries beneath the ocean. When plates move apart, material from the mantle rises and creates long mountain chains. **Volcanic mountains** form from the accumulation of products of volcanic eruptions, such as ash and lava. They often occur singularly, unlike other mountain types that usually exist in chains.

Volcanic Eruptions

A volcanic eruption generally entails a buildup of **magma** (a silicate solution formed of melted rocks) in a magma chamber. Gases present in the magma, such as water vapor, carbon dioxide, and sulfur dioxide, cause increasing pressure in the material. Often, the vent that would enable release of the built-up pressure is blocked by solidified magma. The viscosity of the magma also affects the release of gas pressure; the more viscous the magma, the more pressure will build up. A volcano **erupts** when the pressure becomes too great to be contained and the gases are suddenly and violently released. The freed gases expand, forcing magma and solid materials upward. The products of a volcanic eruption include ash, lava, and solid igneous rocks.

Volcanic Activities at Different Plate Boundaries

Volcanic activity occurs at **divergent plate boundaries** most often under the ocean. Divergent plate boundaries are also known as constructive plate boundaries because new crustal material must be formed to fill the void created by the separation of tectonic plates. As oceanic lithospheric plates pull apart, magma rises from beneath to fill the gap; the increased temperature and magma concentration breeds volcanic activity. At **convergent, or destructive, plate margins**, friction creates the heat energy necessary to melt crustal rocks into magma. Also, the subduction of one plate under another pushes crustal material into the mantle, where temperatures are higher. The presence of volatiles (such as water and carbon dioxide) at subduction zones can force magma out through vents in Earth's surface. Occasionally, volcanic activity occurs at locations far from any plate boundary. These locations, called **hotspots**, are thought to exist over particularly active mantle zones, which shoot "plumes" of molten material up toward the crust.

Earthquake

An earthquake is a sudden movement of a portion of Earth's crust. Strain energy, built up in the lithosphere, is swiftly released in the form of **seismic waves**, which, among other things, cause vibratory ground motion. The majority of these events occur at high-stress tectonic plate boundaries. The **rupture zone** is the total size of the fault that slips; the larger the rupture zone, the greater the effects of the earthquake. The **focus**, or hypocenter, of an earthquake is the location from which the seismic waves seem to emanate. The **epicenter** is the location on Earth's crust above an earthquake's hypocenter. Earthquakes are classified according to their focus depths: shallow (0-70 kilometers below the surface), intermediate (70-300 kilometers below the surface), or deep (below 300 kilometers deep).

Rock Cycle

The rock cycle is the process whereby the materials that make up Earth transition through the three types of rock: **igneous**, **sedimentary**, and **metamorphic**. Rocks, like all matter, cannot be created or destroyed; rather, they undergo a series of changes and adopt different forms through the functions of the rock cycle. **Plate tectonics** and the **water cycle** are the driving forces behind the rock cycle; they force rocks and minerals out of equilibrium and force them to adjust to different external conditions. Viewed in a generalized, cyclical fashion, the rock cycle operates as follows: Rocks beneath Earth's surface melt into magma. This magma either erupts through volcanoes or remains inside the Earth. Regardless, the magma cools, forming igneous rocks. On the surface, these rocks experience weathering and erosion, which break them down and distribute the fragments across the surface. These fragments form layers and eventually become sedimentary rocks. Sedimentary rocks are then either transformed into metamorphic rocks (which will become magma inside the Earth) or melted down into magma.

Formation of Igneous Rocks

Igneous rocks can be formed from sedimentary rocks, metamorphic rocks, or other igneous rocks. Rocks that are pushed under Earth's surface (usually due to plate subduction) are exposed to high mantle temperatures, which cause the rocks to melt into magma. The magma then rises to the surface through volcanic processes. The lower atmospheric temperature causes the magma to cool, forming grainy, extrusive igneous rocks. The creation of **extrusive**, or volcanic, rocks is quite rapid. The cooling process can occur so rapidly that crystals do not form; in this case, the result is a glass, such as obsidian. It is also possible for magma to cool down in Earth's interior; this type of igneous rock is called **intrusive**. Intrusive, or plutonic, rocks cool more slowly, resulting in a coarse-grained texture.

Formation of Sedimentary Rocks

Sedimentary rocks are formed when rocks on Earth's surface experience weathering and erosion, which break them down and distribute the fragments across the surface. Fragmented material (small pieces of rock, organic debris, and the chemical products of mineral sublimation) is deposited and accumulates in layers, with top layers burying the materials beneath. The pressure exerted by the topmost layers causes the lower layers to compact, creating solid sedimentary rock in a process called **lithification**.

Formation of Metamorphic Rocks

Metamorphic rocks are igneous or sedimentary rocks that have "morphed" into another kind of rock. In metamorphism, high temperatures and levels of pressure change preexisting rocks physically and/or chemically, which produces different species of rocks. In the rock cycle, this process generally occurs in materials that have been thrust back into Earth's mantle by plate subduction. **Regional metamorphism** refers to a large band of metamorphic activity; this often occurs near areas of high orogenic (mountain-building) activity. **Contact metamorphism** refers to metamorphism that occurs when "country rock" (that is, rock native to an area) comes into contact with high-heat igneous intrusions (magma).

Review Video: Igneous, Sedimentary, and Metamorphic Rocks
Visit mometrix.com/academy and enter code: 689294

Plate Tectonics Rock Cycle

The plate tectonics rock cycle expands the concept of the traditional rock cycle to include more specific information about the tectonic processes that propel the rock cycle, as well as an evolutionary component. Earth's materials do not cycle endlessly through the different rock forms; rather, these transitive processes cause, for example, increasing diversification of the rock types found in the crust. Also, the cycling of rock increases the masses of continents by increasing the volume of granite. Thus the **tectonic rock cycle** is a model of an evolutionary rock cycle. In this model, new oceanic lithosphere is created at divergent plate boundaries. This new crust spreads outward until it reaches a subduction zone, where it is pushed back into the mantle, becomes magma, and is thrust out into the atmosphere. It experiences erosion and becomes sedimentary rock. At convergent continental plate boundaries, this crust is involved in mountain building and the associated metamorphic pressures. It is eroded again and returns to the lithosphere.

Role of Water in Cycling of Earth Materials

Water plays an important role in the **rock cycle** through its roles in erosion and weathering: it wears down rocks, it contributes to the dissolution of rocks and minerals as acidic soil water, and it carries ions and rock fragments (sediments) to basins where they will be compressed into sedimentary rock. Water also plays a role in the **metamorphic processes** that occur underwater in newly formed igneous rock at mid-ocean ridges. The presence of water (and other volatiles) is a vital component in the melting of rocky crust into magma above subduction zones.

Weathering Terms

The rocks on Earth's surface experience physical, biological, and chemical processes that are much different from the processes ambient during their formations. The operation of these processes on Earth materials is called weathering.

- **Mechanical weathering** causes disintegration of rocks and minerals. In this process, the affected rocks break apart into small fragments but retain their chemical compositions. This type of weathering occurs due to the presence of joints, or cracks, in rocks that allow the penetration of water and vegetative roots. Mechanical weathering occurs most often in cooler climates.
- **Chemical weathering** refers to the processes by which rocks experience chemical changes (such as decomposition and decay) due to the influence of organic acids. Chemical weathering occurs most often in high-temperature, high-humidity climates. The two types of weathering are not mutually exclusive; they often occur side by side.
- **Erosion** also occurs simultaneously with weathering. This term refers to the transportation of Earth materials by wind, water, gravity, and sometimes living organisms.

SUBTYPES OF MECHANICAL WEATHERING

The subtypes of mechanical weathering are pressure release, exfoliation, freeze-thaw, and salt-crystal growth.

- **Pressure release**, or surface unloading, occurs when erosion removes materials overlying rock. Decreased pressure causes the underlying rocks to expand and fracture.
- **Exfoliation** often occurs in regions with some moisture that experience substantial diurnal temperature changes. Rocks are subjected to heat during the day, which causes them to expand. At night, the much cooler temperatures cause the rocks to compact. The repeated expansion and contraction creates stress in the outer layers of the rocks, which eventually begin to "peel" off in thin layers. Exfoliation can also be caused by pressure release.
- **Freeze-thaw** operates when water, which has penetrated the joints of a rock, freezes and expands. The resultant pressure widens the joints and can even shatter the rock. If the rock does not fracture, the thawing of ice in the joints admits water further into the rock. Continuous, long-term freeze-thaw activity weakens rocks.
- In **salt-crystal growth**, the evaporation of saline solutions within rocks leaves salt crystals behind. Pressures accompanying this crystallization can be very high.

SUBTYPES OF CHEMICAL WEATHERING

The subtypes of chemical weathering are hydration, hydrolysis, oxidation, and solution.

- **Hydration** occurs when salt minerals, which are part of a rock, expand and change due to the absorption of water. For example, anhydrite changes to gypsum with the addition of water. Hydration can cause rocks to fragment mechanically.
- **Hydrolysis** involves a chemical reaction between acidic water and a rock-forming mineral. The interaction breaks the rock down into new materials. For instance, the chemical reaction between feldspar and acidic water produces quartz and clay.
- **Oxidation**, or rusting, which results in yellow, brown, or red discoloration, occurs in iron-bearing minerals when they are exposed to the atmosphere.
- **Solution** is the weathering process whereby an organic acid interacts with certain minerals in a rock, producing ions that are then washed away by erosion. Solution, therefore, is a gradual dissolving process. It produces underground channels and caverns.

MASS MOVEMENT

A mass movement (also called mass wasting) is the downward movement of large amounts of rock and debris due to gravitational forces. The speed at which the material will move and the amount of dislodged material are affected by several factors: the amount of water in the affected material, the climate, the type and extent of weathering, the steepness of the incline, the presence or absence of rooted vegetation, the type of bedrock present and its condition, and the presence or absence of seismic activity. **Mass movements** cause changes in the landscape of an area. They can also place humans and animals in the affected area in danger.

ROCKFALL

A rockfall is a mass movement wherein various amounts of rock material fall very rapidly (at speeds of 99 miles per hour or more) from a cliff face. This movement may involve a single rock or boulder or may spur an avalanche of tons of rock. The pile of rocks that results from a rockfall is termed a **talus**. When it occurs at a mountain base, a talus may prevent weathering of the mountain. A **rockfall** may be triggered by an earthquake, excessive rain, ice wedging (common on mountains), or human activity. Such a mass movement may, in turn, spawn an **avalanche**, a rockfall that contributes to a debris flow. The materials in motion in a rockfall often leave "scars" on the slope from which they fall.

Landslide

The term *landslide* may be used to designate several different downslope movements. Normally, a **landslide** involves the movement of soil and rock as a more or less coherent mass down a slope, although either the bedrock itself or the soil which overlays it may move independently. There are two main categories of landslides. **Glides**, or translational slides, entail a large portion of rock detached from its bedrock "gliding" outward and downward along a slope. A **slump** (or rotational slide) involves the motion of a relatively cohesive mass along a concave plane; the upper part of the sliding mass ends up below ground level, and the bottom part of the mass ends up above it.

Flow

Flow is a type of mass movement that entails viscous motion of surface materials. **Flows** are characterized by motion of the internal grains of the moving mass (unlike slides). Also, they do not include a clear barrier between the flow material and a stable surface underneath. The velocity of a flow is widely various, dependent on the slope upon which it travels and the presence or absence of water. Flows generally involve one of three types of material: earth, mud, or debris. An **earthflow** is often initiated at the end of a slump slide, when the block of sliding material breaks apart. A **mud flow** involves the motions of soil and relatively high proportions of water. Increased water content increases the velocity of the moving mass from that of an earthflow. Mudflows are common in deserts. A **debris flow** is similar to a mudflow; often, the only distinction between the two is the size of the particles in motion. The motions of both debris flows and mudflows tend to follow pre-existing channels.

Creep

Creep is another landscape-altering mass movement. It involves a shallow mass of soil material moving slowly downward. This type of movement usually occurs so slowly that no one notices it. **Creep** can be caused by freeze-thaw or wet-dry cycles, depending on the characteristics of the bedrock materials. As with other types of mass movements, the introduction of high amounts of water into creep material will cause it to move more quickly. Though creep does not pose an immediate threat to human or animal life, it can be dangerous through long-term effects on tree roots and the foundations of buildings or other structures.

Solifluction

Solifluction is an intensified form of creep. The existence of permafrost (a layer of earth that remains in a long-term state of freeze that occurs in very cold climates) prevents absorption of surface water. The excess water then enters the topmost "active" layer of soil. That layer is thus more vulnerable to the process of creep than a comparable layer of soil in a warmer climate because of its increased fluidity and the frozen surface over which it slides. **Solifluction** tends to result in a "wrinkled" landscape with smooth terrain.

Erosion Landform

An erosion landform is a landform created by the processes of weathering and erosion. For example, a cliff is an **erosion landform**. Cliffs are formed when relatively strong rocks are exposed to centuries of wind and water, weathering, and erosion. Sandstone, limestone, and basalt are examples of rocks that commonly become cliffs. A **canyon** provides the classic instance of an erosion landform. Canyons are formed from many years of weathering and erosion processes (often water-based), usually operating on a plateau (a mountain that has been eroded down to a flat but elevated surface). Strata of rocks that resisted the destructive processes remain visible in the canyon walls.

Stream Deposition

Stream deposition is the last phase in the weathering and erosion process performed by water, specifically streams. **Stream erosion** occurs when the movement of water in a stream detaches material from the sides and bottom of the channel through which it flows. This can carve out valleys and wide, meandering streams. Streams then carry the weathered material, as well as material deposited in the stream by other erosive processes, out to sea. Streams transport sediment in three ways:

- The **solid load** consists of the suspended load (sediment grains of various sizes floating in the water) and the bed load (the materials dragged along the bed of a channel by the moving water).
- The **bed load** performs much of the erosion of the sides and bottoms of the channel.
- A stream's **dissolved load** is composed of ions produced in the chemical weathering process.
- **Stream deposition** occurs when the stream drops its load of sediment. This can occur due to flooding or intersection of the stream with a larger body of water.

Landscape Evolution Terms

The movement of water in streams and rivers plays a key role in **landscape evolution**. The long-term effect of rivers and streams is to erode the land around them down to sea level, the base level of erosion. There are several theories as to how this occurs:

- **Backwasting** entails the wearing down of river valley slopes parallel to themselves. When the surface between valley slopes is worn down to the base level of erosion, the slopes retreat in parallel layers until all of the land above the widening platform is eroded to the same level.
- **Downwasting** is another theoretical process that explains landscape evolution. This process involves the diminishing of valley slopes through mass movements of soil and rock decomposition.
- A **peneplain** is the result of the erosive process of the land around streams. It is a wide, nearly flat plain of bedrock that exists just above the base level of erosion.
- A **monadnock** is an anomalous portion of especially tenacious rock that rises above a peneplain.

Coriolis Force

The Coriolis force, which gives rise to the Coriolis effect, is not really a force at all. Rather, we experience it only because Earth is a rotating frame of reference that we are observing from. In the atmosphere, air tends to move from areas of low pressure to areas of higher pressure. This air would move in a straight line, but the **Coriolis force** appears to deflect the air and cause it to swirl. Earth actually moves underneath the wind, which creates the impression of swirling air to someone standing on Earth's surface. The Coriolis force causes winds to appear to swirl to the right as they approach the Northern Hemisphere, and to the left as they approach the Southern Hemisphere.

Geomorphology

Geomorphology is a subdiscipline of physical geography. Geomorphologists study the origins and formative processes of **landforms**. Observation of weathering and erosion processes, the movement of tectonic plates, mass movements, and the effects of human activity on the environment all contribute to an understanding of the formation and evolution of landforms. Aerial photography (from within Earth's atmosphere or from space) can aid geomorphologists in their quests. Photos taken at intervals allow them to study, for example, the creative and destructive events that occur at plate boundaries. Landscape photography also enables geomorphologists to observe long-term processes of stream erosion. Geomorphology can be applied to the prediction and prevention of natural hazards such as landslides; it can also be helpful in assessing and rectifying damage to the natural environment by humans.

Chapter Quiz

Ready to see how well you retained what you just read? Scan the QR code to go directly to the chapter quiz interface for this study guide. If you're using a computer, simply visit the online resources page at **mometrix.com/resources719/dssthumculgeog** and click the Chapter Quizzes link.

Spatial Patterns of Culture

Push/Pull Factors

Push and pull factors are features of regions that cause people to want to leave or move to a particular region. **Push factors** are those that encourage residents to depart an area; they are viewed as negative aspects of a region. There are several common factors that "push" people from, for example, rural to urban areas: overpopulation and overgrazing result in scarce resources, which decreases income levels; agricultural endeavors are subject to unpredictable and sometimes harsh physical forces (such as drought or flooding); the possible lack of health and educational services so far from a downtown district; and mechanization of agricultural labor may decrease the number of available jobs. The perceived **pull factors** of urban areas also contribute to urbanization: utilities such as water and electricity may make housing more comfortable, theoretically increasing a migrant's quality of life; food sources are ostensibly more reliable in urban areas than in agricultural rural areas; there are more job opportunities in larger urban regions; and more goods and services are available for purchase in cities.

Population Density

Population density is a measurement of the population per unit (usually miles or kilometers squared). **Population density** may be an indicator of economic development; however, this is not so for many less economically developed countries. There are several factors that commonly influence population density:

- The level of **industrial activity** in an area affects the area's population; major industrial areas provide many job opportunities, which draw people into the region, increasing population density. The climate of a region also affects its population density, as people generally gravitate toward temperate climates rather than extremely cold or hot areas.
- **Urbanization** affects population density in that people often move into cities where resources, services, and employment are readily available because they no longer have to work in agriculture.
- **Natural disaster areas** influence population density as well. Although potential danger exists for residents of these regions, many large population centers are located in or near them; often, this occurs for historical or agricultural reasons. For example, the byproducts of volcanic eruptions can create extremely fertile soil.

Effect of Environmental Factors on Patterns of Human Settlement

Site factors are those taken into consideration by humans in the selection of an ideal location to create a settlement. There are several environmental characteristics weighed by settlers deciding where to place their communities. While many of these factors were more important in the pre-modern past, many of them are still relevant today. **Water supply** is an important site factor. Used for drinking, washing, cooking, and agriculture, settlements cannot thrive without a consistent, adequate supply of water. Settling in an area prone to flooding or on marshy land can also be dangerous for budding towns. Though modern settlements do not rely singularly on natural sources for water supplies, it is still important for communities to be within piping distance of a central water source. A related factor is the proximity of **rivers** to an area. In addition to drinking water, rivers provide transportation or act as natural boundaries. **Aspect** is the direction a site faces; this affects the amount of direct sunlight in an area, which affects temperature and agriculture.

Self-Governing Political Entities

A **country** is a geographical territory. Many countries are independent entities, with their own governments, constitutions, militaries, and tax regulations; however, some are non-sovereign (which means they are governed by a separate government), and some have an overseas dependency (which means that they control the government of a separate country).

A **state** is a political entity that inhabits a specific geographical territory. States have independent governments, through which they exercise internal and external sovereignty. Some social thinkers have offered alternate conceptualizations of a state. For example, Max Weber defined *state* as "a human community that (successfully) claims the monopoly of the legitimate use of physical force within a given territory."

A **nation** is a cultural entity. Historically, the term has been used to refer to a group of people who share a commonality in ethnic ancestry, descent, or parentage. The criteria used to identify members of a nation are widely variable. A state that is recognized as a nation's "homeland" is called a nation-state.

Subdiscipline of Political Geography

Political geography (sometimes referred to as geopolitics) is the branch of geographic study that focuses on the spatial implications of power relations. In other words, political geographers investigate the relationships between political and social power, and geographic location and space. **Geopolitics** examines, among other things, the delineation of Earth's surface into nations, states, cities, and so on, as well as regional alliances, the locations of bases of political power, and the spatial relationships of different areas to central regions. The study of **political geography** can be useful at international, national, and metropolitan levels.

Hegemony

Hegemony is a continuous process whereby a dominant group exercises ideological control over other subordinate groups. By influencing the shared belief and value systems of others, the dominant group attempts to naturalize its own beliefs in other groups. The process of **hegemonic establishment** may or may not involve force or the threat of force; in fact, hegemony is more effective when it exists as a mixture of control (on the part of the dominant group) and consent (on the part of the subordinate group(s)). In practice, hegemony serves to empower certain religious beliefs, ethnic groups, political ideologies, economic systems, and cultural practices; this marginalizes alternative beliefs and practices. The creation of hegemony is both a method of attaining power and a means to maintain that power. Theories of hegemony attempt to explain the ways that dominant groups (referred to as **hegemons**) coerce members of non-dominant groups to accept and internalize the social, cultural, political, and economic norms of the former.

Civil War

A civil war is a conflict that occurs between antagonistic groups in the same country or empire; each faction wishes to secure control of the affairs of the state. Like any conflict, a **civil war** may take place due to differing political or religious views among members of the warring groups, an unequal distribution of wealth among citizens of a country, racial or ethnic prejudices, or the desires of revolutionary groups to change the social organization of a country. For example, the **Nigerian Civil War** (1967-1970) was bred from religious, political, and ethnic tensions between the Hausa, Yoruba, and Igbo peoples. The political boundaries of Nigeria had been created by

European colonial powers with no regard for previously existent cultural boundaries, sparking conflict between the indigenous groups. The **Irish Civil War** (1922-1923) occurred between supporters and opponents of a treaty that created an Irish state (excluding the six counties of Northern Ireland). This state was described as "free" but was actually a non-sovereign dominion of the British Empire.

Causes of Historic International Wars

An international war is a violent conflict between two or more independent states. Such conflicts frequently occur as a result of competition over land, resources, and/or sovereignty. Throughout the late 19th and early 20th centuries, many of the era's great powers competed for colonial territory and trading rights in Eastern Asia. The **Russo-Japanese War** (1904-1905) was fought between Russian and Japanese forces for imperial control of Manchuria and Korea (specifically, the Liaodong Peninsula). The Japanese victory in 1905 marked the first time an Asian country had defeated a European country, and firmly established Japan as a formidable global power. The **Arab-Israeli conflict**, an extended conflict dating back to the late 1800s, is an example of international animosity based on differences in political and religious ideologies. The spectrum of points of view among members of the concerned parties problematizes any simple definition of the cause of the conflict. However, reasons cited for the conflict tend to relate to hostilities between Muslims and Jews and the dispute over Israel's right to self-determination.

Measures of Economic Development

Geographers examine several characteristics of a country in the determination of that country's level of **economic development**.

- A country's per capita **gross national product** (GNP), the total value of all final goods and services (those provided directly to consumers) produced per person in a year, is taken into account. The higher a nation's GNP, the more developed it is assumed to be.
- The annual **population growth** of a country also serves as a measure of its economic development. Generally, poorer countries have relatively rapid rates of population growth.
- The **occupational structure** of a country's labor force (the proportions of people working in the primary, secondary, and tertiary sectors of industry) is considered. In MDCs, most workers participate in tertiary activities; in LDCs, most workers participate in primary activities.
- A country's level of **urbanization** (the proportion of a country's total population living in urban areas) is seen as progress in the process of economic development, as urban areas often provide specialized job opportunities and services.

Subdiscipline of Human Geography

Human geography is the subdiscipline of geography that involves the identification and analysis of the ways humans interact with the physical Earth. It focuses particularly on the causes and effects of the **spatial distributions of humans and human activity** on the planet's surface. **Human geography** draws upon cultural, economic, political, and social data about particular regions to reveal patterns about the ways human beings interact with their environments. This field of study includes several subdisciplines that focus on certain aspects of human life, such as medical geography, feminist geography, military geography, and religion geography. While the focal point of human geography is human activity, it is impossible to discuss such activity without knowledge of the physical landscape upon which it occurs.

Population and Demography

Population refers to the conglomeration of people or organisms of a certain species in a particular area. This variable is especially important in the study of human geography, which deals with (among other things) changes in the **population** of a region and why those changes occur.

Demography is the study of human populations. This field examines the characteristics of a population, such as its size and distribution, the way it changes over time, and the religions, ethnicities, and languages of members of the population. The term *demographic* refers to specific population attributes, especially as used in marketing or opinion research.

Terms

- A **standard of living** is a quantitative and qualitative assessment of the material goods and services available to members of a society. It is often measured through observation of the average yearly income per person (adjusted for inflation); however, variables such as the literacy rate and cultural resources of a society may also be taken into account in the estimation of that society's standard of living.
- The **gross national product** (GNP) of a country is defined as the aggregate value of all goods and services generated by a society in a particular year. When the GNP is divided by the population of the country, the per-capita GNP is revealed.
- The **literacy rate** of a society is the percentage of people in that society who can read and write.
- **Population density** is defined as the number of people per specified unit of area.
- The **life expectancy** of a society is the average lifespan of people living in that society.
- The **birth rate** of a society refers to the number of births per 1,000 people in that society. This figure, usually expressed as the crude birth rate (CBR), is calculated without consideration of the sex or age of the population.
- The **death rate** of a society is figured in the same manner but with regard to deaths rather than births and is expressed as the crude death rate (CDR).
- The **fertility rate** of a society is the average number of children which would be born by a woman during her "childbearing" years. Replacement fertility is the fertility level at which women on the average are birthing just enough children to "replace" themselves and their partners in the population.
- **Population momentum** is the phenomenon whereby a society's population persists after the attainment of replacement fertility. This occurs at the end of Stage 3 in the demographic transition model, due to the relatively high concentration of people of the same age in their "childbearing" years.

Delineation of the Developed/Developing World

The terms *developed world* and *developing world*, when used in human geography and related fields, have a few different definitions. One common delineator is based on education and technology levels in a given country.

The **developed world** refers to those regions of the planet where people were able to cultivate natural and human resources using technology made available by the Scientific Revolution. Developed countries had direct access to the tools and information discovered in this era. These regions share several characteristics. For one, people living in developed countries are generally well-educated and highly literate. Public education systems are relatively sophisticated, and young people spend many years in a structured school environment. Education of a developed society's youth is often seen as a precious human resource. Countries of the developed world also display low rates of population growth; some are experiencing negative growth. Another characteristic of the developed world is that most people work in the service or manufacturing industries (as opposed to the agricultural industry).

The **developing world** refers to regions in which the advancements offered by the Scientific Revolution were either slow to arrive or ignored by the inhabitants. Today, many countries are attempting to **modernize**; however, the process is very expensive and people in developing regions have relatively little money. Several characteristics distinguish this part of the world from the developed countries. For example, many people in developing societies have not had time to receive thorough educations because they must work from a very young age. This means that literacy rates are often much lower in developing countries than in developed countries.

Malthusian Catastrophe

The Malthusian Catastrophe (also referred to as the Malthusian Disaster, Dilemma, or Crisis) is the prediction by English political scientist and demographer **Thomas Malthus** (1766-1834) that the **world population** would eventually surpass the **global food supply**. Malthus's relatively pessimistic views were developed as a rebuttal to the hopeful theorizing of his peers. For one, Malthus believed that the global population would increase exponentially unless methods to check such growth were implemented. He felt that after a certain point, society would return to subsistence-level food production (the level at which people consume only enough food to survive), due to a decrease in the amount of available nourishment per person. Obviously, this catastrophe has not yet come to pass. Malthus underestimated the rate at which agricultural and economic production would increase with technological, scientific, and industrial advancements in those fields. Also, the rate of global population expansion has not undergone continuous growth, as evidenced by the demographic transition model.

Phases of the Demographic Transition Model

The demographic transition model is a representation of changes in population in industrial societies, created by demographer Warren Thompson. This model describes variations (transitions) in birth and death rates in developed nations over the past 200 years. The **demographic transition model** encompasses four transitional phases.

- **Stage 1** is associated with premodern (that is, preindustrialized) society; it characterizes most regions of the world through the 17th century. In this stage (the high stationary stage), birth and death rates are high and nearly equivalent, indicating that population growth is slow. The second stage in the demographic transition model is differentiated by a sharp increase in a society's population due to a dramatic decrease in the death rate. This transition occurred in the late 18th century in Western Europe and spread outward.
- **Stage 2** is associated with advances in public health such as the creation of food handling regulations and sewage disposal, as well as advances in agricultural practices (including crop rotation) that helped to create a stable food source.
- **Stage 3** of the demographic transition model involves a decrease in a society's birth rate (following the rapid population growth in Stage 2). Most developed nations entered this phase late in the 19th century. Many hypotheses have been advanced to explain this phenomenon. For example, some have suggested that the decline in birth rates observed in developed societies is related to urbanization, which dilutes the high value traditionally placed on fertility; also, the costs attendant to urbanization make it less financially desirable for a family to have many children. The decline in birth rates has also been said to relate to medical advancements that decreased the rate of childhood mortality, or to improvements in contraceptive technology (though this occurred later, in the second half of the 20th century).

- In **Stage 4** of the demographic transition model, the populations of societies are either stable or declining. After the decline in birth rates, the general population grows older. If the fertility rate dips below replacement, the population experiences a rapid decline.

Developed vs. Less-Developed Societies

An alternate demographic transition model exists that applies demographic analysis to less-developed nations. There are several differences between the transitions observed in more-developed countries and those observed in less-developed countries, two of which include the following:

- Less-developed societies experienced a more pronounced **decrease in death rates** (about 50 years, as compared to 150 years in more-developed societies) in Stage 2 of the transition model. This is so because of medical advancements as well as increases in the female literacy rate (behavioral changes) due to exposure to more-developed countries. Rather than being "(re)discovered," this type of information was imported by less-developed countries and quickly applied.
- Less-developed societies experienced a **later** (20th century) **Stage 3 transition** (decline in birth rates). This difference stems from the fact that the technological advancements which accompanied the decline of birth rates in more-developed societies were unavailable in less-developed societies at the time.

Human Settlements

A human settlement is defined as any area inhabited by humans. The term may refer to a newly established region of residency for a group of people, or it may refer to a single home. Settlements are described as **nucleated** if residents live very closely together; settlements are described as **dispersed** when people live separately. A village is an example of an agglomerated rural settlement, in which people reside together in small groups. There are several different general types of settlements. The **temporary residences** set up by nomadic peoples (those constantly traveling due to their pastoral responsibilities, or in search of employment or food) constitute a type of settlement. There are also several types of **permanent settlements**.

Rural, Urban, and Suburban Communities

Permanent human settlements are classified by their economic activities and layouts, as follows:

- **Rural settlements** are those in which a majority of land is used for agricultural purposes. Inhabitants of rural areas often work in the agricultural industry, serving their own community.
- An **urban settlement** is typified by many nucleated buildings. Most residents of urban areas work outside of the agricultural industry, serving outside communities. Cities and larger towns are examples of urban areas.
- A **suburban community** is one that exists just outside a large urban area; it is generally smaller and less nucleated than the major urban community it abuts. Often, city workers reside in a suburban area and commute to work, aiming to avoid unsavory elements of urban life, such as crowding and pollution.

Central Place Theory

Central Place Theory is also referred to as Christaller's Theory for its formulator, **Walter Christaller**. This theory describes the typical size and spacing of human settlements. It rests on the idea that centralization is a natural principle of order that manifests itself in human settlement patterns. Christaller's Theory predicts that a large central market will have several smaller towns around it at equal distances; the smaller towns purchase goods and services from the central hub. From several assumptions, Christaller derived laws for the determination of the size, number, and distribution of towns. These assumptions include the even distribution of population and resources; similar purchasing power among all consumers; a flat, expansive surface; and providers of goods and services who cannot earn excess profits. There are three principal laws of **Central Place Theory**:

- The number of settlements is inversely proportional to the size of the settlements.
- The larger the settlements, the greater the distances between them will be.
- As settlements increase in size, services become increasingly specialized.

Order of Settlements

Following Central Place Theory, the goods and services available for purchase in settlements vary depending on a settlement's size. Settlements may thus be classified by these factors. **Settlement order** may be displayed in a hierarchical pyramid, in which lowest-order settlements make up the bottom level (they are most plentiful) and highest-order settlements are at the top of the pyramid (they are fewest). In a **high-order settlement**, such as a conurbation (a large urban city or capital), one might expect to find the following services: government buildings, museums and theaters, churches of various religions, multiple medical centers, transportation terminals, and large shopping complexes. A **middle-order settlement** (a city or town) might house a hospital, multiple retail stores, a few specialized medical practices, a high school football team, and a cathedral. In **low-order settlements**, such as hamlets and villages, one may find a single church, a main store, a tavern, and a small junior high school. The **lowest-order settlements** offer no services whatsoever.

Common Settlement Forms

Study of the shape (form) of a settlement can reveal information about its origins and development.

- An **isolated settlement** is a single structure, such as a farmhouse. This settlement form is often found in areas where physical conditions make survival difficult or uncomfortable. Historically, isolated settlements were common in the early stages of pioneer settlement.
- A **dispersed settlement** consists of two to three buildings that are two kilometers or farther from the next dispersed settlement, possibly forming a hamlet.
- A **nucleated settlement** includes many buildings grouped together for a social, economic, and/or defensive purpose; they often form around crossroads.
- A **loose-knit settlement** is similar to a nucleated settlement, but the buildings are spaced farther apart.
- **Lineated settlements** consist of buildings spread out in lines along a river, canal, or dike, allowing all residents access to the waterway.
- **Planned settlements**, usually made up of crescent-shaped estates housing several small buildings, are typically constructed near one or more major cities that support the workforce.

Human Migration

Human migration is simply the movement of people from one location to another. **Human migration** may be international or internal:

- **International migration** is movement from one country of residence to another. This kind of migration generally covers permanent movements, thus excluding such transitory activities as migrant labor, nomadism, tourism, and commuting. When leaving a country, migrating peoples are referred to as emigrants; when they arrive in a new country, they are called immigrants.
- **Internal migration** occurs when citizens move within a country, such as in the United States when people moved west from adjacent areas in the east.

Migration may also be voluntary or forced:

- **Voluntary migration** (movement based on uncoerced personal decisions) occurs for many reasons: proximity to family and friends, expansion of territory, a search for employment and economic opportunity, an attempt to improve one's quality of life, and the settlement of undeveloped territory.
- **Forced migration** occurs when a person or group of people is compelled to move regardless of their individual preferences. This type of migration has many possible causes: slavery; overcrowding; racial, religious, or political persecution and/or discrimination; natural disaster (such as hurricanes or flooding); and war.

Population Transfer

The term *population transfer* refers to actions taken by a political authority in a state or country to drive large groups of people out of a particular region (forced migration). Historically, **population transfer** has been used to force groups of people with ethnicities and/or religious beliefs different from the dominant norm into isolated regions. This **forced migration** is often detrimental to the well-being of the ousted people, as no consideration is made for the suitability of the new region to the group's way of life. The "Indian Removal" that occurred in the United States in the 1830s is a classic example of population transfer. Native Americans were forced off of their homelands onto isolated, federally owned reservations. The mass expulsions of Jews, Muslims, and Gypsies that took place in various European countries numerous times throughout history are also instances of population transfer. Though these discriminatory practices were considered "humane" resolutions to religious, ethical, and cultural conflicts for centuries, they are considered violations of international law in modern times.

Internal Migration

Internal human migration is the movement of people within a country; this type of migration may be permanent or temporary. **Permanent internal migrations** include urbanization (the migration of people from less developed rural areas to more developed urban areas, which often occurs when people seek access to the wide variety of services usually available in urban areas), urban depopulation (the opposite of urbanization, which occurs when people seek residencies in quieter, less polluted, less crowded areas), and regional migration (a general trend of movement within a country, such as from northern areas to southern areas). Temporary internal movements such as commuting to work or school are referred to as **daily migrations**. **Seasonal migration** is that practiced by transhumant nomads and farmworkers. The movement of people from one region to another for a significant period of time (but with the intent of returning to the original region) is referred to as **semipermanent migration**. Workers on ships and oil rigs engage in this type of movement.

Early Human Migrations

The early human migrations helped to shape the path of human development throughout history. The first anatomically modern Homo sapiens evolved in **Africa** between 100,000 and 150,000 years ago. These prehistoric beings probably practiced hunting and gathering, meaning that they moved constantly in search of food. These communities became more organized, developing more sophisticated tools and cooperative predation tactics. The population grew as they quickly migrated to other regions, inhabiting each of the continents but Antarctica within 50,000 years. Hunting alone could not sustain the increasing population, spurring the transition from hunting and gathering to migratory slash-and-burn agriculture; crops spread across the globe. People began to settle in permanent, stable agricultural communities. The innovation of sailing vessels encouraged human migration, resulting in new settlements bred from colonization and/or conquest. Seafarers and nomadic pastoralists aided in the distribution of new technologies to various regions. The sharing of increasingly specialized knowledge enabled the rise of several early empires. New social circumstances then bred new (increasingly violent) forms of human migration.

Modern Human Migrations

Due to increases in the population, as well as advancements in technology, **modern human migrations** have surpassed earlier movements in terms of size and scope. The many technological innovations associated with the Industrial Revolution facilitated, among other things, transportation over long distances. This factor, combined with economic, cultural, environmental, and political forces, led to many massive migratory movements. The **Great Atlantic Migration**, which involved the relocation of many people from Europe to North America in the mid- to late-1800s, was the largest such migration. This period of mobility began with the immigration of many Irish and German people to the United States; these migrants left their countries in search of ample food after failure of the potato crop in Ireland and southern Rhineland led to famine in those areas. The mass movement of residents of developing countries to more industrialized nations is another major migration that has taken place in modern times.

Population Structure

The population structure of a society is a description of that society in terms of the ages and sexes of its members. The study of **demographic structure** includes, by extension, analysis of crude birth and death rates and infant mortality rates (the number of infants in a society who die before they reach one year of age divided by the number of live births per year). Practitioners in this field also examine **natural increase**, which is the rate at which a society's population grows due to a difference between the birth rate and the death rate. A society's **population structure** is usually represented by a population pyramid. This type of diagram is created through the placement of two bar graphs (one denoting females and one denoting males) side by side. The x-axis shows the percentage of people of each sex who fall into a certain age group as shown on the y-axis.

Population Pyramid of a Developing Country

The population pyramids of developing countries tend to be wide at their bases and increasingly narrow toward the tops of the diagrams, indicating that a sizeable portion of developing countries' populations is made up of young people, due to high birth and death rates. Improvements in the living conditions of many developing nations may decrease the **CDR**, resulting in a youthful population (one in which the majority of the population is teenaged or younger) and a large gap between the **CBR** and **CDR** (a high rate of natural increase). Developing countries often exhibit high birth rates for several reasons, some of which may become less applicable as a society's standard of living improves. For instance, high infant mortality rates in some societies impel parents to bear many children in the expectation of losing some of them. In agricultural societies, members of large families can share farming and household duties. High death rates in developing nations result from insufficient access to medical services and from unsanitary and/or insufficient food and water supplies.

Population Pyramid of a Developed Nation

Generally, the population pyramid of a developed country is slightly narrow at the base, consistently wide through the middle, and narrower at the very top. A **population pyramid** of this shape indicates relatively low birth and death rates—the number of babies born is less than the number of adults, and a majority of children reach late adulthood. The small discrepancy between the **CBR** and **CDR** implies a low rate of natural increase. Decreasing birth rates can result in an aging population, in which a large number of people are over age 65. Developed nations often exhibit low birth rates because women are likely to have access to reproductive and family planning services, which gives them control of their own fertility. Also, it can be expensive to raise a large family in a developed country. Death rates (including infant mortality rates) in developed countries are usually lower than those observed in developing countries because of better access to medical services, clean water, food, and adequate housing in the former.

Study of Population Structure

The study of population structure supplies geographers with useful information about social trends and patterns. On a **national scale**, the examination of **population structure** provides clues as to the economic status and standard of living of a nation, as evidenced by the patterns observed in the population pyramids of developed and developing nations. On a **regional scale**, variations in population structure may result from migratory processes or from the presence of institutions that attract and concentrate people of a certain age in a given area. For example, the existence of a large university in an urban area will decrease the average age of the area's residents. The study of a region's population structure and changes in that structure is helpful in **city planning**, as different age groups have different physical and social needs and engage in different sorts of leisure activities. Also, examination of the number of males and females in each age group can aid in the **prediction of future variations** in population structure.

Culture

Culture is the acquired knowledge that people use to interpret the world around them and to guide them in social behavior. Therefore, **culture** is not behavior itself; rather, it is a body of shared knowledge that causes people to act and interact with others in certain ways. Also, culture is not genetic. From a young age, members of a group learn about the (arbitrary) aspects of that group's culture from observation of and participation in social activity. Culture may be **tacit**, meaning that its transmission occurs unconsciously (for instance, certain linguistic conventions), or **explicit**, meaning that its transmission is purposeful and articulated (for example, religious education). Culture is a complex system of interrelated parts. While some aspects of culture are shared by all members of a particular society, each person in that society is a member of multiple groups with their own cultural knowledge. For example, one is likely to behave differently in the presence of his or her family than in the presence of friends.

Ethnicity

Ethnicity refers to the classification of a group by its distinctive cultural traits; these traits form a comprehensive cultural entity. Members of an **ethnic group** feel strong ties to the group's cultural traditions and knowledge and identify themselves as a "people" rather than simply a statistical population. **Ethnicity** may be expressed through music, dance, dress, kinship patterns, moral and value systems, food, religious beliefs and activities, language, and literature. In an ethnic group, these cultural qualities are common throughout the society and are seen as unique with respect to other ethnic groups. Often, an ethnic group will share a common history and territorial "homeland."

The concept of ethnicity differs from that of race, which divides people into arbitrary categories based on perceived differences in people's physical and biogenetic characteristics. The labeling of a group as a race group versus an ethnic group is thus determined by the criteria used to define it.

Ethnocentrism

Ethnocentrism is the belief that one's own cultural norms are "natural" and therefore superior to other belief systems. Historically, dominant groups have been wary of ethnic diversity, and ethnocentrism tends to occur in less enlightened societies. **Ethnocentric beliefs** have led to the discriminatory and hostile treatment of minority groups throughout history. The actions taken by Nazis against Jews in World War II Germany provide an extreme example of the attempted elimination of a particular ethnic group.

Pluralism

Pluralism is a doctrine that advocates the autonomous participation of differing ethnic, racial, religious, and/or social groups in a common civilization.

Cultural Relativism

Cultural relativism is a theory that suggests it is possible to observe other cultures without making value-based judgments. This can be achieved only through complete detachment from one's own cultural beliefs. **Cultural relativism** proposes that each group's cultural "reality" is equally valid and worth preserving, and that aspects of a particular culture can only be fairly evaluated in terms of that culture as a whole.

Assimilation

Assimilation is the process whereby individuals of a minority ethnic group are absorbed into and internalize cultural characteristics of a dominant group. **Assimilation** may be voluntary or forced. **Voluntary assimilation** often occurs when immigrants arrive in a new country. As they learn about the dominant culture through contact with and participation in their new societies, many immigrants gradually begin to abandon their previously held cultural beliefs and practices in favor of those predominant in those societies; this helps them to thrive in a new culture. For example, learning the dominant language is extremely important in the creation of economic and educational opportunities. **Forced assimilation** occurs when one group invades and conquers the territory of another group. The conquering group forcibly impels the native group to forsake their ethnic beliefs and practices in favor of those of the newly dominant group. Forced assimilation constitutes an attempt to create artificial unity, which may help the invaders retain control of the region.

Amalgamation

Amalgamation, in cultural studies, is the process whereby a society becomes **ethnically mixed**. This process is also known as **hybridization**. Though assimilation is common among new members of a society different from their own, it is rarely complete. More often, assimilating peoples adopt certain useful characteristics of the dominant culture while retaining certain important aspects of their culture. Examination of Mexican culture reveals that nation's amalgamated society. Throughout centuries of contact, certain aspects of Native American cultures and Spanish cultures have been extracted, modified, and synthesized to create a new society. The hybrid nature of this society may be observed in, for example, spoken dialects, religious beliefs and practices, and architectural styles.

Language

A language is a conventionalized system of sounds, gestures, and signs used for communication. It is an important and distinctive aspect of any culture. Human language relies heavily (though not exclusively) on **vocalizations**. The activities that produce vocal sounds are referred to as speech; speech is generated and interpreted through language. In language, words act as **symbols** that refer to something else. We learn to associate particular words with particular referents. For example, the symbol "wall" refers to a barrier between spaces. Symbology in language simplifies the task of communication; it enables us to communicate about things that are not present. Symbols in language may also be **nonlinguistic**. Posture, eye contact, clothing, and material goods are symbols through which information may be communicated. **Sociolinguistic rules** are cultural conventions that govern the ways humans communicate in different social situations. For example, a person is likely to speak differently during a job interview than he or she would among peers at a social gathering.

Subsystems of Language

The subsystems of language are phonology, grammar, morphology, syntax, and semantics.

- **Phonology** deals with the formation and ordering of sounds. Sounds are classified as phonemes, the basic units used in word construction. Phonemic categories are culturally defined. For example, in English, the "t" sound is treated as a single phoneme; in Hindi, the same sound is divided into four distinct phonemes.
- **Grammar** provides categories and rules regarding the combination of vocal symbols.
- **Morphology** combines units of meaning to make words or modify word meaning. Morphemes are categories of the smallest vocal units intrinsic to meaning. They may be words (categorized, for example, as nouns or verbs) or parts of words. For example, "s" is a morpheme when used to pluralize a word.
- **Syntax** provides rules for organizing words into phrases.
- **Semantics** deals with the categories and rules for relating vocal symbols (words) to their referents. Semantic rules tell us how to combine words with what they stand for. For example, the semantics of the English language instruct us to associate the word "chair" with an object upon which we sit.

Sapir-Whorf Hypothesis

The Sapir-Whorf Hypothesis, developed by the linguists **Benjamin Whorf** and **Edward Sapir**, directly contradicts the belief that language mirrors reality, that words are simply symbols for what already exists. One's **native language** is completely embedded in one's consciousness; we use our languages to formulate thoughts and to identify and classify things that we encounter in nature. Also, certain words and concepts cannot be directly translated from one language to another. Whorf believed that humans are only capable of conceptualizing ideas that may be articulated and expressed through language. Therefore, we cannot think about something we do not have the words or structures to express. The Sapir-Whorf hypothesis states that humans dissect and interpret the multitude of stimuli provided by the outside world using the linguistic systems in our minds. Consequently, people's native languages govern their views of reality and determine their perceptions of the world.

Modified Whorfism

"Modified Whorfism," which suggests that language affects but does not dictate the reality experienced by humans, is accepted by many social and linguistic thinkers. The nature of language itself problematizes any attempt to prove the Sapir-Whorf Hypothesis. Since language is such an integral part of human consciousness, it is fruitless to ask a person how the language he or she speaks has affected his or her view of the world; no one could answer such a question objectively. **Euphemistic language**, the use of words that are seen as less offensive in place of more unpleasant, direct, or harsh synonyms, lends credence to the idea that language has some effect on one's perceived reality. Though different languages may not create exclusive worldviews for their speakers, they do influence the thought patterns of native speakers in distinctive ways.

Industrial Location Factors

Industrial location factors are the various issues that industry owners and managers must take into consideration during the selection of an ideal physical location for their businesses. **Human or economic factors** include the availability of a labor source (the proximity of potential workers to the location), the location of leisure facilities for workers, the market (the capital required to keep a business in operation, which depends on the wage demands of laborers in a particular area, the cost of the transportation of goods, and the size of the business's sphere of influence), the relative location of transportation routes (such as seaports, railways, and highways), the government (which may impose laws, restrictions, and/or incentives in a particular area), access to technology (such as manufacturing robots), and geographical inertia (which refers to traditions of producing particular goods in particular areas). **Physical location factors** include the relative locations of natural transportation routes (such as rivers), the relative locations of raw material sources (the primary industrial location factor), and the size and relief of the prospective business site.

Scientific Revolution

The Scientific Revolution was the second period of major change in human history. This period (approximately 1500-1750 AD) involved intellectual and geographic explorations that produced many scientific and industrial advances in human civilization. Geographic expeditions, such as the ones undertaken by Christopher Columbus, were enabled by **technological developments** in the fields of cartography, shipbuilding, and navigation. Such explorations taught Europeans about the physical and human geography of different regions and about the layout of land on Earth's surface. **Scientific exploration**, practiced by noted thinkers such as Isaac Newton and Galileo Galilei, was enabled by inventions such as the microscope and the telescope. With these and other new tools, people made discoveries about our world and its function that are considered fundamental today. The Scientific Transformation eventually gave rise to the **Industrial Revolution**, which produced a plethora of new inventions, factories, and opportunities for the attainment of wealth. It also produced inequalities (still observable today) between societies with these technological capabilities and those without.

Characteristics Defining Independent Countries

An independent country shares four defining characteristics:

- Any independent country inhabits a specific territory (land and water) defined by **boundaries**. The sizes and shapes of countries differ widely.
- Each country has a **population** that occupies its territory. The sizes and constitutions of each country are also extremely variable.
- Any independent country possesses **sovereignty**, which is the freedom to control and protect its territory, population, and foreign interactions without outside influence. The geographic location and landscape of a country's territory may affect its ability to defend its sovereignty. For example, the high mountains surrounding Switzerland have served to protect the country against foreign invasion for centuries.
- Every independent country has a **government**, an institution that creates and enforces laws and policies and acts to further the public good (through protection, the maintenance of order, and provision of certain services). There are several types of government structures and governmental authority.

Types of Government Structures

Governments may be classified by the nature of the relationship between the central governing body and the smaller units (states, provinces, etc.) that make up a country. Three types of government structures include the following:

- A **unitary system** exists when a central governmental body exerts sole control over an entire country. The principal government formulates policies applicable at all levels of government; smaller units exert power only if the central government grants it to them.
- A **federation** exists when certain powers are allocated to a central government and certain powers are given to regional or local governmental units. In a federation (such as the United States), federal, state, and local governments share political power.
- A **confederation** exists when smaller governmental units retain their sovereignties and allow the central government only specific, limited powers (usually regarding national defense or international trade). In this type of structure, states and provinces retain a large degree of independence but still ally to address common concerns.

Type of Government Authority

A government may be classified by the source of its authority. Different kinds of governments are run with various degrees of public participation. In an **anarchy**, every citizen in the population is seen as a qualified participant in decision-making that will affect the country. There is no central governing body; people govern themselves. A **democracy** also involves rule by the people. However, unlike an anarchy, a democracy includes a central government that aims to serve the people. In a representative democracy, citizens exercise their political franchise or suffrage (the right to vote) in the selection of leaders, who, in turn, participate in governmental proceedings and make political decisions. Citizens of a democratic nation also express their opinions about certain issues by voting. In an **oligarchy**, political power is concentrated in the hands of a small group, usually made up of wealthy people with strong military influence and/or familial traditions of power. Often, the most influential participants in an oligarchic government operate outside the public eye in the economic realm.

Types of Authoritarian Governments

An authoritarian government is one in which the country's leaders possess all (or a majority of) political power. Until fairly recently, most countries across the world had authoritarian governments. Today, various forms of democracy are more common. There are different degrees of authoritarianism. A **monarchy** is a type of authoritarian government in which monarchs (for example, queens, shahs, and pharaohs) inherit political power simply by being born into a ruling family. Monarchs may serve as symbols of national unity, or they may rule as dictators. A **dictatorship** (the most common type of authoritarian government) is a system in which political power is held by a small group or even a unitary individual. The dictator exerts control through military force and intimidation, and he or she attempts to control the behavior of their subordinates. **Totalitarianism** is the most extreme form of authoritarianism. In this kind of system, the ruling body tries to control every aspect of society in its territory, from economic activity to people's personal lives.

Boundaries and Frontiers

A boundary is functional though a hypothetical structure that delineates territories of differing political entities or legal domains, such as countries, provinces, and states. Prior to modernized conceptions of territory, nations defined their territories as the area over which they could exert authority. Today, territories are demarcated by **boundaries** that are effectively material and officially designated. A map whose sole purpose is to convey the sizes and shapes of various governmental units is termed a political map. Though boundaries may run alongside physical features of Earth's surface, such as mountains, they are contrived by humans to segregate one area from another. The areas on either side of a boundary are often referred to as borders. A **frontier** is an area of undeveloped land, the edge of civilization; frontiers exist outside of certain boundaries. Throughout history, competition for the control of boundaries and frontiers has been the cause of much military and ideological conflict.

Phases of Boundary Formation

The processes of boundary formation and implementation occurs in four general phases:

- During the **historical precedent phase**, boundaries are established and maintained based on the cultural characteristics (such as religion, language, or ethnicity) of people in an area. Different cultural groups form communities that inhabit particular areas. The recognition of boundaries in this stage may also be based on previous attempts to establish a dividing line.
- The **political definition or delimitation phase** entails the official establishment of boundary lines through the use of legal documents such as treaties. These lines are drawn on official maps. Often, the placement of a boundary is negotiated by representatives from the concerned regions.
- During the **technical demarcation phase**, the boundaries agreed upon during the previous phase are practically implemented. Demarcators analyze the relevant terrain and material markers, or monuments are constructed to display the location of the officially defined boundary.
- Finally, the **characterization phase** entails modification of the demarcated boundary to accommodate population growth in the border areas.

Boundary Terms

A **natural boundary** is a boundary arbitrarily formed by landscape evolution. This type of boundary may be hydrologic (formed by a waterway such as a river) or orthographic (formed by a land formation such as a mountain chain). An **artificial boundary** is an abstract line formulated by humans to aid in identifying specific locations. Geodesic lines and the lines that constitute the graticule are examples of artificial boundaries. A **separation barrier** is a physical construction (for instance, a wall or fence) intended to separate disparate populations or to inhibit movement between two areas. The Great Wall of China, which spans nearly 4,000 miles, provides a classic example of a separation barrier. It was initially built to protect citizens against raids by conquering tribes. Another example is the border of the United States with Mexico, which was created to prevent the free entry of immigrants into the US

Cultural Boundaries

As displayed on maps, boundaries may appear as straight lines, as lines that follow natural landscape features, or as wiggles that seem to twist and turn for no reason. The last of these boundary types is known as a **cultural boundary** and may be attributed to many (perhaps continuous) boundary disputes between cultural and/or ethnic groups on either side of the separating line. For example, the border region between Belgium and the Netherlands is sprinkled with tiny, hamlet-sized areas "belonging" to one country on the other's side of the boundary. This type of boundary is sometimes referred to as a cultural boundary. When conflict along a cultural border ebbs, the formal process of boundary formation often begins, resulting in the wiggles observed along borders across the world.

International Power Relations

International power refers to the ability of one state to exert control or influence over other states. Power is generally defined as the capacity of an individual or group to impose their wills on others. This may be achieved through hegemonies (soft power) or through the use of brute force (hard power). Today, states may be classified by the degree of their influences, especially in relation to the power of other states. **Middle powers** are those states that cannot dominate other states but still possess degrees of international influence. Such states often ally themselves with groups but do not lead them. Canada is an example of a middle power. A **regional power** is a state that exerts control over other states in its region but not necessarily around the globe. **Great powers**, **global powers**, and **superpowers** are terms for strong states that share power with a few other influential states. A **hyperpower** is a singular dominating state in a unipolar world. Many consider the modern United States a hyperpower.

Spheres of Influence

In international politics, the term *sphere of influence* refers to the claim of a powerful state to exclusive or predominant control over foreign territory, often in the surrounding region; this claim may or may not be recognized as legitimate by other entities. States within a powerful state's sphere of influence often function as **satellite states** (states that are officially independent but influenced by the more powerful state in practice). For instance, during its prime, the Japanese Empire exerted much political power over events in the nearby states of Korea, Vietnam, and Manchuria. Historically, the term *sphere of influence* has been used to refer to the respective **colonial territories** of two or more powers in a region. For example, in the 1880s, Great Britain and Germany signed an agreement stating that neither would interfere in the other's (predefined) sphere of influence in the Gulf of Guinea. In regional geography, a major urban area may exert economic influence over the surrounding area; this is also referred to as a sphere of influence.

Monroe Doctrine

In 1823, President James Monroe formulated a foreign policy which is known today as the **Monroe Doctrine**. In his annual address to Congress, Monroe indicated that the Old World (namely Europe) and the New World (namely the United States) were distinct entities with distinct systems, and should therefore exist as separate spheres. His statement included four main points:

- the United States would not participate in conflicts inside or between European nations;
- the United States officially recognized and would not interfere with existing colonies in the New World;
- the Western Hemisphere was off-limits for future colonization; and
- any endeavor by a European power to influence any nation in the Western Hemisphere would be considered a hostile act against the United States.

Though the Monroe Doctrine was militarily unsustainable at the time of its formulation, as the US emerged as a global power in the 1870s, the Monroe Doctrine came to be viewed as a geopolitical definition of the country's **sphere of influence** as the entire Western Hemisphere.

Review Video: The Monroe Doctrine
Visit mometrix.com/academy and enter code: 953021

Cooperation

Cooperation is the practice whereby individuals and groups work together (possibly with common methods) to achieve a **shared goal**. Often, those working in concert accomplish more than those acting independently or against one another (competition), though the impetus to compete against others is often a motivation for individual behavior. In fact, individuals or nation-states may cooperate with a larger group in order to be part of a larger, more competitive entity. There are potentially infinite reasons for collaboration between people and nation-states. For instance, at the local level, a group of citizens may form a group to protest the planned construction of a large shopping center in a rural neighborhood. At the regional and national levels, organizations such as Mothers Against Drunk Driving (MADD) collaborate in attempts to change public policy and spur the passage of legislation aimed at making society safer. Internationally, the governments of nation-states and/or their citizens may join together to promote humanitarian activities such as the International Federation of Red Cross and Red Crescent Societies (IFRCS).

Home Market Effect

The home market effect is a model that exemplifies one type of international governmental cooperation. Trade, the voluntary exchange of goods and/or services, is a vital mechanism by which nation-states that do not have and cannot feasibly produce a particular good can obtain it. In the **home market effect** situation, it is assumed that it is impractical and/or impossible for a single country to produce all of the resources it needs in sufficient quantities. Therefore, it becomes desirable for each country in a system to specialize in the efficient production of **one resource** and trade a surplus of that resource for another material. This process requires **cooperation** among the participating nation-states in discussions of costs and quantities. For example, Arabic countries control a large portion of the world's oil reserves. Western countries in need of that particular resource often share technological information with Arabic countries in exchange for oil. In this manner, each country has the potential to obtain the resources it needs.

Economic Interdependence

Economic interdependence is a situation in which two or more countries depend on one other for any or all of the following: energy, food, manufactured goods, minerals, or labor. Resources (including natural resources, such as minerals and land, as well as human resources), fuel sources, and information are distributed **unevenly** across the globe; no single country possesses all the resources it needs to subsist and thrive. Therefore, each must **trade** its surplus goods and services for those it lacks. The **North American Free Trade Agreement (NAFTA)** was formed among three economically interdependent countries (Canada, the United States, and Mexico) in an attempt to ease trade restrictions on vital imports and exports in the member states.

Burgess's Concentric Zone Model

Burgess's Concentric Zone Model was developed in 1925 by **Ernest Burgess**, based on his observations of Chicago and other American cities. This model of land use and urban development suggested that towns grow outward from a central "downtown" area, creating **concentric circles** (zones) of building and activity; this indicates that the age of structures decreases with distance from the central hub. Burgess's model also implies that inner zones have tendencies to expand into the outer regions. This characterizes **urban growth** as a process of expansion and reconversion of land uses. While this model is less complex than actual cities existing in the twenty-first century, it is still useful as a theoretical approximation of urban growth patterns. The descriptions given of the zones in Burgess's model are based upon observation and analysis of modern city growth.

Inner Zones

The inner zones of the Burgess Concentric Zone Model are Zones A, B, and C.

- **Zone A**, the central zone in the Burgess Concentric Zone Model, is the **central business district (CBD)**. Land in the CBD is more expensive than in any other zone. As the area accessible to the largest number of people, the CBD houses retail shops, banks, health care facilities, and office buildings. This zone tends to be densely developed, with high levels of traffic and a lack of vegetation.
- **Zone B** is referred to as the **Transition Zone** or the **Twilight Zone**. This area may be subdivided into a declining industrial sector and a section of low-class residential housing (older buildings arranged in tight grids with no yard space). In a continually developing city, Zone A's growth, coupled with attempts to renovate older areas of the region, creates constant activity in Zone B, characterizing it as a transition zone.
- **Zone C**, called the **Council Estates**, houses middle-class residencies; there are fewer apartment buildings with more yard space than in Zone B.

Outer Zones

The outer zones of the Burgess Concentric Zone Model are Zones D and E.

- **Zone D** is the region often referred to as the **suburbs** or the **commuter zone**. The suburbs are typified by high-class (expensive) residential buildings. Houses abut garages and other outbuildings; nearly every residency has a yard. Theoretically, the most affluent members of a community are able to reside at a distance from the CBD because they have the means to procure transportation into the downtown area to work and purchase goods and services.
- The **countryside zone** (**Zone E**) was not present in Burgess's original formulation of his model. Rather, it has been added to represent the residents of an area who wish to live as far as possible from the busy CBD while retaining the ability to use the employment opportunities and services available in the innermost zone of the city. The countryside zone is a rural area with large areas of natural vegetation and a less nucleated form than that of zones closer to the CBD.

Hoyt's Sector Model

The Hoyt Sector Model, formulated by **Homer Hoyt** in 1939, is essentially a modification of Burgess's Concentric Zone Model. Based on observations of the development patterns of many American cities, Hoyt deduced that most large urban areas centered around major **transportation routes**, such as railways and seaports. Commercial entities and industrial facilities were often erected around high-access thoroughfares, and low-income housing was often found near railroad lines. Hoyt updated Burgess's model to account for these patterns. He suggested that cities grow outward from the Central Business District in wedged sectors along major transportation routes. In the **Sector Model**, commercial businesses remain in the CBD, while manufacturing and warehousing interests (a portion of Burgess's Zone B) form in a wedge around major paths of transportation. The low-income housing in Burgess's Zone B abuts the wedge of industrial activity (pollution and noise affect the quality of life in this region, decreasing the land value). As in Burgess's model, middle- and high-income housing in Hoyt's model are situated away from the CBD.

Multiple Nuclei Model

The Multiple Nuclei Model was developed by **Edward Ullman** and **Chauncy Harris** in 1945 to explain urban growth patterns that did not fit the somewhat outdated Concentric and Sector Models. By this point in the development of American cities, many suburbs were growing rapidly and operating as small business districts. Ullman and Harris found that land-use patterns formed around these **nuclei** or **nodes of economic activity**, which were specialized to the needs of residents with certain levels of incomes and certain leisure patterns. The **Multiple Nuclei Model** retains the Central Business District as the main commercial region, from which retail and manufacturing companies spanned outward along transportation routes. In this model, heavy industry is located near the outskirts of a city, possibly near areas of low-income housing. The small communities surrounding suburban nuclei filled the urban periphery.

Exerting Control over Resources Using Boundaries

Though boundaries appear as lines along Earth's surface on two-dimensional maps and globes, they do more than separate terrestrial territories. Theoretically, **boundaries** exist as vertical planes, extending below the surface and into the air, effectively separating **underground resources** and **airspace**. For example, disputes about the "ownership" of an underground oil field (inconveniently located beneath the Iraq-Kuwait border and extending into both countries) contributed to the development of a conflict that culminated in the Gulf War. Disputes over the exploitation of other underground resources, such as coal and natural gas, have been and continue to be sources of international conflict. International boundaries also extend above the surface, creating divisions of airspace (the zone above a state's territory where the rights of other states may be limited). Often, commercial aircraft may fly through another state's airspace only with official agreement. During the communist period, for example, Soviets shot down a commercial Korean aircraft that strayed outside the narrow corridor the USSR had delimited for flights over its territory.

Maritime Boundaries

Maritime boundaries were created by seafaring peoples to claim certain fishing grounds or trading ports for themselves. The concept of territorial control of portions of the seas originated centuries ago. The delimitations of these boundaries have become more and more specific as time passes. A critical action by President **Harry Truman** in 1945 hastened the rush to claim **oceanic territory**. Truman claimed all of the potential natural resources located on the continental shelf for the United States. After Truman's declaration, countries across the world scrambled to lay claim to their own oceanic territories. Today, the following conventions exist regarding maritime law: states may claim up to twelve nautical miles of oceanic territory; states may claim up to 200 nautical miles as their **Exclusive Economic Zones**—coastal states have the sole rights to manage and exploit natural resources within these zones; and coastal states possess exclusive rights over the natural resources on and beneath the continental shelf of their respective continents.

Religion

Religion is culturally shared knowledge and beliefs about the **supernatural realm** (that which exists beyond human experience) that people use to explain the relationship between human life and the universe. People tend to feel most at ease when they are sure of themselves and the order of the world around them. When a particularly traumatic or incongruous event cannot be explained intellectually or experientially, people often turn to **religion** for answers. Religion can provide people with worldviews (sets of beliefs and assumptions about the origin of life and the way things work). An important aspect of religion is the **emotional nature** of the dilemmas it addresses. Consequently, religion can unify disparate peoples with similar beliefs or create unbridgeable divisions between different groups. In human geography, the term is often used to refer to **organized religion** (a structured organization of people supporting a particular religion) rather than an individual's belief system. Organized religion may be public (state-supported) or private (funded by donations from those who attend religious functions).

Governmental Policies Regarding Religion

There are three general attitudes taken by governments regarding religion.

- A **secular government** is one that neither advocates nor discourages religious practices and beliefs. Theoretically, in a secular state, a legal separation exists between religious affairs and political affairs. The "separation of church and state" in the government of the United States of America exemplifies a secular standpoint.
- An **atheistic state** is one in which the government attempts to suppress or even prevent religious practices. North Korea is an example of an officially atheistic state, while China allows people to participate in religious practices under state supervision.
- A **religious government** is one with official links to a particular religion or branch of religion. For example, Sweden is considered Evangelical Lutheran, and Nepal is officially Hindu.

Monism, Dualism, and Pluralism

- **Monism** holds that the universe is created of one single substance, energy, essence, or principle. Substantive monism is the belief in one substance; attributive monism is the belief that while there is only one kind of thing, that category is made up of many individual objects or beings; and absolute monism is the belief that there is but one being created of one substance. Monism may also be broadly subdivided into idealistic monism (which holds that only the mind is real), neutral monism (which states that both mental and physical phenomena can be reduced to a third energetic substance), and materialism (which claims that physical reality is the only reality).
- **Dualism** may refer to the belief in two opposing universal forces that are often personified as deities, to the perceived division between mind and matter, or to the belief that the entire world may be divided into two categories.
- **Pluralism** holds that the universe is made up of many different substances.

Monotheism and Polytheism

Theism is the belief in a divine being.

- **Monotheism** is the belief in a single, all-powerful, universal deity. Zoroastrianism, Islam, and Judaism are examples of monotheistic religions. Deism, a subtype of monotheism, is the belief that although there is one God, this deity does not intervene in human affairs and may be understood only through observation of nature. Monistic theism is a type of monotheism that includes monistic and pantheistic elements as well as the belief in a universal divine being. Substance monotheism, an aspect of some indigenous African religions, claims that the many gods are manifestations of a single God. Inclusive monotheism holds that all polytheistic deities are simply alternate names for the one Supreme Being, while exclusive monotheism asserts that there is one true God and that all others are false.
- **Polytheism** holds that there are many deities; these gods are believed to exist in a pantheon (a set of divine beings with complex, human-like personalities and varying degrees of power in different realms).

Pantheism vs. Panentheism

Pantheism, in its original Greek translation, literally means "all is God and God is all." It is thus a type of monotheism that holds the single divine being and the universe are one. In classical pantheism, God personifies natural order and natural law. Natural pantheism, on the other hand, equates nature with a non-sentient divinity.

Panentheism is the belief that the universe was created by a single immanent God; unlike pantheism, panentheism does not view God and the universe as one. Rather, God is seen as more powerful than and outside of the universe.

Generally, faiths that are considered classically pantheistic may also be described as panentheistic. However, natural pantheism and panentheism are not equivalent concepts—natural pantheists do not believe in the existence of a conscious being that is more powerful than nature.

Largest Religious Bodies in India

Hinduism is the oldest religion practiced in India in modern times, dating to approximately 4,000 years ago. Those who adhere to the principles of Hinduism are referred to as Hindus. Today, each of the several sects of Hinduism relies on the **Vedas** (sacred hymns and verses) as the absolute authority on fundamental truths about the universe. Also, the majority of Hindus believe in **Brahman**, the ultimate universal power. Reincarnation, karma, and the caste system are ideas prevalent in Hinduism. Different branches of Hinduism espouse belief systems that may be described as monistic, dualistic, or pantheistic. In principle, Hindus support religious tolerance and consider different doctrines inadequate rather than wrong.

Buddhism, which grew out of Hinduism during a period of social change in India, was founded by **Siddhartha Gautama** (Gautama Buddha). The goal of Buddhists is to attain the blissful state of **nirvana**. This can be accomplished through the purification of one's thoughts via strictly defined behavior. Buddhism may be described as a polytheistic faith, though any otherworldly powers of Buddhist deities are de-emphasized.

Largest Religious Bodies in Eastern Asia

Confucianism was founded by Confucius (551–479 BC), who lived around the same time as Buddha. This faith was designed to relieve conflict in all arenas, from that which existed among families to that between Heaven and Earth. Confucius defined "appropriate" social roles for people of different ages, sexes, and social ranks; by assuming these roles, Confucians attempt to create a more peaceful world.

Taoism originated in China at approximately the same time as Confucianism. Taoism strives to create harmony between humans and the natural world. Unlike Confucianism, which has a significant political aspect and is largely monistic, Taoism values natural goodness and expressiveness over social order and is largely dualistic.

Note that both Confucianism and Taoism are considered traditional Chinese religions. In fact, most adherents to Chinese religious tradition build their faiths upon a fusion of Confucianism, Taoism, and Buddhism.

Shinto is an ancient Japanese religion. A polytheistic belief system, Shinto espouses a belief in many spirits of nature called **kami**. **Animism**, the belief that all things possess consciousness, is another tenet of Shintoism.

Largest Religious Bodies in Western Asia

Judaism, Christianity, and Islam, all of which originated in Western Asia, are the largest monotheistic religions practiced today.

- **Judaism** is nearly as old as Hinduism. This religion centers on the belief that faithfulness to God and the Ten Commandments will ensure blessings for His followers. The **Torah** is the Jewish religious text, though the **Talmud** in practice is their main authority.

- **Christianity** has its roots in Judaism; like Judaism, Christianity claims the existence of a single, omnipresent, omniscient God. Unlike Jews, however, Christians believe that **Jesus Christ** was the son of God. Christian doctrine asserts that Jesus was crucified to atone for the sins of humanity and rose again three days later to ascend to Heaven. Currently, Christianity has more followers worldwide than any other religion. The **Bible** is the Christian religious text.
- **Islam**, practiced by Muslims, is based upon the guidance of the Prophet **Muhammad**, who advocated the existence of one all-powerful God (**Allah**). The **Koran**, the Islamic religious text, calls for daily prayer, an annual month of fasting, and almsgiving. Islam, like Christianity, has roots in Judaism.

Methods of Religious Diffusion

As evidenced by, for example, the existence of Buddhism in the United States and the presence of Christianity in Africa, all bodies of religious thought have been **diffused** across the globe. As different belief systems come into contact, religious ideas are discarded, changed, and fused, branching existing religions into sects and creating new religions altogether. Some of the factors that influence religious diffusion include the following:

- **Military campaigns** have been an important vehicle in religious diffusion. The Crusades (11th to 13th centuries), a series of military forays by Catholics striving to "recapture" Jerusalem from Muslims, provide an example of religious imperialism (an approach to spreading religion to different people through the use of warfare, oppression, and persecution).
- **Colonization** has often involved religious imperialism.
- **Trade routes** have played a key role in the diffusion of religions. Missionaries, those who attempt to convert others to their faith, often traveled along these routes with traders and explorers.
- **Migration** has also served to bring groups with different religious beliefs together; in fact, religious persecution has spurred many mass human migrations throughout history.

Non-Governmental Organizations

A non-governmental organization, or **NGO** (sometimes referred to as a private voluntary organization) is, as its title suggests, a cooperative group formed independently of any state government. Usually, a group of this type forms for reasons other than commercial gain, such as the advocation of social or environmental policy; non-governmental organizations are often non-profit. There are two general types of NGOs:

1. **Advocacy non-governmental organizations** are formed to promote awareness of and/or support for a certain issue, which they accomplish through lobbying activities, orchestration of awareness-raising events, and press work.
2. **Operational NGOs** participate in the organization and execution of relief-oriented or development-oriented projects. Most development-related groups evolve in three stages: first, the group concentrates on relief and welfare activities; next, on the development of self-reliant activity in affected areas; and lastly, on the implementation of sustainable development activities at local, state, and national levels.

United Nations

The United Nations (**UN**) is a group of nation-states (including nearly every independent country) that defines itself as a "global association of governments facilitating cooperation in international law, international security, economic development, and social equity." This organization was founded after World War II in 1945 by the victorious countries, which possessed the shared aim of **preventing future conflicts and wars** between nations through the establishment of a situation of **collective security**. This means that any aggression against any of the member states is viewed as an attack on the entire organization, which will respond as a whole. Today, the United Nations consists of several specialized agencies that deal with issues such as human rights, arms control, global health, economic development, and humanitarian assistance. As a large organization made up of nearly 200 member states, the UN does not always function perfectly. However, the group has achieved more through international cooperation than any single nation-state could accomplish alone.

Sustainable Development and Agenda 21

Sustainable development is a developmental process that satisfies the needs of those living in the present without impairing the abilities of those in future generations to attain the same degree of comfort; it is development that does not exhaust the global supply of natural resources. In other words, sustainable development refers to a balance achieved between economic development, social development, and environmental protection.

Agenda 21 is a UN program that strives to reach sustainable development. It consists of four sections:

- The **social and economic dimensions section**, which stresses the importance of addressing global poverty in developing nations through health education, promotion of sustainable settlement patterns, and altering destructive consumption patterns;
- The **conservation and management of resources development section**, which includes information on environmental protection and the preservation of biodiversity;
- The **section on strengthening the role of major groups**, which aims to empower groups at the individual and local levels; and
- The **means of implementation section**, which describes educational, technological, financial, and international procedures for the attainment of the program's goals.

Conflict

Conflict is a situation of discord and/or opposition between two or more individuals or groups. In political science, **conflict** is defined as a continuing state of hostility between groups of people, which often involves physical violence. Conflict must be distinguished from **competition**, which involves two or more groups possessing mutually exclusive goals, meaning that attempts by one party to achieve its goal compromises the ability of the other group to attain its goal. Competition (and occasionally cooperation) may lead to conflict. Individuals and nation-states may become involved in conflicts for a variety of reasons at a variety of scales. For example, two local groups may have conflicting views on a proposed tax increase. At the regional level, different religious or ethnic groups may exist in a state of conflict. Internationally, competition for scarce resources or ideological disagreements may lead to a war between countries.

Class Conflict

Class conflict refers to discord that usually exists between members of different classes. **Social classes** may be defined and differentiated using various criteria. An individual's membership in a particular class may be based on his or her income, education level, possessions, reputation, manners, relationship to a means of production, or any combination of these and other factors. **Class conflict** may be overtly manifested through, for instance, physical violence, worker strikes, or protests. Class conflict may also be expressed more subtly, through, for example, informal "slowdowns" in production or prejudicial treatment of members of an oppositional class. Ironically, conflict between different classes may increase the level of cooperation within a single class, as members ally to lobby public policy makers.

Indigenous Peoples, Colonialism, and Imperialism

Indigenous peoples is a term that describes distinctive cultural groups whose historical associations with an area or region predate that area's colonization, annexation, or integration into a nation-state. **Indigenous societies** are often non-urbanized and are frequently based on agricultural, pastoral, or hunting and gathering production methods.

Colonialism is the practice whereby a nation-state asserts sovereignty over territories outside of its boundaries, usually in order to gain control of an area's resources (natural and human) and potential markets. Colonization may occur violently, through the forcible suppression and domination of indigenous peoples, or it may occur relatively peacefully, through the hegemonic promotion of ideologies designed to imply that the colonizers are spreading superior (and thus beneficial) values and systems to colonized areas.

Imperialism is similar to colonialism in that each practice involves the extension of a nation's control over foreign territories. However, imperialism refers more specifically to the creation and/or maintenance of an empire, a set of regions officially ruled by a single emperor.

Factors of Production

Classical economics identifies three main factors in the production of consumable goods and services:

- **Land** refers to the physical location at which production occurs, as well as material goods (including natural fuel resources, such as coal, as well as materials such as minerals and soil that are used in production). Rent is the monetary compensation paid for the use of land owned by a separate party.
- **Labor** refers to the work executed by humans in the production of goods and the performance of services. The quality of labor is affected by education and training levels.
- **Capital goods** are manmade goods that are used, in turn, to produce other goods and services. Capital goods are also referred to as means of production. This factor includes tools, buildings, and machinery.

Types of Economic Systems

The term *economic system* refers to the way in which goods and services are produced, distributed, and consumed in a society. Three types of **economic systems** are traditional, market, and command.

- In a **traditional economy**, determinations of the types and amounts of goods produced, methods of production, and distribution of goods are based on long-established customs and habits. Such economies are sometimes referred to as subsistence economies because little surplus is produced, which negates the need for markets.
- In a **market economy**, producers of goods and services are free to trade them as they see fit. The types and amounts of goods and services produced (and their prices) are determined by the laws of supply and demand, and by private individuals and organizations.

- In a **command economy**, nearly every aspect is controlled by a central government. The government often makes economic decisions based on social and political goals; for instance, a government may set the price of a gallon of milk at 25 cents, even if it costs one dollar to produce, so that everyone can afford to purchase it.

INDUSTRY

The term *industry* refers to a method of economic production, namely manufacturing, that involves the investment of large amounts of capital prior to production. An **industry** may also be defined as a group of businesses that produce similar products; for example, all of the businesses that participate in film production constitute the "film industry." Industries in general may be classified into four sectors based on the resources needed for production and the type of goods produced.

- The **primary sector of industry** is made up of businesses that transform natural resources into raw materials used in other industries. Agriculture, mining, and forestry are examples of activities related to the primary sector of industries.
- The **secondary sector of industry** involves the manufacture of goods suitable for sale to consumers and other businesses. Businesses in this sector often make use of the materials produced in the primary sector. The clothing, tobacco, and energy industries are considered to be in the secondary sector.
- The **tertiary sector of industry** is also referred to as the service industry or sector. Businesses in this industrial category provide services to consumers and other businesses. Hair salons, hospitals, and restaurants are examples of tertiary businesses that provide services directly to consumers. Members of the tertiary industry may also provide services to other businesses, such as the transportation, distribution, wholesale, or retail of goods produced by businesses in the secondary sector. While the provision of services may involve the alteration of the secondary product (like the preparation of raw foods in the restaurant industry), the focus of the tertiary sector is on interaction with consumers.
- The **quaternary sector of industry** is a relatively new categorization, having been recently distinguished from the tertiary sector. The quaternary sector involves the provision of specialized "intellectual" services, such as education, scientific research, and the distribution of information technology.

LABELS CLASSIFYING LEVELS OF DEVELOPMENT

Economic geographers use different terms to classify countries by their levels of economic development. Most broadly, countries may be classified as either **more developed countries (MDCs)** or **less developed countries (LDCs)**. In this system of classification, distinctions are made often made based on political factors as well as economic factors. Geographers may also categorize the level of a country's economic development as **First World** (capitalist), **Second World** (communist or socialist), **Third World** (underdeveloped), **Fourth World** (severely underdeveloped), or **Fifth World** (poorest). Currently, the **World Bank** (an international organization that monitors the economic status of countries) classifies countries as high income, upper-middle income, lower-middle income, or low income. Any of these categorizations may be misleading when applied to an entire country. Most of the world's countries exhibit highly developed cores as well as peripheral regions stricken by poverty. Therefore, averages of national economic statistics have lost some of their meaning. It is useful to consider the relative advantages (geographic location, resources, political stability, etc.) of certain countries over others.

MEASURES OF ECONOMIC DEVELOPMENT

A country's **consumption per capita** is observed as a measure of the country's level of economic development. Naturally, the higher a nation's level of economic development, the wealthier its citizens will be and, therefore, the more they can afford to consume. A country's **infrastructure** is studied in the assessment of its economic status. Transportation systems, urban centers, distribution mechanisms, industrial businesses, communication systems, and service facilities such as hospitals and police stations are all considered aspects of a country's infrastructure. A country's **social conditions** are also used as measures of economic development. These conditions include the literacy rate, the infant mortality rate, and the availability of health care. The United Nations Development Program has developed a **human development index** based on the national averages of three figures: life expectancy, education (assessed through examination of the adult literacy rate and the combined rates of enrollment in secondary and tertiary schools), and per capita income. A higher human development index is seen as an indicator of a higher level of economic development.

Chapter Quiz

Ready to see how well you retained what you just read? Scan the QR code to go directly to the chapter quiz interface for this study guide. If you're using a computer, simply visit the online resources page at **mometrix.com/resources719/dssthumculgeog** and click the Chapter Quizzes link.

Regional Geography

Subdiscipline of Regional Geography

Regional geography is the subdiscipline of geography that involves the study of how human and physical characteristics combine to form **geographic regions**. Geographers use a regional concept to organize Earth's surface into sections based on the presence of at least one shared characteristic. The classification of groups of places into regions enables geographers to examine the associations between historical, cultural, organizational, economic, and environmental factors within a particular region. Geographers then investigate the effects of these associations on that region's development and interrelationships with other regions. Regions may be studied at many levels, from the local to the international.

Review Video: Regional Geography
Visit mometrix.com/academy and enter code: 350378

Impact of Oil Production and Sale on Oil-Exporting Countries

The production of oil and its sale have had significant effects on the countries of the North Africa/Southwest Asia realm that export it. These effects illustrate the impact of trade patterns on participating regions in a number of ways:

- The high demand for oil across the globe creates higher incomes among the populations of oil-exporting countries, which tend to place these countries among those in the upper-middle income category (in contrast to those in peripheral regions of the realm).
- Large oil revenues have led to increased modernization in certain countries.
- Oil-exporting countries have experienced increased industrialization as an effect of oil production and sale.
- Many workers from peripheral areas of the realm migrate to core countries; thus intra-realm migration is an effect of oil.
- Oil-exporting countries also experience inter-realm migration.
- Concentrated oil production in the realm has heightened regional disparities, both economic and cultural.
- Oil-exporting countries of the realm have begun to receive foreign investment, which creates further international relationships.

Geographic Regions

A geographic region is a demarcated area of the Earth. The classification of areas into **geographic regions** is more refined than the classification of realms. A region is a smaller spatial unit than a realm; each realm is subdivided into one or more regions. There are several properties that all regions have in common:

- All regions have **area**. While they are indeed theoretical constructions, regions are materially present in the real world, occupying space on the surface of the globe.
- All regions have **boundaries** that delineate their spatial territories. Like the boundaries of nation-states, regions' boundaries are defined by a synthesis of natural and human factors. They are occasionally rather sharp but generally function more like transition zones. Regional geographers may make use of political boundaries to aid in the designation of regions within realms.
- All regions also have **location**, both absolute and relative. The names of some regions (for example, Equatorial Africa) convey information about their locations.

Formal Geographic Region

A formal geographic region is one that is identified based on physical and/or human characteristics shared throughout the area. In other words, **formal regions** exhibit a high degree of homogeneity or similitude. Formal regions may be based on political or cultural characteristics or physical homogeneity:

- A **political region** is defined by shared governmental/legal systems, as in the cases of states, countries, and cities.
- A **cultural region** is based on population information (including factors such as typical industrial or agricultural production techniques, ethnic heritage, per capita income, or density and distribution). For example, several large American cities include cultural regions characterized by high concentrations of people of Chinese descent practicing their cultural and social traditions, referred to as "Chinatowns."
- **Physical homogeneity** defines a formal region in, for instance, the areas of climate, topology, and vegetation. For instance, the steppe region of Northern Eurasia is typified by temperate grasslands with rich soils.

Functional Geographic Region

A functional geographic region consists of a central node and the surrounding areas affected by it. Often, the focal point and the proximate areas are linked by economic activities such as manufacturing, retail trading, and transportation and communication systems. However, like formal geographic regions, **functional regions** may be identified through the application of several different criteria. The New York metropolitan area provides an example of a functional region. This region includes parts of four states (New York, New Jersey, Connecticut, and Pennsylvania), associated by common media distribution, commuting patterns, and trade flows.

Balance of Trade

The term *balance of trade* refers to the relationship between the values of imported goods and services and exported goods and services. The exchange of raw materials, manufactured goods, agricultural goods, transportation, and travel are all considered in the determination of a country's **balance of trade**. If the value of a country's imports exceeds that of its exports, the balance of trade (the trade deficit) is said to be **negative**. Conversely, if the value of a country's exports is higher than that of its imports, the balance of trade (the trade surplus) is considered **positive**. A nation's balance of trade must be distinguished from its balance of payments; this term covers any international flow of money, including investment income and transfer payments.

Trade Pacts

A trade pact is a broad agreement between two or more nations that specifies which forms of production and consumption are ideal and which are undesirable. This type of agreement attempts to increase productive efficiency through the facilitation of free trade (the international exchange of goods and services without tariffs or trade barriers, such as import quotas). **Trade pacts** often come under political scrutiny for their roles in increasing economic interdependence between entities or altering traditional economic customs. There are several different types of trade pacts.

Types of Trade Pacts

Four types of trade pact are the following:

1. A **Trade and Investment Framework Agreement (TIFA)** institutes an agenda aimed at the resolution of conflicts and expansion of trade between two or more nations.
2. A **Bilateral Investment Treaty (BIT)** establishes the requisites for the foreign direct investment of nationals/companies of one state in another.
3. A **preferential trade area** is a group of nations that gives preferential access to particular goods from other countries in the area. A trade pact that identifies this type of agreement usually reduces tariffs without eliminating them.
4. A **free trade area** is a zone whose component states have agreed to do away with trade barriers such as quotas and preferences on most goods exchanged between them.

Trade Blocs

A trade bloc is a large free trade area delimited by one or more trade pacts. **Trade blocs** are usually regionally based. Occasionally, a state may act as a member in more than one bloc. For instance, Venezuela is a part of both the Andean Community and the Mercosur trading blocs. Generally, such pacts name formal adjudication panels, such as NAFTA's, which may allow differing degrees of member participation. The European Union, for instance, includes a democratically elected parliament, which acts as a decision-making body. A trade bloc may decide to eliminate visa requirements and (at least theoretically) borders between its member states, enabling free travel in the region. NAFTA and the EU are two of the most active trade blocs on the globe. The Caribbean Community and Common Market (CARICOM) is another active group with a state-like governing structure. There are currently 15 full members of CARICOM. The Economic Community of West African States (ECOWAS) is a regional trade bloc aimed at furthering economic integration among its member states.

Stages of Economic Integration

The six stages of economic integration are the following:

1. The first stage is the existence of a **preferential trading area**, which is the weakest form of economic integration between economies.
2. The second stage of economic integration is a **free trade area**.
3. The third stage, a **customs union**, is a free trade area whose participating states have agreed upon a common external tariff, which involves the application of the same customs duties, quotas, and preferences on all goods entering the union.
4. The fourth stage of economic integration may be referred to as a **common market** or a single market. A single market exists when all states in a customs union share common policies on product regulation, and when all factors of production (goods, services, labor, and capital) move freely between them.
5. The fifth stage is the creation of an **economic and monetary union**, a single market with a common currency.

6. **Complete economic integration** is reached when integrated units have no individual control over economic policy. Complete economic integration is more common within countries than in supranational organizations.

Intensive and Extensive Agriculture

Intensive agriculture or **intensive farming** is a type of agricultural production system that involves the use of high levels of chemical inputs, such as fertilizers, pesticides, and growth regulators, on relatively small plots of land to maximize the output of that land. This method of agricultural production is associated with modern farming techniques, including mechanization. While the use of intensive farming techniques can assist in the maintenance of a stable food supply, it often occurs at the expense of the environment. For example, the clearing of land eliminates local vegetation and therefore the natural habitat of the area's fauna, and can lead to soil erosion. Also, the use of chemicals creates pollution, which may affect the local ecosystem and the area's water supply.

Extensive agriculture, in contrast, involves the production of crops over large areas of low-cost land without the use of pesticides and fertilizers. While this type of agricultural production is not harmful to the environment, it cannot produce crops at the same volume as intensive agriculture.

Agrarian Revolution

The term *agrarian revolution* is used to refer to the period of transformation of agricultural production methods in Europe from the 16th to mid-19th centuries. These improvements enabled European farmers to sustain a rapidly growing population during this time. The resultant increase in urbanization and growing markets served as impetuses for improved organization of land ownership and agrarian activities, in the forms of land enclosure and consolidated farmland; higher crop prices encouraged farmers to move from subsistence levels of agricultural production to production for a capitalist market. Other advancements included the introduction of new crops (such as potatoes from the Americas) in the realm, crop rotation (which increased the variety and amount of crops produced and also improved the quality of the soil), and the improvement of storage and distribution systems. The products of the later **Industrial Revolution** contributed to the ongoing process of agricultural advancement. Ultimately, the agrarian revolution marked the development of improved agricultural practices that eventually diffused throughout the realm and world.

Geographic Realm of Europe

The geographic realm of Europe is made up of five geographic regions: Western Europe, the British Isles, Northern Europe, Southern (Mediterranean) Europe, and Eastern Europe. It is home to one of the largest population clusters in the world. Despite the relatively small size of its territory, Europe's people and their actions have affected (and continue to affect) all the world's realms. Technological innovations, political revolutions, and vast empires have influenced the behaviors of people on each continent. European colonial endeavors have established communities and impacted the formation of ideologies the world over. Europe's natural and human resources have helped the realm to survive and grow throughout the years. For approximately the last 50 years, Europe has been engaged in a unification program known as the **European Union**. Currently, 27 of the realm's 48 nation-states are members of the Union.

General Economic Geography of Europe

The **economy of Europe** is dominated by the **European Union**, which, if considered as a whole, has the largest economy in the world. Though the functional region of Western Europe has historically been the hub of economic activity in the realm, this situation is changing with the development of other core regions, productive complementarities, and interregional/international trade markets. Levels of economic development tend to decline as one moves from west to east across the realm; this too is changing with the growth of the economies of former member countries of the Soviet Union and their increasing interactions with other regions and realms. Europe's agricultural and fishing sectors are highly developed and still center on Western Europe. Europe's manufacturing sector is also quite developed. While many of the realm's industries are concentrated in Western Europe, deindustrialization in the region has resulted in the outsourcing of labor to areas such as Eastern Europe and China. Financial activity in the realm is concentrated in several cities, with London as the largest.

Geographic Realm of Russia

Russia, the largest territorial state on Earth, is an example of a geographic realm that has undergone tremendous amounts of change throughout its existence. Tsars conquered and dominated Russian territory, which was subsequently inhabited by Soviets, who then shaped the domain and its peoples into the Soviet Union. Though World War II tested the empire, it also validated the USSR's status as a global superpower, which it retained until the late 1980s. Internal factors (such as mismanagement of a communist government) and external factors (including the Second World War, pressure from anti-communist leaders, and the global decline of colonialism) eventually led to the dissolution of the Soviet Union in 1991. Consequent cultural, economic, and social diversity have given rise to the establishment of **four geographical regions** (each of which contains subregions): the Russian Core, the Eastern Frontier, Siberia, and the Far East.

General Economic Geography of Russia

The economic geography of Russia is highly varied and is characterized by discrete core and peripheral regions of **economic activity**. Despite the presence of substantial natural resources (such as gas and oil) and a well-educated labor force, the effects of the transition from a failed centrally planned economy during the Soviet Era to a free market continue to hinder the development of the economies in certain regions. In the agricultural sector, production has decreased drastically with attempts at the privatization of collective farms and restructuring of the economy. Also, the harsh climate in the realm has had an effect on agricultural production. The levels of meat, milk, vegetables, and grains have decreased yearly since 1989. This has had negative ramifications in a country that is largely dependent on its own food production. The inefficiencies and inadequacies held over from the Soviet Union continue to disturb Russia's industrial sector, particularly in the extraction of raw materials and the distribution of goods. Still, Russia is the most industrialized of all the former Soviet republics.

Geographic Realm of North America

The geographic realm of North America is home to two countries, Canada and the United States (which is currently considered a global superpower). This realm is characterized by **pluralistic (diverse) societies** which, unfortunately, are often plagued by **social inequalities**. It is also a **postindustrial realm**, which means that the economies of Canada and the United States each experienced increases in the amount of available information technology and rapid expansions of the tertiary (service) sector of industry after the industrialization processes in those countries. The eight regions of North America (many of which stretch across the US-Canada boundary) are largely differentiated by differences in the various economic activities practiced in different areas. These regions include the Continental Core, the South, the Southwest, the West Coast, the Agricultural Heartland, French Canada, the New England/Maritime Provinces, and the Marginal Interior.

General Economic Geography of Canada

As one of the world's wealthiest nations, **Canada** has a largely **postindustrial economy**, with employment concentrated in the **service sector** (particularly retail). However, unlike many developed countries, primary economic activities (specifically logging and oil production) are important aspects of the country's economy. Canada has a large and varied (though regionally variable) supply of natural resources, such as oil, nickel, and lead. Canadian agricultural products (especially wheat and grains) are exported in high levels to the United States, Europe, and East Asia. Another unusual aspect of Canada's economy (as compared to those of other highly developed nations) is the historical secondary status of the manufacturing sector of industry. Though it is certainly not unimportant, manufacturing has never been as vital to the nation's economy as primary or tertiary activities. Many of Canada's industrial firms are branches of US companies. Regional disparities in wealth and economy strength have increased regionalism throughout the region.

General Economic Geography of the United States

As a current superpower, the **United States** has one of the most advanced economies in the world. Like Canada, the United States contains many deposits of **natural resources**. For instance, the North American realm has more coal reserves than any other. The spatial organization of regional agricultural production in the United States exists within the framework of a modified Von Thunen model, with the "megalopolis" of New England at its center and belts of specialized activity extending westward. Though the **manufacturing** sector is less important in a postindustrial economy, this type of activity is still practiced in the United States and tends to cluster around several urban-industrial nodes, especially within the Manufacturing Belt (located in the Northeast United States). Increased mechanization and advancements in technology have eliminated many "blue-collar" jobs in this region. Most laborers in the US workforce are employed in **quaternary economic activity**. States offering noneconomic amenities (such as weather and proximity to urban centers and universities) have experienced higher levels of growth than other regions.

Geographic Realm of Central America

The geographic realm of Central America, which is sometimes referred to as **Middle America**, covers the territory between southern North America and the boundary between Panama and Colombia. The exact demarcations of the realm vary from source to source; however, the economic subregion recognized by the United Nations includes all mainland states of North America south of the US-Mexico border in the realm. Basically, this definition counts Mexico and Belize as members of the Central America realm, while other definitions assign these countries to the North American realm. Due to the influence of Spanish and Portuguese colonialism in Central America, this realm and South America are often jointly referred to as **Latin America**. Central America is divided into four regions: Mexico, the seven states of Central America (Belize, Costa Rica, El Salvador, Guatemala, Honduras, Nicaragua, and Panama), the larger islands of the Caribbean (the Greater Antilles), and the smaller islands of the Caribbean (the Lesser Antilles).

General Economic Geography of Central America

The economic geography of Central America includes the least developed territories in the Americas, with the exception of Mexico. Under the **Mainland-Rimland framework**, Central America is divided into a **Euro-Amerindian Mainland** (made up of mainland Middle America from Mexico to Panama, excluding parts of the Caribbean coast) and a **Euro-African rimland** (consisting of the coastal zone and the Caribbean islands). Economic activity on the Mainland has historically been oriented around **haciendas** (privately owned estates maintained more for prestige and self-sufficiency than maximum production), and is therefore less dependent on trade with other nations. Governmental and social pressures have led to the forced specialization of productive activity in or the parceling out of haciendas in this area. The Rimland's economy has traditionally focused on **plantation production**, characterized by efficient production of one crop specifically for export and the importation of labor. The Rimland's economy is thus more dependent on the fluctuating global market. Plantation systems, like hacienda systems, continue to metamorphose under internal and external pressures; still, their effects remain visible in the region.

Geographic Realm of South America

The geographic realm of South America is made up of four regions: Brazil, the Northeastern countries, the West, and the Southern Cone. South America and Central America are often collectively referred to as **Latin America**, due to the enduring cultural and social influences of former Spanish and Portuguese colonial presences in these areas. These influences are most visible in the languages, architecture, music, and visual arts of the peoples of South America. Roman Catholicism and traditional systems relating to land ownership, also transmitted from European countries, continue to be major factors in the evolution of South American societies. In addition, the cultural practices and beliefs of Native Americans have been and continue to be vital shaping forces in the realm.

General Economic Geography of South America

The economic geography of South America is characterized by high levels of regional disparity. In many of the realm's countries (such as Brazil, Bolivia, and Venezuela), the richest 20% of the population may control over 60% of the nation's wealth, while the poorest 20% may own less than 5% of that wealth. Although several South American nations have become involved in the mining of oil, coal, and valuable minerals in high amounts, the realm's main economic focus is **agriculture**. The South American realm is unusual, because subsistence farming and commercial farming exist side by side; generally, a geographic realm is dominated by one or the other. **Commercial farmers** in this area tend to be involved in cattle ranching, wheat farming, grain farming (in a "Corn Belt" zone similar to that in the United States), or plantation-type agriculture. Commercial agricultural endeavors tend to be located near the coasts of the South American continent, with small pockets of activity in the interior. **Subsistence-level farming** takes place on all other arable land.

Geographic Realm of North Africa/Southwest Asia

The size and geographic diversity of the geographic realm of North Africa/Southwest Asia have spawned a number of different labels for the region, none of which are completely satisfactory. These labels include the Islamic realm, the Arab World, the dry world, and Afrasia. Though Islam and aridity do dominate the religious and climatic aspects of the realm, that domination is not complete, and the heterogeneity within these groups alone problematizes the notion of referring to the realm by a single characteristic. The use of relative location is seen as less divisive. The **North Africa realm** is composed of three regions (Egypt, North Africa, and the Southwest), and **Southwest Asia** is composed of four (the Middle East [this label is also disputed, due to what some see as the pejorative connotations of the term], the Arabian Peninsula, the North, and the East).

Mesopotamia

Mesopotamia, a major historic culture hearth, is located in the Tigris-Euphrates lowland, from the northern edge of the Persian Gulf to present-day Turkey. **Mesopotamia** (literally the "land between the rivers") was an area of fertile alluvial soils and plentiful sunshine and water. This zone saw the development of **advanced farming techniques**, such as planned sowing and harvesting, irrigation, and the distribution of surplus crops for later consumption. Unfortunately for residents of the realm, much of the area's land is now **desert**; this climate change is thought to be related to glacial recession in the late Pleistocene era. However, this realm is still home to the Nile and the fertile Tell Atlas mountain range area (the northern coast of Morocco, Algeria, and Tunisia).

General Economic Geography of North Africa/Southwest Asia

The economic geography of the realm of North Africa/Southwest Asia is primarily **agricultural**. Though much of the fertile farmland associated with Mesopotamia and the Fertile Crescent (another ancient culture hearth characterized by its advanced agricultural activity) has dried up, many residents of this realm continue to produce resilient crops (particularly cereals), mostly at subsistence levels. Another important aspect of the economic geography of this realm is the vast **oil reserves** located on the southern Arabian Peninsula, in North Africa, and near the Caspian Sea. While oil is considered one of the most important natural resources on our planet, its presence in North Africa/Southwest Asia has improved the quality of life for only a small portion of the population. This realm exhibits a large gap between the rich and the poor.

Geographic Realm of Sub-Saharan Africa

The geographic realm of Sub-Saharan Africa is composed of the territory between the southern border of the Sahara Desert and the southernmost coast of the country of South Africa. The boundary between the North Africa realm and the Sub-Saharan realm is a prime example of a **transition zone**; several states straddle this hypothetical divide. This area of the globe constitutes a fairly distinctive cultural realm, due to a fusion of traditional African beliefs and cultures with the influences of European colonialism. Many countries in this realm exhibit export-oriented transport systems and European concepts of political geography while retaining their traditional languages, religions, and social practices. The realm of Sub-Saharan Africa is the least developed realm in the world, and the majority of its residents engage in agricultural production. This realm is made up of four regions: West Africa, East Africa, Equatorial Africa, and Southern Africa.

General Economic Geography of Sub-Saharan Africa

The **economic geography of the realm of Sub-Saharan Africa** is primarily **agricultural**. Though many raw materials useful to industrialized countries (such as oil and diamonds) are located within this realm, most residents of Sub-Saharan Africa have little or no access to the technology needed to extract these resources, or to the world economy. Agriculturalists in this realm generally produce at the subsistence level (partially due to the harsh physical conditions—hot, dry weather—of the realm). Grain crops are produced more easily in drier areas, while root crops are grown in relatively wetter areas. Peoples in Sub-Saharan Africa also depend on **pastoralism** (especially the raising of goats, cattle, and chicken) and fishing for their livelihoods. Though this realm is the least developed in the world, farmers are attempting to better their situations by introducing cash crops to their land. Still, many in the area (which has the highest rate of population growth in the world) remain malnourished.

Geographic Realm of South Asia

The geographic realm of South Asia, which is one of the world's largest population agglomerations, has **India** at its center. This realm is delineated by **natural boundaries**: the Himalayan Mountains to the north and east, and the Arabian Sea and the Bay of Bengal to the south. India was once the cornerstone of civilization, and later a key part of the British colonial empire. Violent conflicts over the control of territory within South Asia have culminated in the creation of six states. This realm, with its many languages and variety of religious affiliations, contains deep cultural divisions. It contains five regions: the Ganges Plain, Pakistan, the mountainous North, Bangladesh, and the Dravidian South (including the island of Sri Lanka).

General Economic Geography of South Asia

The economic geography of South Asia is **low-income**, as the area continues to experience the effects of former British colonialization. When they came to South Asia, European powers changed trade patterns in the realm; Europe replaced India as the provider of manufactured goods for the realm. This caused a decrease in South Asian industry. Colonialists also exploited raw materials in the realm. Today, each of the states in South Asia has a low-income economy, due largely to the fact that these economies tend to center on inefficient and relatively less productive agricultural methods. Most residents of this region live in villages and survive directly on their parcels of land (often measuring less than an acre). Low-technology production methods keep crop yields (both per acre and per worker) at the **subsistence level**. Also, local traditions of inheritance often subdivide already undersized plots, preventing the organization of progressive measures, such as cooperative farming and shared irrigation in many states. The lack of a strong official agricultural development policy at the state and federal levels also inhibits the maturation of agricultural production.

Geographic Realm of East Asia

The geographic realm of East Asia has **China** at its center; this realm houses the largest concentration of human population in the world. Culturally, the 1.4 billion Chinese people dominate this realm, while the Japanese dominate economically. In fact, the economic activity and success of Japan have recently led to the tentative identification of the **Pacific Rim region**, a functional region with Japan as its anchor. The conceptualization of this region, as well as its practical development in the real world, continues to affect several realms and regions facing the Pacific Ocean. East Asia contains five regions: China Proper (eastern and northeastern China), which includes (somewhat precariously) North Korea, the mountains and plateaus of Xizang (the former Tibet), the deserts of Xinjiang, Mongolia, and the Pacific Rim (including Japan, Taiwan, South Korea, Thailand, and sometimes Malaysia), most of which was formerly referred to as the **Jakota Triangle**.

General Economic Geography of East Asia

The economic geography of East Asia is highly variable: Japan is one of the **most developed** countries on the globe, while Mongolia is one of the **least developed**. The wide inter- and intraregional variations in this realm's development level, therefore, demonstrate that it is inappropriate to label entire realms as "developed" or "underdeveloped." **Agriculturalists** in the realm tend to inhabit the fertile basins of the great rivers of the east, and produce grains such as wheat. East Asia is also home to large deposits of **raw materials** such as coal and natural gas. Economic development in the nations of the Jakota Triangle (Japan, South Korea, and Taiwan) is thought to presage the future growth and modernization of the other political entities in the region. Japan, in particular, has experienced rapid growth in all **industrial** sectors and possesses long-established trading relationships with nations across the globe. China, the other giant of the realm, has developed a mixed-market economy that displays both capitalistic and communistic characteristics.

Geographic Realm of Southeast Asia

The geographic realm of Southeast Asia contains ethnic and linguistic groups that are particularly diverse. The high occurrence of conflicts for territory and/or power in this realm throughout history has led some to refer to the realm as "the Eastern Europe of Asia." Some use the term **Indochina** synonymously with Southeast Asia, which is appropriate because it conveys the identities of the two major cultural contributors to the realm. The ethnic affinities of those in this realm tend to lie with China, while cultural influences (specifically religious) arrived in the region from India. The two major regions of Southeast Asia are differentiated by their spatial separation. Indochina is the eastern, mainland part of the region; the archipelagoes of the **Philippines** and **Indonesia** make up the other region.

General Economic Geography of Southeast Asia

The economic geography of Southeast Asia resembles that of East Asia. It is a study in **economic contrasts**; like Eastern Europe, this realm is a shatter belt. Singapore, for example, has the second-busiest port in the world and is a major banking and financial center. Indonesia, Thailand, and the Philippines have grown from foreign direct investments (a manner of transferring capital across political boundaries, in which the investor exercises control over the acquired asset) in local industries. Also, the islands of Southeast Asia contain large petroleum reserves. Countries such as Vietnam and Cambodia, on the other hand, are some of the least developed countries in the world. This is partially due to the effects of the transition from a planned economy to a market economy. Levels of unemployment tend to be high in both urban and rural areas, as masses of people leave their farmlands (typically rice and/or grains) for crowded cities with limited job opportunities. The lack of a cohesive infrastructure, coupled with political instability, continues to problematize economic growth in these countries.

Geographic Realm of Australia

The geographic realm of Australia is formed by the regions of **Australia** and **New Zealand**. This realm is distinguished from other areas of the world by its **continental isolation** and the strong influence of Western culture among its peoples, who are demographically unique. Today, the furthest northwestern points of Australia may be considered part of the Pacific Rim region of East Asia. Australia is anomalous alongside Southeast Asia and the regions of the Pacific, due to its relatively high level of economic development. Still, some of the peoples of New Zealand remain traditional societies. The realm of Australia is made up of four regions. Australia the state is divided into an urbanized core and an arid interior, and New Zealand is made up of two large islands that are physically and culturally distinct.

General Economic Geography of Australia

The economic geography of Australia, as well as New Zealand, relies principally on the exportation of **livestock products**; Australia also participates in farming (especially wheat) and mining activities. Dependence on a constantly fluctuating world market places this realm's economy in a **precarious** position. Despite the plethora of advantages enjoyed by residents of the realm (plentiful farmlands, diverse mineral deposits, access to waterways, and underground water resources, as well as political stability), the Australian economy's growth has declined. Though it is considered one of the most developed realms in the world, Australia must now compete with the emerging Pacific Rim for trade opportunities. Australia has attempted to integrate itself into the Pacific Rim by exporting raw materials to countries in that region. Agriculturalists in this realm produce grains, rice, and certain fruits, while pastoralists produce wool and meat raising sheep. Manufacturing in Australia remains oriented to local domestic markets, partially due to the high costs of shipping and transportation to and from the relatively isolated realm.

Geographic Realm of the Pacific

The geographic realm of the Pacific is made up of the thousands of islands (large and small) that are situated in the Pacific Ocean, between Asia and Australia to the west and the Americas to the east. This geographic realm is more fragmented than any other; it is also culturally heterogeneous. The Pacific Realm is traditionally subdivided into three regions: **Melanesia** (the most populous Pacific region), which is associated with New Guinea; **Micronesia** (so named for the small sizes of this region's constituent islands), which is located to the north; and **Polynesia**, which extends from the Hawaiian archipelago southward to Easter Island and southwestward to New Zealand. The regions of Melanesia and Polynesia meet in New Zealand (the residents of which are descended from Polynesian peoples) and Australia (whose indigenous population is Melanesian).

General Economic Geography of the Pacific Realm

The economic geography of the Pacific Realm is based on **tourism**. Though this realm covers a larger total area than any other, it possesses the least land area. Coral atolls, ancient volcanoes, open sea, and tropical vegetation offer travelers one spectacular view after another. The region of Melanesia produces valuable export items such as palm oil, coffee, and cocoa, in addition to the subsistence-level production of root crops and bananas. Melanesia also houses large mineral deposits. Micronesia is also involved in agriculture; fertile soils in this region help to diversify crop production. Polynesia, the region that includes the Hawaiian Islands, has a highly developed tourism economy. Most states in the Pacific Realm have high or upper-middle-income economies.

Place

In geography, a place is a space on Earth's surface that has been given particular meaning by humans. A **place** may be as small as a room or as large as a continent. Places are differentiated by the unique combination of human and physical properties exhibited by each and are often bounded and named. The human characteristics of a place include political systems, economic systems, languages, population statistics, and cultural norms. A place's physical characteristics include climate, vegetation types and distributions, landforms, animal life, and soils. Constant changes in these qualities affect entire places; therefore, places never stay the same for long. They may thrive or ebb, become simpler or more complex, or become altered in organization.

Enclaves

An enclave is a piece of territory that is completely surrounded by another political territory of which the former is not a part. For example, the sovereign country of Vatican City is enclaved within Italy. There are several kinds of enclaves:

- A **true enclave** is one that can be entered only via another country.
- A **practical enclave** is one that may be more easily accessed through another country, even though it is not completely detached from the "mother" country, due to, for example, its topography or available transportation routes.
- A **subnational enclave** is a territory that belongs to one political subdivision of land, yet is attached to another. For instance, Long Island is considered part of the city of Boston, but is road-accessible only from Quincy, Massachusetts.
- An **ethnic enclave** is a community of members of a minority ethnic group that is situated in the midst of a larger ethnic group (such as a Chinatown).

Exclaves

An exclave is a territory belonging to, yet detached from, one political entity and surrounded by other political entities. The term is similar in meaning to enclave. However, the two are not synonymous; an **exclave** is not necessarily an enclave. For instance, if area C, whose motherland is country B, is located in the center of country A, area C may be referred to as B's exclave and A's enclave. If, however, area C is located along the boundary between country B and another foreign country (D), it is no longer referred to as an enclave, but it is still appropriate to describe it as B's exclave. Like enclaves, exclaves may be subnational, true, or practical.

Irredentism

Irredentism refers to any nationalist policy that seeks to extend cultures and possibly expand political territories through the incorporation of territories ruled by foreign entities. Originally, the term referred to the nationalist Italian movement that advocated the annexation of certain territories (which were officially held by Austria but populated by a majority of Italians) to Italy. An example of **irredentism** can be found in Hungary. While the population of Hungary proper is close to 10 million, there are large concentrations of Hungarians living in Romania, Slovakia, Croatia, Serbia, and Slovenia (holdovers from a time when Hungary was more powerful and held more territory on the Balkan Peninsula). The Hungarian government appeals to these "ethnic cohorts" and seeks to protect them, if needed, from the government of the states in which they live; this behavior is referred to as irredentism.

Globalization

Globalization is the process whereby regional differences are reduced due to the increased exchange of cultural, economic, and political ideas and practices among traditionally isolated nations. Advancements in technology have bred increased interdependency among the world's countries and enabled people to interact with others on a global scale. Time-space convergence is the increasing nearness of people and places due to the technological reduction of the travel/communication times and distances between them. Social theoriest Arjun Appaduri has identified five categories of **global connectivity**:

1. **Ethnoscapes** are the movements of people from one region to another.
2. **Financescapes** are the movements of money around the world.
3. **Ideoscapes** are the global movements of ideas and belief systems.
4. **Mediascapes** are the mass distributions of images through the media.
5. **Technoscapes** are the movements of technologies around the globe.

Some view the changes associated with globalization as positive steps toward the development of a fully multicultural global society. Others see globalization as a synonym for **imperialism**.

Processes of Spatial Diffusion

Spatial diffusion is the mechanism whereby ideas, practices, and innovations spread through a population over time and space. Study of the processes through which **spatial diffusion** takes place allows geographers to hypothesize the dispersal of cultural and economic ideas in the past and future. There are four processes associated with spatial diffusion:

1. **Expansion diffusion** is the type of diffusion in which a strong central source area emanates propagation waves in all directions. These waves affect ever-growing populations and places.
2. **Contagious diffusion** is a method of expansion diffusion that relies on local proximity to spread phenomena.
3. **Hierarchical diffusion** involves the diffusion of phenomena from a high leader such as a king or chief.
4. **Relocation diffusion** occurs when a phenomenon spreads after the movement and resettlement of a source population; expansion from the relocated source area typically follows.

Economic Geography

Economic geography is the subfield of geography that investigates the ways in which people support themselves and their families, and the ways in which the goods and services they produce are spatially organized. For example, the types of goods produced in a particular geographic region may be influenced by the region's climate, political and/or social organization, infrastructure, and geology. Scholars of **economic geography** seek to explain how the interaction of these and other factors creates the patterns of **diverse economic activity** observed across the surface of the globe. Recognition of these relationships can help geographers make predictions about past and future events and to postulate solutions to the problems of **unequal economic development** among the nations of the world.

Medical Geography

Medical geography is the subfield of geography that studies the **health** of the global population in a spatial context. Most diseases that affect human beings originate in the natural environment. Certain environmental qualities facilitate the spread of **disease**. Tropical Africa, for instance, with its hot, humid climate, is the ideal habitat for carriers such as mosquitoes and flies. Cultural factors, such as personal hygiene, sexual behaviors, and food preparation techniques, can also contribute to disease diffusion. One virus that has its roots in the environment is the Ebola virus, which periodically breaks out randomly and violently in the region of Equatorial Africa. These viruses are born in **source (core) areas** and diffuse throughout the surrounding population through **hosts**. Analysis of the spatial patterns of diseases and the geographic characteristics of the affected regions can provide vital information about the nature, prevention, and cure of diseases.

Cultural Landscapes

A cultural landscape is a geographic area that includes cultural and natural resources associated with a historic event, activity, person, or group of people. People of every cultural group transform the lands upon which they live. They erect buildings, create transportation routes, till soil, and subdivide their territories into smaller parcels. The ways in which humans interact with the natural environment often differ from culture to culture. For example, industrialized societies may ignore the presence of certain vegetation or even see it as an obstacle to development, while traditional societies may view the same vegetation as an important natural resource. **Carl Sauer**, a geographer who focused his cultural studies on the concept of **cultural landscapes** provides a straightforward definition: cultural landscapes are "the forms superimposed on the physical landscape by the activities of man." The term *sequent occupance* refers to the stages of evolution undergone by an area when different cultural groups successively occupy that particular landscape. The presence of a distinctive cultural landscape is a major criterion in the delineation of a cultural region.

Epochs of Metropolitan Evolution in North America

Analysis of advancements in transportation technology and industrial energy reveals five epochs of metropolitan evolution in North America:

1. The **Sail-Wagon Epoch** (1790-1830) was characterized by basic overland and waterway methods of transportation. North America depended on overseas trade, which was more plausible than trade with the largely inaccessible western periphery.
2. The **Iron Horse Epoch** (1830-1870) was dominated by railways. The completion of the transcontinental railroad near the close of this epoch heralded the start of the creation of national urban systems.
3. The **Steel-Rail Epoch** (1870-1920) was greatly affected by the US Industrial Revolution, with the associated increases in production levels and railway efficiency.
4. The **Auto-Air-Amenity Epoch** (1920-1970) saw the invention of the gasoline-powered internal combustion engine and a consequent rise in automotive and air transportation. Much of the American workforce entered the service industry.
5. The **Satellite-Electronic-Jet Propulsion Epoch** (1970-present) has thus far shown increased levels of international interaction, specialization, and constraints on expensive energy sources, and the development of a global village.

Eras of Intraurban Structural Evolution in North America

Developments in transportation technology and industrial energy affected urban areas in North America on a local scale. **Intraurban growth**, like national urban evolution, may be organized into stages:

- During the **Walking-Horsecar Era** (prior to 1888), cities had to be compact due to the time required for long travel by pedestrians.
- The **Electric Streetcar Era** (1888-1920) saw the invention of a motor that could be attached to horsecars; this decreased travel time significantly and thus enabled urban expansion. This, in turn, enabled more specialized land use.
- The **Recreational Automobile Era** (1920-1945) was characterized by increased accessibility to the outer metropolitan ring, due to the impact of automobiles and highway expansion. The city core reached its peak during this era, which also saw an increase in suburbanization and the partitioning of residential space.
- The **Freeway Era** (1945-present) has demonstrated the full effect of individual automobile transportation on high-speed expressways; urban sprawl has resulted in distances up to 30 miles between the city's center and outskirts.

Rostow's Model of the Development Process

In the 1960s, economist **Walt Rostow** formulated a model of the process of economic development (the **Rostovian take-off model**). Rostow asserted that each of the world's countries follows a five-stage path toward development:

1. In the first stage, **traditional society**, people engage in agricultural production at subsistence levels. Nations in the first stage tend to adhere to a rigid social structure and resist technological change.
2. The second stage, **preconditions for take-off**, involves the introduction of a progressive leader (or leaders) who steers the nation toward greater diversification and flexibility. Traditional beliefs and practices are discarded, agricultural activity and birth rates decline, and infrastructure improves.
3. The third stage, **take-off**, generally involves an industrial revolution as well as urbanization and technological advancements.
4. The fourth stage, **drive to maturity**, is reached when technology disperses throughout a nation, enabling industrial specialization and increased trade.
5. A nation in the fifth stage, **high mass consumption**, exhibits high income levels and a majority of workers in the third and fourth sectors of industry.

Neolithic Revolution

The Neolithic Revolution was a period of conversion from hunting and gathering methods of subsistence to **agricultural** methods of production; this transition began approximately 10,000 years ago. This "revolution" is so named because of the long-lasting effects of social and economic changes in human society that resulted from this conversion. The causes of these changes are **climatic changes** associated with the end of the last ice age (namely, warmer, drier climates), which led hunter-gatherers to settle near stable water sources, and a food crisis perpetuated by the extinction of several species of large mammals during the late Paleolithic era. The transition to agricultural production involved the development of permanent settlements (as well as a decrease in nomadic lifestyles), the domestication of plants and animals, human modification of the natural environment, the evolution of notions of land ownership, economic specialization, and the development of trading systems. Many of the characteristics of present-day "**civilization**" (for instance, social hierarchies, advanced, specialized technologies, and cities) began with the **Neolithic Revolution**.

Industrial Revolution

The term *Industrial Revolution* generally refers to the conversion from an economy based on **manual labor** to one supported by **industry and machine manufacture**, which took place in Britain during the late 18th and early 19th centuries (though other countries experienced industrial revolutions after Britain's). The numerous causes of this revolution are complex. They include the presence of a large workforce, due to improvements in disease control; the agrarian revolution, which made agriculture a less labor-intensive endeavor and forced workers into other spheres; colonial expansion, which improved Britain's international trade market and increased its available capital; the existence of a sizeable domestic market; and the availability of abundant natural resources. Developments of the Industrial Revolution included improvements in iron smelting, based on the use of coal (converted into carbon-rich coke) as an energy source, and the invention of the steam engine, adapted for use in the textile, mining, manufacturing, and transportation industries. Innovations developed during the Industrial Revolution spread through Europe and to North America and eventually diffused across the globe.

Review Video: The Industrial Revolution
Visit mometrix.com/academy and enter code: 372796

Dust Bowl

The Dust Bowl (1930-1941) was a period of American history characterized by a high incidence of dust storms in the Oklahoma Panhandle region. The instability of the world agriculture market during World War I led to **overproduction** in the 1920s. Even lands previously considered unsuitable for agricultural use were leveled and developed. This excessive activity devastated the plains of the Oklahoma Panhandle, eliminating the natural vegetation that could have prevented the massive soil movement that occurred during the drought and strong winds of the 1930s. Thus, this ecological disaster occurred in large part due to the activities of humans in the region. In turn, the **Dust Bowl** led to a large intra-realm **migration** of humans in North America; hundreds of thousands of people migrated from Oklahoma to California. The events before, during, and after the Dust Bowl, as well as the environmental event itself, provide key examples of the complex processes of interaction between humans and their environments.

Perceptual Region

A perceptual geographic region is one that is shaped by people's shared feelings and attitudes about an area. **Perception** is the process whereby individuals use their senses to collect information about their situation or environment. A person's perception is affected by his or her past experiences and cultural background. The delineation of a **perceptual geographic region** is thus a subjective process. Perceptual geographic regions are often influenced by people's **mental maps**. The theoretical organization of parts of Earth's surface into perceptual regions may help to develop an individual's sense of the world's structure; however, since such regions are delineated based on personal viewpoints, they may reflect inappropriate (and sometimes prejudicial) stereotypes.

Geographic Realms

A geographic realm is the largest geographical unit into which Earth's surface can be divided. **Geographic realms** are sometimes referred to as "**global neighborhoods**." All places within a realm share at least one **overarching characteristic**, whether that factor is physical (such as climate type) or human (such as mode of production). Realms are also distinguished by the type of **interaction** that takes place between human society and the natural environment. In other words, the ways in which humans alter the land on which they live, including the features they erect upon it, affect the area's position in the global regionalization scheme. Finally, a geographic realm must encompass a "**great cluster**" (population concentration) of humans. China, for example, exists at the center of one such cluster. Like all regional classifications related to human activity, geographic realms change over time. Today, geographers identify twelve realms: Europe, Russia, North America, Middle America, South America, North Africa/Southwest Asia, Sub-Saharan Africa, South Asia, East Asia, Southeast Asia, Australia, and the Pacific Rim.

Earth's Three Largest Population Clusters

Earth's three largest population clusters are East Asia, India, and Europe.

1. **East Asia**, centered on China, is home to the world's largest population cluster, incorporating the eastern coastal zone from the Korean Peninsula to Vietnam. Population density is highest near the coast and ebbs as one moves inland; members of this cluster are also concentrated in the valleys of China's major rivers. The majority of people in East Asia lives in rural areas and engages in agricultural production.
2. **India** exists at the center of South Asia, the second-largest population cluster, which also includes Pakistan and Bangladesh. The highest concentration of humans in this region is located near the Ganges River. This realm is also largely agricultural. High levels of population growth in South Asia have problematized sustainable production.
3. **Europe** is the third-largest of the world's population clusters. In contrast to the other two largest clusters, the highest population density in this cluster runs along an east-west axis, corresponding to a zone of raw industrial materials. As one of the most industrialized realms, Europe is highly dependent on these resources.

Transition Zones

A transition zone is an area of spatial change between global neighborhoods. Such zones are characterized by gradual changes in the physical and human characteristics which differentiate one realm from another. Like other geographic boundaries, the divisions between geographic realms are often blurred. As these boundaries are theoretical, it not surprising that they do not practically differentiate adjacent realms. **Cultural amalgamation** and **international economic activities** often take place in transition zones. The high degree of interaction between residents of neighboring realms that takes place in these areas often leads to regional change.

Culture Hearth, Cultural Mosaic, Transculturation

A culture hearth is a principal source area and center of cultural innovation from which migrating peoples transport traditions and beliefs to their new homes. Mesoamerica, a region that spans the area between central Mexico and the northwestern boundary of Costa Rica, is an example of a **culture hearth**. Populations from this hearth expanded and worked for advancements in the spheres of, for instance, science, architecture, agriculture, and religion; these advancements spread to other regions and influenced further developments. The term *cultural mosaic* is used to describe a society in which distinct ethnic, language, and culture groups exist side by side. This concept is largely synonymous with the idea of cultural pluralism and is the opposite of a culturally assimilated society. **Transculturation** is the process whereby different cultures merge and converge. It refers specifically to the tendency of humans to work toward the resolution of conflicts, be they political, ethnic, or social.

Culture Spheres

A culture sphere is a cultural region within a larger region. The identification of general culture spheres may be useful in the description of the cultural mosaic of a pluralist society. For instance, geographers have delineated five generalized **culture spheres** within the South American realm. The tropical-plantation region is characterized by a dispersed settlement pattern, a high level of plantation agriculture, and a culture dominated by the descendants of African slave laborers who were brought over to work on those plantations. The European-commercial region is populated largely by Europeans, specifically those with affiliations to Hispanic culture. This region is economically more developed than the rest of the realm. The Amerind-subsistence region is characterized by a feudal socioeconomic structure, a holdover from former Spanish conquerors. This region contains some of the realm's poorest areas. Culture in the Mestizo-transitional region is a fusion of Amerind and European elements. It is also a zone of transition between the commercial and subsistence economic areas. The undifferentiated region consists of regions with unclassifiable cultural characteristics.

Balkanization, Shatter Belt, Ethnic Cleansing

There are several geographic terms with roots in the region of Eastern Europe that are used to describe the collapse of established order; these terms are so designated due to the complex, transitory nature of the area.

- **Balkanization**, named after the Balkan Peninsula, is defined as the breaking down of a society (such as a region) into smaller and more hostile units.
- A **shatter belt** is a region, such as Eastern Europe, located between two or more stronger, oppositional cultural-political forces. A shatter belt region is often pressured, taken over, and divvied up by outside, rival forces.
- **Ethnic cleansing** is another term coined from events in Eastern Europe. The phrase is a euphemism used to designate the forcible elimination of people of a certain ethnic group from their homeland by more aggressive groups in search of power. The term has been used historically by the Soviets (in reference to the "resettlement" of Poles) and by Serbs in Yugoslavia (in description of the policies of Albanians against Serbs).

Centripetal and Centrifugal Forces

In political geography, centripetal forces are forces within a state which act to unify and strengthen it. For instance, an outside threat (actual or perceived) on a state often binds that state's political system and may consequently make it stronger. A particularly important and enduring **centripetal force** is the belief of the state's citizens in the state's governmental system and their committed support of that system. Historically, certain charismatic leaders, such as Charles De Gaulle in France and Mao Zedong in China, have inspired this type of loyalty. **Centrifugal forces** are those that act against centripetal forces, tending to divide or degrade states. These forces are usually internal. Interracial hostilities, religious and/or ethnic conflicts, and political strife are key factors in the disunification of states. For example, clashes among ethnic groups in Yugoslavia led to much fighting and the eventual breakup of the state in 1991. The proportion of centripetal to centrifugal forces in a state affects its stability and strength.

Urban Geography

Urban geography is the subfield of geography that involves the spatial analysis of city-centered settlements with high population densities. This area of study has been organized into four main sections:

- **Urban evolution geography** (the historical evolution component of urban geography) is interested in the forces behind urban development during each period of human development since the city's founding.

- **Interurban geography** is concerned with the interactions and relationships between urban systems at a national level. Areas of interest include city types, city functions, and spheres of influence.
- **Intraurban geography** deals with the internal spatial organizations of highly urbanized settlements. This includes study of the infrastructure of a city as well as observation of the distribution and activities of different population groups in that city.
- **Urban social geography** is the component of urban geography that investigates the spatial arrangements of people in a metropolis, with a focus on their residences.

A related field, urban economic geography, examines the distribution of commercial and recreational activities in urban areas.

Principles of Spatial Interaction

A spatial interaction is a realized movement of people, freight or information between an origin and a destination. Human contact and interaction in the realm of economics and trade is organized around three principles:

1. **Complementarity** comes about when one area produces a surplus of a certain commodity that is needed in a second area. This principle thus occurs due to spatial variations in the supply and demand of particular resources, both natural and human.
2. **Transferability** is the ease of transportation of goods between two areas. Distance (including costs and travel time) and accessibility (including travel routes and the character of the relevant terrain) are factors in the transferability of a commodity. Therefore, complementarity alone does not ensure trade between regions.
3. **Intervening opportunity** states that trade between two areas, even if the conditions of complementarity and transferability are met, will occur only through the lack of a more proximate (intervening) supply source.

Areal Functional Specialization

Areal functional specialization is a phenomenon that occurs due to variations in amounts of available resources (natural and human), levels of industrialization, and amounts of available technology, which leads certain areas and peoples to specialize in the production of certain goods. Europe, for example, exhibits a high degree of **areal functional specialization**; particular ores, minerals, manufactured goods, and agricultural products tend to be produced (in surplus) in particular areas. The needs of these specialized regions of production tend to be complementary, so each area satisfies its needs through trade with other areas. Europe, therefore, is a realm of areal (economic) interdependence.

Core Areas and Peripheral Areas

Core areas of a region or nation, which may also be referred to as heartlands, are the hubs of human and economic activity in those areas. These central regions usually exhibit at least one substantive urban area, a large population cluster, and high levels of accessibility and connectivity, which grant them influence over entire regions. **Peripheral areas** (also referred to as hinterlands, a term that literally means "countries behind") are those surrounding core regions. These areas depend on goods and services produced in those core regions, which are key influences on urban development along the periphery. Heartlands and hinterlands develop due to the presence or absence of natural resources, the degree of availability of those resources, regional variations in climate, and the degree of a region's connectivity to other regions. Contrasts in development levels exist at several different scales: local, regional, national, and global.

Core-Periphery Relationships

The structure of core-periphery relationships causes already powerful and developed core areas to continue to grow and evolve, while peripheries remain undeveloped and often unstable. Uneven development is, sadly, a fact of life on Earth. Certain countries (and regions within those nations) have advantages that other countries and regions do not have, and the gap between these haves and have-nots continues to grow. These core and peripheral regions are functionally tied together. Citizens of the periphery contribute labor and taxes to the development of the core. In other words, **core regions** would not be as they are without the contributions of **peripheral regions**. Hinterlands begin to depend on heartlands for employment (though workers from the periphery generally receive lower wages than workers in the core), specialized goods and services, and even military protection. This situation negates the possibility of economic growth in the hinterlands.

Assumptions Behind Von Thünen's Isolated State Model

In 1826, economist **Johann Heinrich von Thünen** created a geographic model to explain the effects of distance and cost of transportation on the location of productive activity. Thünen's **Isolated State Model** is so titled because he wanted to develop a secluded community with no outside influences on its economic activity in order to ascertain the basic factors in the spatial organization of an agricultural region. He based his model on four assumptions:

- That soil quality and climate characteristics were homogeneous throughout the area;
- That the area was flat and contained no divisive landforms (such as river valleys or mountains);
- That the region consisted of a centrally located city surrounded by wilderness; and
- That farmers within the Isolated State would move their own products directly to the central city (meaning that transportation costs would be directly proportional to distance).

Though Thünen's theoretical model did not represent real economic areas in Europe, the distorting factors could be applied individually to the idealized representation of agricultural economy.

Thünen's Isolated State Model

Thünen's Isolated State Model seeks to identify the ideal spatial arrangement of agricultural activities in an isolated community. It consists of a central market city surrounded by **concentric rings**. The innermost ring is a zone of intensive production (including dairying), the second zone houses a forest from which firewood and timber (an important building material in Thünen's time) can be extracted, the third area produces extensive field crops, and the fourth zone is characterized by ranching and animal husbandry. In other words, the crops that yield the highest returns and perish most easily (such as vegetables) are grown closest to the city. Extensive crops such as potatoes and grains are grown further away (outside the forest zone); ranching activities take place just inside the boundary marking the distance at which transportation costs make market agricultural production uneconomical. Today, due to improvements in transportation technologies, Thünen's model can be expanded to a **macroscale**, meaning that it centers on an entire urban area rather than a single city.

Chapter Quiz

Ready to see how well you retained what you just read? Scan the QR code to go directly to the chapter quiz interface for this study guide. If you're using a computer, simply visit the online resources page at **mometrix.com/resources719/dssthumculgeog** and click the Chapter Quizzes link.

DSST Practice Test

Want to take this practice test in an online interactive format?
Check out the online resources page, which includes interactive practice questions and much more: **mometrix.com/resources719/dssthumculgeog**

1. Through which of the following does the prime meridian NOT pass?

a. Equator
b. Middle of the Pacific Ocean
c. Greenwich, England
d. Tropic of Cancer

2. What is the name for a line that connects points with equal total rainfall?

a. Isotherm
b. Isoline
c. Isobar
d. Isohyet

3. The apparent distance between Greenland and Norway is greatest on a(n)

a. Mercator Map
b. Conic Projection Map
c. Contour Map
d. Equal-Area Projection Map

4. On a globe, the distance between Buenos Aires and Tokyo is 35 cm. If the globe has a scale of 1 cm for every 516 km, what is the real distance?

a. 18,060 km
b. 35 km
c. 21,080 km
d. 14,740 km

5. The shortest distance between New York and Paris goes:

a. Over Florida and Spain
b. Along the 42nd parallel
c. Near Labrador and Greenland
d. Over Philadelphia and London

6. On which type of map are different countries represented in different colors, with no two adjacent countries sharing a color?

a. Physical map
b. Political map
c. Climate map
d. Contour map

7. Which of the following is a possible absolute location for New Orleans?

a. 30° S, 90° E
b. 30° N, 90° E
c. 30° S, 90° W
d. 30° N, 90° W

8. On a map of Africa, there is a small box around Nairobi. This city is depicted in greater detail in a box at the bottom of the map. What is the name for this box at the bottom of the map?

a. Inset
b. Legend
c. Compass rose
d. Key

9. Which map describes the movement of people, trends, or materials across a physical area?

a. Political Map
b. Cartogram
c. Qualitative Map
d. Flow-line Map

10. How many intermediate directions are there?

a. 2
b. 4
c. 8
d. 16

Refer to the following for question 11:

For a geography unit, students are learning about the state of Wisconsin. To help better understand the climate of the state, students are asked to record how the elevation of certain regions correlates to temperature. They are also expected to locate and label the major cities of the state, such as Madison and Milwaukee.

11. Which of the following gives the clearest relative location of Milwaukee?

a. In Wisconsin
b. On Lake Michigan
c. 44° N, 88° W
d. 100 miles north of Chicago

12. Antarctica will appear the largest on a

a. Mercator projection
b. Robinson projection
c. Homolosine projection
d. Azimuthal projection

13. Which of the following is NOT a method of representing relief on a physical map?

a. Symbols
b. Color
c. Shading
d. Contour Lines

14. Which of the following countries are separated by a geometric border?

a. Turkish Cyprus and Greek Cyprus
b. North Korea and South Korea
c. France and Spain
d. England and Ireland

15. On which type of map would Nigeria be bigger than Australia?

a. Contour map of elevation
b. Flow-line map of the spice trade
c. Mercator projection
d. Cartogram of population

16. On which of the following maps would the scale be largest?

a. A map of Benelux nations
b. A map of Senegal
c. A map of Rio de Janeiro
d. A map of Greenwich Village

17. Tracy needs to determine the shortest route between Lima and Lisbon. Which of the following maps should she use?

a. Azimuthal projection with the North Pole at the center
b. Azimuthal projection with Lisbon at the center
c. Robinson projection of the Eastern Hemisphere
d. Robinson projection of the Western Hemisphere

18. Which type of chart is best at representing the cycle of demographic transition?

a. Pie chart
b. Political map
c. Line graph
d. Flow-line map

19. What kind of chart would be best for representing the major events of World War I?

a. Timeline
b. Bar graph
c. Pie chart
d. Political map

20. On a political map of India, the northernmost part of the border with Pakistan is represented as a dotted line. Why is this so?

a. Pakistan does not have control of this border.
b. This area has never been comprehensively mapped.
c. Indian Sikhs are threatening to secede.
d. The borders of the Kashmir region remain in dispute.

21. Which part of a hurricane features the strongest winds and greatest rainfall?

a. Eye wall
b. Front
c. Eye
d. Outward spiral

22. What is the most common type of volcano on Earth?

a. Lava dome
b. Composite volcano
c. Shield volcano
d. Cinder cone

Refer to the following for question 23:

A biome featuring scrubby plants and small evergreen trees has a hot, dry summer followed by a wetter winter. The following food chain exists in the biome:

$$tree \rightarrow caterpillar \rightarrow frog \rightarrow snake \rightarrow hawk \rightarrow vulture \rightarrow worm$$

23. Which biome is this?

a. Taiga
b. Coniferous forest
c. Chaparral
d. Savanna

24. Which type of rock is formed by extreme heat and pressure?

a. Limestone
b. Metamorphic
c. Sedimentary
d. Igneous

25. What is the name for a brief interval of coolness in between warm periods in the Pacific Ocean?

a. La Niña
b. Tropical gyre
c. El Niño
d. ENSO

26. The rocks and landmasses that make up the earth's surface are called the

a. atmosphere
b. biosphere
c. hydrosphere
d. lithosphere

27. Which of the following landmasses is *not* part of the Ring of Fire?

a. Japan
b. Cascade Mountains in Washington
c. Andes Mountains in South America
d. Mount Kilimanjaro

28. In the plate movement known as ____, an oceanic plate slides underneath a continental plate.

a. faulting
b. spreading
c. subduction
d. converging

29. Which of the following statements about loess is true?

a. It is primarily carried by water.
b. It has low mineral content.
c. It is very dense.
d. It has been essential to the success of farming in the American Midwest.

30. Which of the following currents is responsible for the climate of the British Isles?

a. North Equatorial Current
b. Canary Current
c. Gulf Stream
d. Labrador Current

31. What is the name for the pile of rocks and debris left behind by a glacier?

a. Iceberg
b. Col
c. Fjord
d. Moraine

32. According to Alfred Wegener, the earth originally had one continent called:

a. Pangaea
b. Eurasia
c. Transcontinentia
d. Africa

33. Which of the following is an example of an isthmus?

a. Panama
b. The Aleutian Islands
c. Northern Greenland
d. Florida

34. Which of the following statements about the equator is true?

a. It intersects four continents.
b. It is to the north of both horse latitudes.
c. It is located at 0° longitude.
d. It is not very windy.

35. Which soil horizon consists of weathered rock?

a. A horizon
b. C horizon
c. O horizon
d. R horizon

36. What causes the motion of glaciers?

a. Gravity
b. Erosion
c. Wind
d. Temperature change

37. Which of the following is an example of chemical weathering?

a. Frost wedging
b. Heat expansion
c. Acid rain
d. Salt wedging

38. Which of the following statements about tropical rain forests is false?

a. There are tropical rain forests on only two continents.
b. The largest tropical rain forest is the Amazon River basin.
c. Over half of the world's plant and animal species are found in the tropical rain forest.
d. Tropical rain forests cover less than 10 percent of the earth's surface.

39. Which of the following layers of the atmosphere is the furthest from the ground?

a. Thermosphere
b. Troposphere
c. Stratosphere
d. Mesosphere

40. Which of the following soil types has the smallest grains?

a. Sand
b. Silt
c. Clay
d. Loam

41. Which type of precipitation results when warm, wet air is forced over mountains?

a. Orographic precipitation
b. Dorsal precipitation
c. Convectional precipitation
d. Frontal precipitation

42. During one year in Grassley County, there are 750 births, 350 deaths, 80 immigrations, and 50 emigrations. What is the natural increase rate for this year?

a. 400
b. 830
c. 430
d. More information is required.

43. Which of the following is NOT one of the world's four major population agglomerations?

a. North Africa
b. Eastern North America
c. South Asia
d. Europe

44. Thai food has become increasingly popular in the United States, though it is prepared in slightly different ways here. This is an example of:

a. Cultural divergence
b. Assimilation
c. Cultural convergence
d. Acculturation

45. Which government system vests almost all control in a central government?

a. Federation
b. Democracy
c. Unitary system
d. Confederation

46. To which language family does English belong?

a. Romance
b. Indo-European
c. Amerindian
d. Papuan

47. What is the name for the traditionally Arab district in a North African city?

a. Souk
b. Medina
c. Wadi
d. Bazaar

48. Which of the following languages is *not* alphabetic?

a. Spanish
b. Russian
c. Chinese
d. Arabic

49. Where is the area of greatest corn production?

a. South Africa
b. Kazakhstan
c. United States
d. Mexico

50. What has been one result of NAFTA?

a. The border between the United States and Mexico has opened.
b. There has been significant migration from Canada to Mexico.
c. Trade barriers between the United States and Canada have increased.
d. Mexico has sought to enter other trade agreements.

51. Last year, 4 residents of Henrytown died. The population of Henrytown is 500. What is the death rate of Henrytown?

a. 1
b. 4
c. 8
d. 12

52. Which of the following locations would be considered a modern cultural hearth?

a. New York City
b. Baghdad
c. Auckland
d. Edmonton

53. According to Mark Jefferson, which of the following would be considered the primate city of England?

a. London
b. Manchester
c. Brighton
d. Salisbury

54. The popularity of hockey in Canada and the northern United States is an example of

a. Expansion diffusion
b. Indirect diffusion
c. Forced diffusion
d. Direct diffusion

55. Which of the following is NOT one of the criteria for nationhood?

a. Defined territory
b. Elections
c. Government
d. Sovereignty

56. Which form of religion includes the belief that the natural world is imbued with spirits?

a. Monotheism
b. Pantheism
c. Animism
d. Polytheism

57. When a foreign power has some political and economic control over a region in another country but does not directly govern, it is said to have a(n)

a. Colony
b. Sphere of Influence
c. Settlement
d. Enclave

58. The town of Hamilton has 400 citizens living in 12 square miles. The town of Burrsville has 300 citizens living over 10 square miles. Which town has the greater population density?

a. Hamilton has the greater population density.
b. Burrsville has the greater population density.
c. The towns have the same population density.
d. The answer cannot be determined based on the information given.

59. When a person grows only enough food to feed himself and his family, he is engaged in

a. Nomadic herding
b. Commercial farming
c. Sharecropping
d. Subsistence farming

60. Which of the following exemplifies the multiplier effect of large cities?

a. The presence of specialized equipment for an industry attracts even more business.
b. The large population lowers the price of goods.
c. Public transportation means more people can commute to work.
d. A local newspaper can afford to give away the Sunday edition.

61. In which stage of demographic transition does fertility remain high while mortality declines?

a. High stationary stage
b. Early expanding stage
c. Late expanding stage
d. Low stationary stage

62. During which stage of spatial diffusion does the process slow to a stop?

a. Primary
b. Diffusion
c. Condensing
d. Saturation

63. In the United States, what is the correct term for a settlement with fewer than 100 inhabitants?

a. Village
b. Town
c. Hamlet
d. City

64. To communicate, traders from distant regions of the world settle on a(n):

a. Lingua franca
b. Pidgin language
c. Conurbation
d. Activity space

65. Juan has a mill, which he uses to grind wheat into flour. This is an example of

a. Primary economic activity
b. Secondary economic activity
c. Tertiary economic activity
d. Quaternary economic activity

66. Which of the following is *not* one of the necessary characteristics of a geographical region?

a. Area
b. Location
c. Homogeneity
d. Population

67. Stephen travels to the city every morning for work. Every evening, he returns to his home in the suburbs. What kind of movement is this?

a. Cyclic movement
b. Migratory movement
c. Cross-boundary movement
d. Periodic movement

68. Which of the following is NOT one of the demographic variables?

a. Fertility
b. Diversity
c. Mortality
d. Migration

69. Which of the following is an example of indirect diffusion?

a. The Dutch and the Belgians both love soccer.
b. Iran forbids its citizens from watching Western television programs.
c. Japanese anime comics are popular in the United States.
d. Many Native Americans have struggled with alcoholism.

70. Which of the following most closely resembles a communist society?

a. Colony
b. Ghetto
c. Shtetl
d. Kibbutz

71. The Russian city of St. Petersburg is crucial to the economy because of its

a. timber reserves.
b. access to the Baltic Sea.
c. historic architecture.
d. location on the Volga River.

72. Which of the following nations is NOT a member of OPEC?

a. Saudi Arabia
b. Venezuela
c. Yemen
d. Iraq

73. Which of the following was a consequence of the Mexican Revolution of 1910?

a. Land redistribution
b. National sovereignty
c. Two-party rule
d. The creation of railroads

74. For thousands of years, Africans have cultivated the grasslands south of the Sahara Desert, an area known as the

a. Qattara Depression.
b. Great Rift Valley.
c. Congo Basin.
d. Sahel.

75. What are the two regions of the Czech Republic?

a. Chechnya and Slovakia
b. Moravia and Slovakia
c. Bohemia and Chechnya
d. Bohemia and Moravia

76. Egypt is plagued by the sandstorms arising from a spring wind known as the

a. Khamsin
b. Sirocco
c. Zephyr
d. Fellaheen

77. What is the name of the highest habitable region in Middle and South America?

a. *Tierra fria*
b. *Puna*
c. *Tierra helada*
d. *Templada*

78. Identify one consequence of Zimbabwe's first free election in 1980.

a. The government outlawed private property.
b. The policy of apartheid was ended.
c. The country ceased to be known as Rhodesia.
d. The British government acknowledged the nation's sovereignty.

79. What do Marseilles and Genoa have in common?

a. They are national capitals.
b. They both border Germany.
c. They are both in the south of France.
d. They are both important ports on the Mediterranean.

80. Indian women often cover their faces in public, a tradition known as

a. burqa.
b. hijab.
c. sari.
d. purdah.

81. What is the most popular religion in Japan?

a. Shinto
b. Buddhism
c. Confucianism
d. A blend of these three religions

82. Why was Aksum able to become a powerful empire in Africa 2,000 years ago?

a. It had access to major waterways.
b. It was a Muslim nation.
c. It had access to oil reserves.
d. It was located in the center of the continent.

83. Which of the following is the name of a prominent Muslim ethnic group living in northwestern China?

a. Tibetans
b. Mandarin
c. Falun Gong
d. Uighurs

84. Which religious group does NOT consider Jerusalem a holy city?

a. Christians
b. Buddhists
c. Muslims
d. Jews

85. Which of the following is *not* one of the Baltic states?

a. Moldova
b. Latvia
c. Lithuania
d. Estonia

86. Where do most Pakistanis live?

a. Farming villages
b. Karachi
c. Baluchistan Plateau
d. Khyber Pass

87. What is the best description of the Mongols?

a. Grain farmers
b. Nomadic herders
c. Industrialists
d. Tradesmen

88. Which state covers the most area?

a. New York
b. Texas
c. California
d. Alaska

89. Which of the following is a true statement about the Yucatan Peninsula?

a. It is densely populated.
b. It is more mountainous than the rest of Mexico.
c. It was once inhabited by Aztecs.
d. It has a number of large sinkholes.

90. Which two nations share the longest undefended border in the world?

a. Chile and Argentina
b. Canada and the United States
c. Kazakhstan and Russia
d. Egypt and Sudan

91. The reorganization of the USSR's economy under Gorbachev was known as

a. glasnost.
b. rubles.
c. soviets.
d. perestroika.

92. What is the best description of the pampas in Argentina and Uruguay?

a. Migrant workers
b. Jagged peaks
c. Temperate grasslands
d. Wild horses

93. Conflict between Sinhalese and Tamils has simmered for thousands of years in what is now

a. Sri Lanka.
b. Bhutan.
c. Burma.
d. Thailand.

94. Which of the following is NOT an official language of Switzerland?

a. Italian
b. Dutch
c. French
d. German

95. Which of the following statements about Kemal Ataturk is true?

a. He increased the influence of Islam on the Turkish government.
b. He outlawed English.
c. He diminished the civil rights of women.
d. He westernized Turkey in many ways.

96. What are the Atlantic provinces of Canada?

a. Labrador, Prince Edward Island, New Brunswick, and Nova Scotia
b. New Brunswick, Nunavut, Nova Scotia, and Labrador
c. Prince Edward Island, Nova Scotia, Quebec, and Newfoundland
d. Manitoba, Nunavut, Ontario, and Saskatchewan

97. Which country controlled Hong Kong before China?

a. Japan
b. United States
c. Great Britain
d. Korea

98. What is the name for a shantytown in Brazil?

a. *Barrio*
b. *Favela*
c. *Maquiladora*
d. *Ciudad*

99. In Holland, the lands reclaimed through a network of dikes and canals are known as

a. polders.
b. cantons.
c. grabens.
d. moors.

100. Which of the following countries has the least amount of arable land by percent of total landmass?

a. China
b. Italy
c. Germany
d. Japan

Answer Key and Explanations

1. B: The prime meridian does not pass through the middle of the Pacific Ocean. It is 0°, the line from which longitude is measured. There is no special reason why it passes through Greenwich, other than that the observatory there was one of the first to devise a system for measuring longitude and therefore put itself at the base of the system. The international date line is 180° longitude; it passes through the middle of the Pacific Ocean. Both the equator and the Tropic of Cancer are lines of latitude and therefore intersect the prime meridian. The equator circles the earth at its broadest circumference, equidistant from the North and South poles. The equator has a latitude of 0°. The Tropic of Cancer, 23°26′22″ North latitude, represents the northernmost point at which the sun is directly above the earth. In other words, at no point during the year will the sun be directly above any point north of the Tropic of Cancer. This line is mirrored in the Southern Hemisphere by the Tropic of Capricorn.

2. D: An isohyet is a line that connects points with equal total rainfall. On an isohyetal map then, a series of lines will indicate areas of greater or lesser rainfall. This is a form of contour map, the most common of which uses a series of lines to indicate changes in elevation. The other answer choices represent lines used in other forms of contour maps. An isotherm connects points with the same temperature. An isoline connects points with an equal value, as, for instance, on a contour map illustrating iron production. An isobar connects points with identical atmospheric pressure.

3. A: The apparent distance between Greenland and Norway will be greatest on a Mercator map. The Mercator map is a type of cylindrical projection map in which lines of latitude and longitude are transferred onto a cylindrical shape, which is then cut vertically and laid flat. For this reason, distances around the poles will appear increasingly great. The Mercator map is excellent for navigation because a straight line drawn on it represents a single compass reading. In a conic projection map, on the other hand, a hemisphere of the globe is transposed onto a cone, which is then cut vertically (that is, from rim to tip) and laid flat. The apparent distances on a conic projection will be smallest at the 45th parallel. A contour map uses lines to illustrate the features of a geographic area. For example, the lines on an elevation contour map connect areas that have the same altitude. An equal-area projection map represents landmasses in their actual sizes. To make this possible, the shapes of the landmasses are manipulated slightly, and the map is interrupted (divided into more than one part).

4. A: The distance between Buenos Aires and Tokyo is approximately 18,060 km. The process of converting a scaled distance to a real distance is fairly simple. In this case, multiply the number of centimeters by the number of kilometers represented by each of these centimeters. The calculation can be expressed as (35 cm) (516 km/1 cm). Because centimeters are in the numerator of the first term and the denominator of the second term, they cancel out, leaving kilometers as the unit.

5. C: The shortest distance between New York and Paris goes near or over Labrador and Greenland. This is not apparent on a projection map, in which a straight line drawn between the two cities would extend straight out across the Atlantic Ocean, roughly along the 42nd parallel. The illusion that this straight line is the shortest path is a result of the distortions inherent in projection maps. On a globe, it would be easier to see that a plane flying from New York to Paris would cover the least ground by carving an arc, first up through eastern Canada and Greenland and then back down through the British Isles and northern France. This sort of path is known as a great circle route because it looks like an arc when it is drawn on a projection map.

6. B: On a political map, countries are represented in different colors, and countries that share a border are not given the same color. This is so that the borders between countries will be distinct. Political maps are used to illustrate those aspects of a country that have been determined by people: the capital, the provincial and national borders, and the large cities. Political maps sometimes include major physical features like rivers and mountains, but they are not intended to display all such information. On a physical, climate, or contour map, however, the borders between nations are more incidental. Colors are used on these maps to represent physical features, areas with similar climate, etc. It is possible that colors will overrun the borders and be shared by adjacent countries.

7. D: The only answer choice that represents a possible absolute location for New Orleans is 30° N, 90° W. When a location is described in terms of its placement on the global grid, it is customary to put the latitude before the longitude. New Orleans is north of the equator, so it has to be in the Northern Hemisphere. In addition, it is west of the prime meridian, which runs through Greenwich, England, among other places. So, New Orleans must be in the Western Hemisphere. It is possible, then, to deduce that 30° N, 90° W is the only possible absolute location for New Orleans.

8. A: A smaller box in which some part of the larger map is depicted in greater detail is known as an inset. Insets provide a closer look at parts of the map that the cartographer deems to be more important (for instance, cities, national parks, or historical sites). Often, traffic maps will include several insets depicting the roads in the most congested area of the city. Legends, also known as keys, are the boxes in which the symbols used in the map are explained. A legend, or key, might indicate how railroads and boundaries are depicted, for example. A compass rose indicates how the map is oriented along the north-south axis. It is common for cartographers to tilt a map for ease of display, such that up may not be due north.

9. D: A flow-line map describes the movement of people, trends, or materials across a physical area. The movements depicted on a flow-line map are typically represented by arrows. In more advanced flow-line maps, the width of the arrow corresponds to the quantity of the motion. Flow-line maps usually declare the span of time that is being represented. A political map depicts the man-made aspects of geography, such as borders and cities. A cartogram adjusts the size of the areas represented according to some variable. For instance, a cartogram of wheat production would depict Iowa as being much larger than Alaska. A qualitative map uses lines, dots, and other symbols to illustrate a particular point. For example, a qualitative map might be used to demonstrate the greatest expansion of the Persian Empire.

10. B: There are four intermediate directions. They are northwest, northeast, southwest, and southeast. The intermediate directions are midway between each set of adjacent cardinal directions. The cardinal directions are north, south, east, and west. On a compass rose, the cardinal directions are typically indicated by large points, while the intermediate directions are represented by smaller points.

11. D: A relative location for Milwaukee is 100 miles north of Chicago. Relative location is a description of placement in terms of some other location. The latitude and longitude of Milwaukee are its absolute location because they describe its placement relative to an arbitrary but inalterable system of positioning. To say that Milwaukee is in Wisconsin or on Lake Michigan does not provide as much detail as answer choice D because Wisconsin is a big state and because Lake Michigan is a large body of water.

12. A: Antarctica will appear the largest on a Mercator projection. This projection map converts the globe into a rectangle, such that lines of longitude and latitude are perpendicular to one another.

This type of map depicts landforms near the equator at nearly their normal size but increasingly stretches out distances as it reaches the poles. A Robinson projection, on the other hand, rounds the edges of the Mercator projection, such that the polar regions are not so large. A homolosine projection renders the sizes and shapes of landmasses correctly, but it distorts the distances between them. An azimuthal projection represents one hemisphere as a circle, such that a straight line from the center to any point on the map would also be the shortest distance in the real world.

13. A: Symbols are not used to represent relief on a physical map. A physical map is dedicated to illustrating the landmasses and bodies of water in a specific region, so symbols do not provide enough detail. Color, shading, and contour lines, on the other hand, are able to create a much more complicated picture of changes in elevation, precipitation, etc. Changes in elevation are known in geography as relief.

14. B: North Korea and South Korea are separated by a geometric border, meaning that the boundary between the two nations is a straight line drawn on a map, without respect to landforms. Specifically, the boundary between the Koreas is the 38th parallel. Another example of a geometric border lies between the continental United States and Canada. The Turkish Cyprus–Greek Cyprus border is anthropogeographic, or drawn according to cultural reasons. The border between France and Spain is physiographic-political, a combination of the Pyrenees Mountains and European history. The Irish Sea separates England from Ireland.

15. D: On a cartogram of population, Nigeria would be bigger than Australia. Even though the area of Australia is several times greater than that of Nigeria, Nigeria has a much larger population. A cartogram is a map on which countries or regions are sized according to a certain variable. So, in a cartogram of population, the country with the most people will be the biggest. The countries would be depicted at their usual size in a contour map of elevation or in a flow-line map. On a Mercator projection, Nigeria would actually be smaller relative to Australia because it is closer to the equator.

16. D: The scale would be largest on a map of Greenwich Village. Scale is described as large when it is closer to life-sized; the smaller the region being depicted, the closer to actual size the map can be. Of the four answer choices, Greenwich Village, a neighborhood in Manhattan, is the smallest. Therefore, it must be depicted in the largest scale. Incidentally, Benelux is the name for the region of northern Europe that includes Belgium, the Netherlands, and Luxembourg.

17. B: To determine the shortest route between Lima and Lisbon, Tracy should use an azimuthal projection with Lisbon at the center. An azimuthal projection depicts one hemisphere of the globe as a circle. A straight line drawn from the center of the map to any point represents the shortest possible distance between those two points. Tracy could obtain her objective, then, with an azimuthal projection in which either Lisbon or Lima were at the center. If the North Pole were at the center, the map would not include Lima because this city is in the Southern Hemisphere. A Robinson projection approximates the sizes and shapes of landmasses but does distort in some ways, particularly near the poles.

18. C: The cycle of demographic transition is best illustrated by a line graph. Demographic transition is a phenomenon in which a region's growth rate increases rapidly, peaks, and then decreases slowly over a long time. In the early phase of a region's development, both the birth and death rates are high, which can cause the population to fluctuate. As the people of the region become settled, the growth rate calms down, and the region enters a period of rapid increase. Political maps are better at depicting borders and the locations of cities, while pie charts are better at representing proportions. Flow-line maps are good for illustrating the movement of people, goods, or trends across a physical area.

19. A: A timeline would be the best way to represent the major events of World War I. Timelines place events in chronological order, with the distance between the events correlated to their interval on the line. A timeline can run in any direction. A thematic map or a flow-line map might also be good at representing this subject, but a political map is restricted to borders and cities; therefore, it would not be able to suggest the changes caused by the war. Bar graphs and pie charts are used to depict quantities and proportions rather than sequences of events.

20. D: The northernmost border between India and Pakistan is represented on political maps as a broken line because the borders of the Kashmir region remain in dispute. Both nations lay claim to this mountainous region, which has great water resources. This has been just one of the issues to complicate relations between these neighbors in South Asia. Although India controls most of Kashmir at present, the boundaries have not yet been fully resolved, and, on a political map, such undefined borders are usually represented with dotted lines.

21. A: The eye wall of a hurricane has the strongest winds and the greatest rainfall. The eye wall is the tower-like rim of the eye. It is from this wall that clouds extend out, which are seen from above as the classic outward spiral pattern. A hurricane front is the outermost edge of its influence; although there will be heavy winds and rain in this area, the intensity will be relatively small. The eye of a hurricane is actually a place of surprising peace. In this area, dry and cool air rushes down to the ground or sea. Once there, the air is caught up in the winds of the eye wall and is driven outward at a furious pace.

22. D: The cinder cone volcano is the most common type of volcano on Earth. A cinder cone has steep sides made of fallen cinders, which themselves are made of the lava that intermittently shoots into the air. A composite volcano, sometimes called the stratovolcano, has steep sides, so the explosions of ash, pumice, and silica are often accompanied by treacherous mudslides. Indeed, it is these mudslides that cause most of the damage associated with composite volcano eruptions. Krakatoa and Mount Saint Helens are examples of composite volcanoes. A lava dome is a round volcano that emits thick lava very slowly. A shield volcano, one example of which is Mt. Kilauea in Hawaii, emits a small amount of lava over an extended period of time. Shield volcanoes are not known for violent eruptions.

23. C: The chaparral biome features scrubby plants and small evergreen trees and also has a hot, dry summer followed by a wetter winter. This biome is mainly found around the Mediterranean Sea, though there are also chaparrals in Australia, South Africa, and the American Southwest. The taiga is a colder biome found primarily in northern Europe and Asia. The vegetation of the taiga is mainly scattered stands of coniferous trees. A coniferous forest, meanwhile, is a warmer forest composed of trees that have needles and cones rather than leaves. These trees are better suited for a cold climate than are deciduous trees. A savanna is a tropical grassland with only a few trees. Savannas are clustered around the equator.

24. B: Metamorphic rock is formed by extreme heat and pressure. This type of rock is created when other rocks are somehow buried within the Earth, where they are subject to a dramatic rise in pressure and temperature. Slate and marble are both metamorphic rocks. Metamorphic rocks are created by the other two main types of rock: sedimentary and igneous. Sedimentary rock is formed when dirt and other sediment are washed into a bed, covered over by subsequent sediment, and compacted into rock. Depending on how they are formed, sedimentary rocks are classified as organic, clastic, or chemical. Igneous rocks are composed of cooled magma, the molten rock that emerges from volcanoes. Basalt and granite are two common varieties of igneous rock.

25. A: La Niña is a brief interval of coolness in between warm periods (El Niño) in the water of the Pacific Ocean. For a long time, La Niña was considered only in terms of its relation to El Niño. Increasingly, however, it is being studied as a climate event in its own right. A tropical gyre is a circle of winds made up of equatorial currents in one direction and countercurrents in the other direction. There are tropical gyres in both the Northern and Southern hemispheres. El Niño is an annual event, though some years it is considerably more pronounced. It is an increase in the temperature of coastal Pacific water, sometimes by as much as 2° Celsius. El Niño has a great impact on fishing and weather in the areas that border the Pacific Ocean. The El Niño–Southern Oscillation (ENSO) occurs during a particularly intense El Niño; the flow of equatorial wind and water during an ENSO actually reverses course.

26. D: The rocks and land formations that make up the earth's surface are collectively known as the lithosphere. The lithosphere does not include the core or mantle of the earth. The atmosphere is the air, water, and particles that are above the surface of the earth. The biosphere encompasses all the living things of the earth, such as animals, plants, fungi, and bacteria. The hydrosphere is all the water on and beneath the surface of the earth, including all the lakes, oceans, rivers, and creeks.

27. D: Mount Kilimanjaro is not part of the Ring of Fire, a circle of volcanoes that stretches around the Pacific Ocean. The Ring of Fire extends from islands east of Australia through Indonesia, Japan, the Aleutian Islands connecting Russia to Alaska, and down the western coast of the Americas. It includes such famous volcanoes as Mount Saint Helens and Krakatoa. Over 90 percent of earthquakes and over 80 percent of volcanic eruptions occur along the Ring of Fire.

28. C: In the plate movement known as subduction, an oceanic plate slides underneath a continental plate. Oceanic plates are denser, so they tend to go beneath when they are pressed against lighter continental plates. The edge of the oceanic plate will be melted by the earth's mantle and may reemerge as a volcano. The Cascade Range of the northwest United States was formed by subduction. In faulting, the edges of two plates grind against each other laterally. The San Andreas Fault in California is perhaps the most famous example of this process. In spreading, plates pull apart from each other, typically creating a rift valley and the potential for earthquakes. In converging, two plates of similar density press against each other, creating mountain ranges where they meet.

29. D: Loess, a form of silt or dust, has been a major reason for the success of farming in the American Midwest. Loess is rich in minerals and is light enough to be moved by the wind. It has a very low density and is porous enough to retain a great deal of water. All of these attributes make it an ideal base for farm soil. There are also great deposits of loess in China, with similar benefits for agriculture.

30. C: The climate of the British Isles is mild for its latitude because of the Gulf Stream, an air current originating in the Gulf of Mexico. As this current of warm air makes its way northeast across the Atlantic, it divides, with the North Atlantic Current bringing moisture and mild temperatures to Ireland and the United Kingdom. Even though the latitude of the British Isles is roughly the same as that of Alaska, the land is arable, and the temperature remains warm for the most part. The North Equatorial Current, on the other hand, is a current of warm air that runs west just above the equator. The Canary Current brings cool air from western Europe down around the western tip of Africa, which includes the Canary Islands. The Labrador Current moves cool air from the water in between Canada and Greenland south to the northeastern United States.

31. D: A moraine is a pile of rocks and debris left behind by a glacier. As a glacier moves across the earth's surface, it churns up the ground beneath. The piles that remain after the glacier is gone become significant landmasses in their own right. For instance, Long Island off the coast of New York is the moraine of a long-ago glacier. An iceberg, meanwhile, is a mass of floating ice that has broken off of a glacier, typically near one of the poles. A col is a mountain pass, that is, the trough between two mountain peaks. A fjord is a narrow waterway cut out of the land by a glacier. A fjord typically has high walls on either side.

32. A: Alfred Wegener was a German scientist credited with developing the idea of Pangaea, the original supercontinent from which today's large landmasses were formed. Wegener created this name from the Greek words for *all* and *earth*. The continental drift theory asserts that Pangaea began to break up approximately 180 million years ago. Wegener was inspired in part by his observation that many of the continents seemed to fit together. He also discovered a number of prehistoric fossils that suggested similarities between animals and plants from different continents.

33. A: An isthmus is a narrow strip of land connecting two larger landmasses. The strip of land should be bordered by water on either side. The nation of Panama is the most classic example of an isthmus in Central America because it is so narrow. This is why it was chosen as the site for a great canal connecting the Atlantic and Pacific Oceans. The Aleutian Islands are an example of an archipelago, or cluster of islands in an ocean. Northern Greenland is an example of a tundra, the coldest of the biomes. There are no trees in the tundra. Florida is an example of a peninsula, a strip of land extending out into a large body of water, in this case the Atlantic Ocean.

34. D: Around the world, the area around the equator is known for a relative lack of wind. Indeed, the equatorial belt is sometimes called the doldrums because the constant warm water encourages the air to rise gently. To the north and south, however, there are trade winds that can become quite violent. The equator only intersects three continents: Asia, Africa, and South America. It is in between the north and south horse latitudes, which are belts known for calm winds. Finally, the equator is located at 0° latitude, not longitude, though the 0° line of longitude does intersect the equator.

35. B: The C horizon of soil consists of weathered rock. A soil that has been in the same place for a long time will begin to develop unique layers known as horizons. The bottom layer is called the R horizon; it consists of unweathered bedrock. Just above is the C horizon, which is composed of weathered rock fragments. Next up is the B horizon, made up of minerals and drier soil. Above that is the A horizon, or topsoil, which has a great deal of organic matter in it. The top layer is known as the O horizon. It is a thin layer of humus.

36. A: Glaciers move because they are incredibly heavy, and the force of gravity slowly pulls them lower. Erosion is a result rather than a cause of glacier movement. Although large glaciers may only move a few inches a year or may not move at all, some valley glaciers in Europe move as much as 600 feet annually. The result is a rounded valley and a trail of rock and soil debris known as a moraine. The Great Lakes in the United States were formed by the passage of glaciers long ago.

37. C: Acid rain is an example of chemical weathering. When acidic chemicals are evaporated and fall as rain, they can have devastating effects on plant and animal life. Although human activity is the primary cause of acid rain, weathering chemicals can also get into the atmosphere through oceanic bacteria and volcanoes. The other three answer choices are examples of mechanical weathering. Frost wedging occurs when water seeps into a narrow space within a rock formation and then freezes. Because water takes up more space as ice and frost than it does in its liquid state, this process can cause structural damage to the rock. Heat expansion occurs when rapid changes in temperature cause rocks to expand, leading to cracks and fissures. Salt wedging occurs when water flowing into a rock brings salt in with it. The water evaporates, but the salt is left behind, and over time the deposits of salt can create pressure within the rock.

38. A: There are tropical rain forests on all the continents except Europe and Antarctica. Indeed, the Congo River Basin in Africa is the site of the second-largest tropical rain forest. There are also tropical rain forests in Central America, northern Australia, and Southeast Asia. Of course, all these rain forests are close to the equator, where there is abundant heat and precipitation. All the other answer choices are true statements, though it could be said more specifically that tropical rain forests cover approximately 6 percent of the earth's surface.

39. A: Of the options listed, the thermosphere is the furthest from the ground. There is very little air in the thermosphere. The stratosphere lies just above the troposphere and includes the ozone layer. The mesosphere is in between the stratosphere and the thermosphere, 30 to 50 miles above the surface of the earth.

40. C: Clay soil has the smallest grains. This is somewhat counterintuitive because clay tends to clump together when it is exposed to any moisture. However, the individual constituent parts of clay are finer than grains of sand. In fact, silty soils have smaller grains than sand as well. Loam is a combination of sand, silt, and clay. In most cases, loam is the best soil for agriculture. Most soils are comprised of some mixture of sand, silt, and clay.

41. A: Orographic precipitation is caused by warm, wet air being forced upward so that it can pass over high landforms. The air cools rapidly as it gains elevation, and snow and cold rain begin to fall. This phenomenon occurs in the Andes Mountains, where warm air flowing over the Pacific Ocean is forced upward. The land on the other side of a range that receives orographic precipitation usually gets very little precipitation. There is no such thing as dorsal precipitation. Convectional precipitation results when warm air rises slowly and cools. As it cools, it expels some of its moisture. This kind of rainfall is common over tropical jungles. Frontal precipitation results when warm air encounters cooler air and is forced up.

42. D: More information is required to calculate the natural increase rate for Grassley County during this year. Natural increase rate is the growth in population measured as the surplus of live births over deaths for every thousand people. The calculation of natural increase rate does not take account of immigration or emigration. The natural increase rate for Grassley County cannot be calculated because the original population of the county is not given. As an example, if the beginning population of the county had been 10,000, the natural increase rate would be 40; $400 \times 1{,}000/10{,}000 = 40$.

43. A: North Africa is not one of the world's four major population agglomerations. These are eastern North America, South Asia, East Asia, and Europe. The largest of these is East Asia, which encompasses Korea, Japan, and the major cities of China. The second-largest population agglomeration is South Asia, which includes India and Pakistan. Most of the population in this area is near the coasts. The European agglomeration is spread across the largest piece of land, while the much smaller agglomeration in eastern North America is primarily focused on the string of cities from Boston to Washington, DC.

44. C: The increasing popularity of Thai food in the United States is an example of cultural convergence, or the intersection of traits or customs from two distinct cultures. Thailand's cuisine has been introduced to the United States, but it has undergone subtle changes as a result of the desires and practices of the American consumer. The phenomenon of cultural convergence is credited with much of the innovation in any society. Cultural divergence, on the other hand, is the practice of shielding one culture from the influence of another. France, for instance, seeks to limit the influence of American culture on its citizens. Assimilation is the process by which a minority group gradually adopts the culture of the majority group. For example, many Native Americans assimilated into the European-style culture of the early American settlers. Acculturation is the process of obtaining the practices and ideas of a culture. A child undergoes acculturation, wherein he or she learns to think and act appropriately for his or her setting.

45. C: In a unitary system of government, almost all control is held by the central government. The central government makes the laws, and the local governments are not allowed to overrule them. Although the unitary system is often associated with repressive regimes like that of North Korea, it also exists in countries like Japan and Great Britain. A unitary system tends to work better in countries with homogenous populations and relatively little cultural difference between regions. A federation, meanwhile, is a system in which the central government has some powers but grants others to local governments. The United States is a federation. A democracy is a system in which the people elect government officials. A democracy could be a unitary system, but it does not have to be. In a confederation, the central government has much less power than the regional and local governments. In such a system, the central government is usually only responsible for defense and trade with other nations.

46. B: English is part of the Indo-European language family. This language family has its origins in the language spoken over 5,000 years ago by the inhabitants of what is now eastern Europe. Greek, Latin, and Sanskrit are all members of this language family. Romance languages are those derived from Latin. Spanish, French, and Italian are Romance languages. Latin is a member of the Indo-European language family, but it is not considered a direct antecedent of English. Amerindian languages are those of the indigenous peoples of the Americas. Navajo is one example of an Amerindian language. Finally, the Papuan language family includes all the dialects spoken by the inhabitants of Papua New Guinea and surrounding islands in the Pacific Ocean.

47. B: The Arab districts in North African cities are known as medinas. These are typically old neighborhoods surrounding a large mosque. Many Arabs who made their living in trade eventually settled in countries like Algeria, Tunisia, and Libya. There, they influenced culture by bringing Sunni Islam to the indigenous people. A souk, meanwhile, is a market area surrounding the mosque in the medina. A wadi is a dry North African creek bed, which becomes an essential source of water during the sporadic rains. The location of wadis has been a crucial factor in the political and economic history of North Africa. A bazaar, finally, is an open-air market in the Middle East.

48. C: Chinese is not an alphabetic language, which means that it is not written as a series of different sequences of letters. In English, for instance, all the words are made up of combinations of 26 letters. There are upper-case and lower-case forms of these letters, but these forms are constant. The same is true of all alphabetic languages, including Spanish, Russian, and Arabic. Chinese is a logographic language that uses characters that typically represent syllables or morphemes rather than individual letters. Learning to read a logographic language requires the mastery of thousands of ideograms. Functional literacy in Chinese typically requires knowledge of a few thousand characters, although large dictionaries list over 20,000 characters.

49. C: The greatest area of corn production is in the United States, specifically in the so-called Corn Belt that runs from northern Florida and eastern Texas all the way up to Iowa and Pennsylvania. Corn has traditionally been the specialty grain of the Americas, although it is now grown as a subsistence crop all over the world. Indeed, all the incorrect answer choices are areas that produce significant amounts of corn, though not as much as the Corn Belt. Corn is useful because it can grow in various climates and can be converted into a number of different products.

50. D: One result of NAFTA, the North American Free Trade Agreement, has been that Mexico has sought to enter into other trade agreements. After the implementation of NAFTA in 1993, trade barriers among Canada, the United States, and Mexico were removed. The goal was to encourage economic activity within all three countries. There continues to be a lot of controversy over NAFTA's success, and it was eventually replaced with USMCA, United States-Mexico-Canada Agreement.

51. C: The death rate of Henrytown is 8. Death rate is calculated as the number of deaths every year for every thousand people. Of course, the population of Henrytown is only 500, so it requires a quick calculation to obtain the death rate. This can be accomplished with the following equation:

$$\frac{4}{x} = \frac{500}{1000}$$

This equation basically means "4 is to 500 as x is to 1000." The equation is solved by first cross multiplying, which yields $4{,}000 = 500x$. Then, both sides are divided by 500 to isolate the variable. This indicates that x is equal to 8.

52. A: Of the four answer choices, New York City is the most likely to be considered a modern cultural hearth. A cultural hearth is an area from which cultural trends emanate. Geographers suggest that there were seven original cultural hearths, including Mesoamerica and the Indus River Valley. The modes of living that originated in these areas emanated out into the rest of the world. These days, the cultural hearths tend to be the cities and countries with the most economic power. Of the four answer choices, New York City is clearly the wealthiest and the most influential. The styles and trends that originate in New York City find their way into communities all around the world.

53. A: According to Mark Jefferson's definition of a primate city, London would be considered the primate city of England. In 1939, Jefferson published an influential article, "The Law of the Primate City," in which he defined the primate city as that which most completely represents the culture of the nation it lies within and also houses a disproportionately large percentage of the population. So, for instance, Paris would be the primate city of France, and Beijing would most likely be the primate city of China. In some cases, it can be difficult to name the primate city; for example, in the case of the United States, it might be hard to choose between Washington, DC and New York City. Many of the candidates for primate city status in Africa and South America are somewhat diminished by the heavy influence of foreign powers.

54. D: The popularity of hockey in Canada and the northern United States is an example of direct diffusion. Direct diffusion is the transfer of cultural practices and ideas between two groups living in close proximity to each other. Expansion diffusion, also known as forced diffusion, is the transfer of cultural practices from a subjugating culture to a subjugated culture. One example of expansion diffusion was the Western imposition of trading practices on China during the nineteenth and early twentieth centuries. Indirect diffusion is the spread of cultural traits over a long distance without there necessarily being any direct contact between the cultures. The popularity in the United States of henna tattoos, which originated in India, is an example of indirect diffusion.

55. B: Elections are not necessary to be recognized as a nation. Indeed, many nations are ruled by individuals or cabals who never allow elections to be held. Geographers assert that there are four criteria for nationhood: defined territory, government, sovereignty, and population. A nation must have land and other natural resources to exist. A nation also must have some form of government, whether it be tyrannical or democratic. Some level of central administration indicates the unity of the nation. A nation must have sovereignty; that is, it must not be directly controlled by some other country. Finally, and perhaps most obviously, a nation must have a population.

56. C: Animistic religions include the belief that the natural world is imbued with spirits. Animists believe, for example, that trees, rocks, and animals are divine in some way. This sort of belief system is typical of Native Americans and the indigenous peoples of West Africa (for instance, the Asante). Many sociologists have noted that animist cultures often demonstrate greater reverence for the natural world. Monotheism is a belief that there is only one God. Christianity, Judaism, and Islam are all monotheistic religions. Pantheism is the belief that everything is a manifestation of the Divine Spirit. Polytheism is a belief in multiple gods. Hinduism is the most popular polytheistic religion.

57. B: A sphere of influence is a region in which a foreign power has some political and economic control but does not directly govern. One classic example is the sphere of influence held by European nations in China in the nineteenth and early twentieth centuries. These regions were ostensibly still part of China but had their politics and trade manipulated by the governments of foreign nations. Spheres of influence are less formal than colonies or settlements, which are directly under the control of the foreign government. An enclave, meanwhile, is a country that is entirely surrounded by some other country.

58. A: Hamilton has the greater population density. Population density is a measure of the number of people living in a particular area. It is usually calculated in units of citizens per square mile or square kilometer. The respective population densities of these two towns, then, can be calculated by dividing the number of citizens by the number of area units. So, the population density of Hamilton is 400 / 12 = 33 citizens per square mile, and the population of Burrsville is 300 / 10 = 30 citizens per square mile.

59. D: When a person grows only enough food to feed himself and his family, he is engaged in subsistence farming. The peasants of undeveloped countries are often forced to rely on subsistence farming because they lack the equipment and water resources to expand their crop. Of course, subsistence farming is not an ideal arrangement because a drought or monsoon can wipe out an entire crop and endanger the lives of the farmers. Nomadic herding is constant migration accompanied by livestock, particularly cows or sheep. Commercial farming is large scale enough to allow some or all the crops to be sold in a market. Sharecropping is a system wherein a landowner allows tenant farmers to use his or her land in exchange for a portion of the harvest.

60. A: One example of the multiplier effect of large cities would be if the presence of specialized equipment for an industry attracted even more business. Large cities tend to grow even larger for a number of reasons: they have more skilled workers, they have greater concentrations of specialized equipment, and they have already-functioning markets. These factors all make it easier for a business to begin operations in a large city than elsewhere. Thus, the populations and economic productivity of large cities tend to grow quickly. Some governments have sought to mitigate this trend by clustering groups of similar industries in smaller cities.

61. B: In the early expanding stage of demographic transition, the fertility rate remains high, while the mortality rate declines sharply. Demographic transition is a model for how the population growth rate of a region changes over time. It consists of four stages. In the first, the high stationary stage, fertility and mortality rates are high, so the population rate varies, and there is little growth. In the second stage, some of the problems causing mortality have been solved, but fertility continues at the same rate. This means that the population begins to expand at a greater rate. In the third stage, the late expanding stage, the fertility rate begins to decline, but because the mortality rate remains low, there is continuing growth. In the low stationary stage, there are low rates of fertility and mortality, and consequently there is a low rate of growth.

62. D: In the saturation stage of spatial diffusion, the process slows down and eventually stops altogether. The Swedish geographer Torsten Hägerstrand outlined four stages in spatial diffusion, which is the spread of innovation throughout a geographical region. In the primary stage, the innovation first appears and is adopted in the immediate vicinity. In the diffusion stage, the innovation is used in increasingly far-flung areas. In the condensing stage, any areas that had not already received the innovation do so. In the saturation stage, the innovation is either replaced or abandoned because it is no longer believed to have utility.

63. C: In the United States, geographers typically define a hamlet as a settlement with fewer than 100 inhabitants. A hamlet may have a few businesses, but it is unlikely to have a post office or a government office. A village is slightly larger than a hamlet; it may contain about 500 to 1,000 people. A village is likely to have a grocery store. A town is larger than a village. It usually has about 2,500 inhabitants. A city is larger than a town.

64. A: Traders from distant regions of the world adopt a lingua franca, or a shared vocabulary of terms. The lingua franca used by ancient merchants often included words from many different languages. These days, English often serves as the lingua franca for global businessmen. There is no conscious organization of a lingua franca; it, like other languages, emerges in response to the communication needs of the people who use it. Pidgin languages are contact languages used between two groups, such as traders, who do not share a common language. These languages typically have smaller vocabularies and less sophisticated grammar than standard languages. A conurbation is a combination of two urban areas. Finally, in geography, an activity space is the physical place in which a person performs his or her daily tasks.

65. B: Grinding wheat into flour is an example of secondary economic activity. A secondary economic activity is one in which raw materials are converted into a more valuable product. Another secondary economic activity would be weaving cotton into yarn. A primary economic activity is a direct use of natural resources. Hunting is one example of a primary economic activity. Service jobs are considered to be tertiary economic activities. These jobs do not necessarily entail the acquisition and use of raw materials. Lawyers and bus drivers are just two examples of tertiary economic actors. Quaternary economic activities entail the acquisition, synthesis, and production of information. Teachers and writers are among those who make up the quaternary level of economic activity.

66. D: Population is not one of the necessary characteristics of a geographical region. A geographical region does not require people. Indeed, such regions as the Hindu Kush or Death Valley have few if any inhabitants. A region does need to have area and location, however. It must be capable of being mapped, and it must be able to be found by travelers. A region also needs homogeneity, which means that it needs some sort of consistent features. It makes sense for a region to include a group of nearby mountains, but it does not make sense for it to include a mountain and an island hundreds of miles away. In human geography, it is necessary for the inhabitants of a region to share some cultural characteristics, such as religion or language.

67. A: Stephen's routine is considered by geographers to be cyclic movement. This type of movement happens regularly, does not involve traveling over a great distance, and does not require a change of residence. Because Stephen returns home every evening, he cannot be said to be changing residence. A migratory movement is a permanent change of residence, especially from one country or region to another. A cross-boundary movement is any change in location that involves crossing a national border. A periodic movement is similar to a cyclic movement, except it takes place over a longer time. Going to college for a semester is an example of periodic movement.

68. B: Diversity is not one of the demographic variables. Demographers, or those who study population, rely on fertility, mortality, and migration to determine the number of people in a region. The general equation is *Total Population = Original Population + Births – Deaths + Immigration – Emigration*. The natural increase, on the other hand, is calculated only with the number of births and deaths. The diversity of a population may be relevant to subsequent research performed by the demographer, but it is not considered one of the essential three demographic variables.

69. C: The popularity of Japanese anime comics in the United States is an example of indirect diffusion. Indirect cultural diffusion is the spread of ideas or practices from one culture to a distant culture. Indeed, the primary difference between direct and indirect diffusion is distance, or adjacency. Because the United States and Japan are not close to each other, trends that begin in Japan and take root in the United States are examples of indirect diffusion. The Internet has made indirect diffusion a much more common phenomenon.

70. D: A kibbutz is a collective farm in Israel in which the economy closely resembles that of a communist society. Those who live on a kibbutz do not own private property; rather, they share living space with one another. Children are raised by the entire community. Although the kibbutz has become slightly less popular in recent years, there are still many of these arrangements in Israel. A colony is any settlement controlled by the government in another country. A colony could be administered like a communist society, but it need not be so. A ghetto is an impoverished urban district primarily populated by people of a certain race, religion, or ethnicity. A shtetl is a Jewish community, especially one in eastern Europe, that existed over the past few centuries.

71. B: St. Petersburg is crucial to the Russian economy because of its location along the Baltic Sea. Access to the Baltic has been a driving force throughout Russian history. Peter the Great finally conquered lands adjacent to the Baltic in the early eighteenth century, and he built there the magnificent city that bears his name. After the Russian Revolution and the creation of the USSR, St. Petersburg became known as Leningrad. The name reverted to St. Petersburg after the fall of the Soviet Union. The city remains an essential outlet to the rest of the world.

72. C: Yemen is not a member of OPEC, the Organization of Petroleum Exporting Countries. Yemen has some deposits of oil, but the nation has only recently begun developing them. This, along with a desperate water shortage, accounts for Yemen's position as the poorest nation in the Middle East. OPEC was established in 1960 to set oil prices and production. Until the formation of OPEC, many oil-producing nations felt they were being exploited by Western oil companies. This organization has obtained a great deal of power and is held responsible for the gas shortages that wracked the United States during the late 1970s.

73. A: Land redistribution was one consequence of the Mexican Revolution of 1910. Up to that point, all the arable land in the country was controlled by a select group of aristocrats. There were approximately 8,000 haciendas, which could only be farmed by certain people. After the Mexican Revolution ended in 1920, the newly formed government moved to purchase these haciendas and provide access to peasant farmers. Much of this land is distributed in what are called *ejidos*, or collective farms owned and operated by several people. Nevertheless, to date, the Mexican government has only succeeded in redistributing about half of the original haciendas. As for the other answer choices, Mexico had already become a sovereign nation in 1821 after a long struggle with Spain. The Mexican Revolution did not usher in a period of multi-party rule; in fact, it was not until the election of Vicente Fox in 2000 that the country had a president who was not a member of the Institutional Revolutionary Party. Finally, the massive construction of railroads in Mexico had already taken place during the late 19th century, mainly to provide foreign economic interests with access to Mexico's natural resources.

74. D: The Sahel, a belt of grasslands just south of the Sahara Desert, has long been a focus of agricultural efforts in Africa. This semiarid region has provided sustenance to people and animals for thousands of years. In the last thousand years, stores of salt and gold were found there, giving rise to empires in Ghana and Mali. Changes in climate have expanded the Sahara, however, and pushed the Sahel farther south. The Qattara Depression is a low-lying desert in Egypt. The Great Rift Valley is a region of faults and rocky hills that extends along the southeastern coast of Africa. The Congo Basin is a repository of sediment from the Ubangi and Congo rivers. It is in the northern half of what is now called the Democratic Republic of the Congo.

75. D: The two regions of the Czech Republic are Bohemia and Moravia. Bohemia is the western half of the country, including Prague. Moravia is the eastern half of the Czech Republic. Czechoslovakia became two separate nations, the Czech Republic and Slovakia, in 1993. This separation was spurred by Slovak resentment of the domination of the government by the Czech majority.

76. A: In the early spring, a desert wind known as the khamsin stirs up sandstorms throughout Egypt. These storms can be so strong that they effectively blot out the sky. The possibility of these storms makes it extremely difficult for any serious agriculture or animal husbandry to be performed. They are another reason why 99 percent of the Egyptian population lives in the Nile Valley. A sirocco is any hot and dry wind originating in North Africa but felt in the southern Mediterranean nations of Europe. A zephyr is a gentle western wind. The fellaheen are the peasant farmers of Egypt.

77. B: The highest habitable region in Middle and South America is known as the *puna*, or *páramos*. This region ranges in altitude between 12,000 and 15,000 feet and lies primarily in the Andes Mountains. Only sheep and other rugged livestock can be herded at this height, so there is very little economic activity. *Tierra fria* lies just below the *puna*, between 6,000 and 12,000 feet in elevation. It is possible to cultivate wheat at this height. The *tierra helada* is an uninhabitable region over 15,000 feet high, just above the *puna*. This region is always covered in snow and ice. The *templada*, also known as the *tierra templada*, is a moderate region between 2,500 and 6,000 feet high. Coffee, corn, and tobacco can all be grown in this region.

78. C: Shortly after holding its first free election in 1980, the country formerly known as Rhodesia officially became Zimbabwe. Rhodesia was the name given to this land by the British colonizers. Rhodesia had declared independence from Britain in 1965, but the country continued to be controlled by a white minority. After considerable pressure from the United States and Britain, Rhodesia finally democratized and elected a black president, Robert Mugabe. Unfortunately, under Mugabe, the country now known as Zimbabwe has slid into dictatorship and endured an almost total economic collapse.

79. D: Both Marseilles and Genoa are important ports on the Mediterranean. Marseilles is on the southern coast of France. It is known for its lively mix of French and North African cultures. Marseilles is the second busiest port in western Europe. Genoa, meanwhile, is a thriving port on the western coast of Italy. The shipping traffic in Genoa has increased in the past few decades, as the surrounding region, known as the Po Valley, has become a center of manufacturing.

80. D: In the Indian tradition known as purdah, women cover their faces in public. This veiling originally was limited to the Muslim community but subsequently spread to the Hindus as well. The other answer choices are terms related to this topic. A burqa is a whole-body covering worn by Muslim women. Only the eyes and hands are visible when a woman is wearing a burqa. A hijab is a head covering worn by Muslim women. There are many styles of hijab, though many are simple scarves. A sari is a traditional Indian garment composed of a long piece of cloth, which is wrapped around the body and draped over the shoulder.

81. D: The religious practice of most Japanese people incorporates elements of Shinto, Buddhism, and Confucianism. Shinto is the oldest religion in Japan; it focuses on the divinity of the natural world and the importance of honoring ancestors. Shinto has been influenced heavily by Buddhism and Confucianism, both of which were imported from China. The Zen school of Buddhism originated in China and later became highly influential in Japan. It emphasizes meditation and realization of life's impermanence. Japanese religion and culture are affected by Confucianism, which asserts the importance of hierarchical relationships between people and the natural world.

82. A: Aksum became an imperial power in Africa 2,000 years ago in large part because of its access to major waterways. Specifically, the lands held by Aksum, in what is now Ethiopia, bordered the Red Sea to the east and the Blue Nile to the west. This enabled Aksum to trade with Arabs, Persians, other Africans, and even Europeans. The growing economic power of Aksum was mirrored by military and political success. One major hindrance, however, was religion: Aksum became a Christian nation in the fourth century, and in the centuries that followed, influential Arabs preferred to deal with fellow Muslims.

83. D: The Uighurs (pronounced WEE-gurs) are a minority group of Muslims in northwestern China. This group is discriminated against by the Chinese government; they are not allowed to practice their religion freely, and they are paid lower wages than the majority Han Chinese. Some Uighurs have declared a desire for independence, but this is unlikely to happen. Xinjiang Province, where most of the Uighurs live, is rich in natural resources, so the Chinese government will not let it go without a fight. The Tibetans are Buddhists from a region in what is now southwestern China. China's conquest of Tibet was frowned upon by most of the rest of the world. Mandarin is the official dialect of Chinese. It comes from the northern part of the country. The Falun Gong is a religion that combines Daoism, Buddhism, and other spiritual disciplines. It has been outlawed by the Chinese government.

84. B: Buddhists do not consider Jerusalem a holy city. Christians, Muslims, and Jews all do, though for different reasons. Christians honor Jerusalem as the city near which Jesus was crucified. For Muslims, it is the city from which Mohammed ascended into heaven. For Jews, Jerusalem is the former site of the Temple, which was originally built by King Solomon around 960 B.C. The struggle for control of Jerusalem has been going on for thousands of years. Currently, the city is divided between Israel and the Palestinian territory on the West Bank of the Jordan River.

85. A: Moldova is not one of the Baltic states. Latvia, Lithuania, and Estonia all border the Baltic Sea, which has enabled them to become major traders. Unfortunately, the smallness and advantageous locations of these nations has made them attractive to invaders. The Soviet Union took over these lands in 1939, and it was not until 1991 that they regained independence. All three of these nations are now struggling to establish themselves as viable economic actors.

86. A: Most Pakistanis live in farming villages. Indeed, the total population of the 68 largest cities in Pakistan is only about one quarter of the nation's citizenry. Karachi is the most populous city in Pakistan; it has approximately 12 million citizens. The Baluchistan Plateau encompasses most of southern Pakistan, but it is tough terrain and mainly unsuitable for farming. The Khyber Pass is one of the world's most famous mountain passes. It winds through the Hindu Kush mountains, connecting Peshawar in Pakistan with Kabul in Afghanistan. The winter climate of the Khyber Pass is much too forbidding to allow many permanent residents.

87. B: The Mongols are known as nomadic herders, meaning that they do not build permanent villages but move about the land with animals, usually sheep and goats. Mongolia is an enormous, dry country that is dominated by the Gobi Desert in the south and grasslands in the north. Mongols traditionally lived in portable tents, known as yurts. In recent decades, however, more Mongols have begun to migrate to the large cities of China and to the capital of Mongolia, Ulan Bator.

88. D: Alaska is the largest state in terms of area. It is about 660,000 square miles, while the second-largest state, Texas, is about 270,000 square miles. Despite its immensity, however, Alaska is sparsely populated, with fewer than 630,000 permanent residents. Much of the state is covered in ice year round, and there are several months during the winter in which the sun barely rises at all. Nevertheless, Alaska is an incredible source of natural resources for the continental United States. In particular, Alaska supplies large amounts of oil, timber, and fish to the rest of the nation. There is a continuous conflict between environmentalists and those who want to harvest the state's natural resources more aggressively.

89. D: One of the unique features of the Yucatan Peninsula in Mexico is its collection of sinkholes created by the collapse of limestone caverns beneath the surface. Unlike most of the rest of Mexico, which has firm bedrock, the Yucatan is supported by porous limestone. When this limestone becomes too weak, it creates deep sinkholes that can be used as wells. The other answer choices are all false statements about the Yucatan Peninsula. This region of Mexico is relatively unpopulated; the largest city, Merida, has only about 500,000 citizens. The Yucatan is much flatter than the rest of Mexico; indeed, it is this absence of prehistoric volcano sites that accounts for the difference in soil. Finally, the Yucatan was once inhabited by Mayans, not Aztecs. Some scholars believe that the modern name of the peninsula is derived from the Mayan words for "I do not understand your words," which was merely the unrelated reply to questions from Spanish explorers.

90. B: The United States and Canada share the longest undefended border in the world. It is more than 5,000 miles long, stretching from the Atlantic to the Pacific. The fact that there is no fence or military guard on this border is evidence of the strong, friendly bond between these two nations. Indeed, Canada and the United States are also major trading partners. The United States buys about 85 percent of all Canadian exports, and Canada buys about a quarter of everything sold abroad by the United States. There has never been a significant problem with illegal migration between the United States and Canada, though there has been considerable smuggling.

91. D: Under Gorbachev, the Union of Soviet Socialist Republics (USSR) began a program of economic reorganization known as perestroika. This program included a shift in power from central bureaucrats to local governments. Glasnost was the general policy of openness and transparency adopted by the Soviet government under Gorbachev. Formerly, government actions had been shrouded in secrecy and were often marked by corruption. Rubles are the unit of currency in Russia, as they were in the USSR. Soviets were the legislative assemblies that represented communities, regions, and the nation during the existence of the USSR.

92. C: The pampas in Argentina and Uruguay are temperate grasslands. These enormous stretches of interior space feature rolling hills, mild temperatures, and fertile soil. For many years, cattle farming was the dominant economic focus on the pampas. The cowboys who worked this land were known as gauchos. In recent decades, however, the pampas have increasingly been used for the cultivation of wheat. Although the winters in this region can be cold, the pampas manage to supply more than 80 percent of the grain used in Argentina.

93. A: The South Asian nation of Sri Lanka, formerly known as Ceylon, has been the site of almost constant fighting between Sinhalese and Tamils. Sri Lanka is an island nation off the southeast coast of India. The Sinhalese arrived from northern India in about 500 BC, and soon after, the Tamils arrived from southern India. Ever since, they have been in competition for control of the island. For the most part, the Sinhalese have remained in control of the government. However, the Tamils maintained a guerilla campaign against the government for decades. In late 2009, the Sri Lankan military finally succeeded in quashing this insurgency.

94. B: Dutch is not one of the four official languages in Switzerland, a nation unique in Europe for having several distinct cultures within its borders. The official name of the country is the Swiss Confederation. The majority of Swiss speak German, and cities like Zurich and Bern are predominately German in architecture and culture. Geneva, on the other hand, is a largely French-speaking city. There is a local Swiss dialect, known as Romansch, which is spoken by many people. Some areas, such as Ticino, have considerable Italian-speaking populations.

95. D: Kemal Ataturk was responsible for the rapid westernization of Turkey in the early twentieth century. He had spent considerable time in western Europe, and in 1923, soon after becoming president, he threw out the Islamic government structures and declared Turkey a republic. He went on to replace the Arabic alphabet and calendar with the Western versions. He also added to the rights of women, giving them the power to divorce their husbands, vote, and seek office. Even today, Turkey remains the Muslim nation with the closest similarities to the nations of western Europe.

96. A: The Atlantic provinces of Canada are Labrador, Prince Edward Island, New Brunswick, and Nova Scotia. All of these provinces have a coastline on the Atlantic Ocean. Although these four provinces represent only about 5 percent of Canada's total landmass, they have played a major role in the development of the nation. In particular, the fishing industry off the coasts of Nova Scotia and Newfoundland has long been a solid component of the Canadian economy. There is also a great deal of agriculture in Nova Scotia and Prince Edward Island.

97. C: Before China took control of Hong Kong in 1997, the island was administrated by Great Britain. This transfer of power had been planned for a long time. One of the conditions for the transfer was that Hong Kong will retain political and economic independence from China. Hong Kong is referred to as a Special Administrative Region of China, and its citizens are given much more leeway than other Chinese citizens. To date, China has been successful in harnessing the economic power of Hong Kong and allowing two systems of governance to coexist within one nation.

98. B: A *favela* is a shantytown in Brazil. These communities begin when a parcel of vacant or abandoned land is taken over by squatters. Over time, small villages crop up, featuring rudimentary architecture and local government. In many cases, *favelas* are outside of the control of the Brazilian government and are instead managed by criminal syndicates and gangs. The problem of the *favela* is one of the greatest facing modern Brazil as it attempts to join the top tier of nations. A *barrio* may be just a neighborhood, but it typically refers to a low-income district in Central or South America. A *maquiladora* is an industrial district in northern Mexico. These areas manufacture goods for sale mostly in the United States. Finally, *ciudad* is the Spanish word for *city*.

99. A: The Dutch lands reclaimed through a network of dikes and canals are known as polders. This process has been ongoing since the 1200s when the Dutch first began using windmills to dry the land. About a third of Holland is below sea level, so it has taken a great deal of engineering ingenuity to keep the land inhabitable. The entire country is dotted with dikes, or thick earthen embankments that keep back the encroaching waters. Cantons are the states in Switzerland and Austria. Grabens are the narrow, sunken strips of land that lie between faults. There are a number of grabens in Greece. Moors are treeless, boggy patches of land.

100. A: Despite its size, China has only 11 percent of usable land for farming, or just a little over 1 million square kilometers. For this reason, China consistently remains one of the largest importers of food in the world.

How to Overcome Test Anxiety

Just the thought of taking a test is enough to make most people a little nervous. A test is an important event that can have a long-term impact on your future, so it's important to take it seriously and it's natural to feel anxious about performing well. But just because anxiety is normal, that doesn't mean that it's helpful in test taking, or that you should simply accept it as part of your life. Anxiety can have a variety of effects. These effects can be mild, like making you feel slightly nervous, or severe, like blocking your ability to focus or remember even a simple detail.

If you experience test anxiety—whether severe or mild—it's important to know how to beat it. To discover this, first you need to understand what causes test anxiety.

Causes of Test Anxiety

While we often think of anxiety as an uncontrollable emotional state, it can actually be caused by simple, practical things. One of the most common causes of test anxiety is that a person does not feel adequately prepared for their test. This feeling can be the result of many different issues such as poor study habits or lack of organization, but the most common culprit is time management. Starting to study too late, failing to organize your study time to cover all of the material, or being distracted while you study will mean that you're not well prepared for the test. This may lead to cramming the night before, which will cause you to be physically and mentally exhausted for the test. Poor time management also contributes to feelings of stress, fear, and hopelessness as you realize you are not well prepared but don't know what to do about it.

Other times, test anxiety is not related to your preparation for the test but comes from unresolved fear. This may be a past failure on a test, or poor performance on tests in general. It may come from comparing yourself to others who seem to be performing better or from the stress of living up to expectations. Anxiety may be driven by fears of the future—how failure on this test would affect your educational and career goals. These fears are often completely irrational, but they can still negatively impact your test performance.

Elements of Test Anxiety

As mentioned earlier, test anxiety is considered to be an emotional state, but it has physical and mental components as well. Sometimes you may not even realize that you are suffering from test anxiety until you notice the physical symptoms. These can include trembling hands, rapid heartbeat, sweating, nausea, and tense muscles. Extreme anxiety may lead to fainting or vomiting. Obviously, any of these symptoms can have a negative impact on testing. It is important to recognize them as soon as they begin to occur so that you can address the problem before it damages your performance.

The mental components of test anxiety include trouble focusing and inability to remember learned information. During a test, your mind is on high alert, which can help you recall information and stay focused for an extended period of time. However, anxiety interferes with your mind's natural processes, causing you to blank out, even on the questions you know well. The strain of testing during anxiety makes it difficult to stay focused, especially on a test that may take several hours. Extreme anxiety can take a huge mental toll, making it difficult not only to recall test information but even to understand the test questions or pull your thoughts together.

Effects of Test Anxiety

Test anxiety is like a disease—if left untreated, it will get progressively worse. Anxiety leads to poor performance, and this reinforces the feelings of fear and failure, which in turn lead to poor performances on subsequent tests. It can grow from a mild nervousness to a crippling condition. If allowed to progress, test anxiety can have a big impact on your schooling, and consequently on your future.

Test anxiety can spread to other parts of your life. Anxiety on tests can become anxiety in any stressful situation, and blanking on a test can turn into panicking in a job situation. But fortunately, you don't have to let anxiety rule your testing and determine your grades. There are a number of relatively simple steps you can take to move past anxiety and function normally on a test and in the rest of life.

Physical Steps for Beating Test Anxiety

While test anxiety is a serious problem, the good news is that it can be overcome. It doesn't have to control your ability to think and remember information. While it may take time, you can begin taking steps today to beat anxiety.

Just as your first hint that you may be struggling with anxiety comes from the physical symptoms, the first step to treating it is also physical. Rest is crucial for having a clear, strong mind. If you are tired, it is much easier to give in to anxiety. But if you establish good sleep habits, your body and mind will be ready to perform optimally, without the strain of exhaustion. Additionally, sleeping well helps you to retain information better, so you're more likely to recall the answers when you see the test questions.

Getting good sleep means more than going to bed on time. It's important to allow your brain time to relax. Take study breaks from time to time so it doesn't get overworked, and don't study right before bed. Take time to rest your mind before trying to rest your body, or you may find it difficult to fall asleep.

Along with sleep, other aspects of physical health are important in preparing for a test. Good nutrition is vital for good brain function. Sugary foods and drinks may give a burst of energy but this burst is followed by a crash, both physically and emotionally. Instead, fuel your body with protein and vitamin-rich foods.

Also, drink plenty of water. Dehydration can lead to headaches and exhaustion, especially if your brain is already under stress from the rigors of the test. Particularly if your test is a long one, drink water during the breaks. And if possible, take an energy-boosting snack to eat between sections.

Along with sleep and diet, a third important part of physical health is exercise. Maintaining a steady workout schedule is helpful, but even taking 5-minute study breaks to walk can help get your blood pumping faster and clear your head. Exercise also releases endorphins, which contribute to a positive feeling and can help combat test anxiety.

When you nurture your physical health, you are also contributing to your mental health. If your body is healthy, your mind is much more likely to be healthy as well. So take time to rest, nourish your body with healthy food and water, and get moving as much as possible. Taking these physical steps will make you stronger and more able to take the mental steps necessary to overcome test anxiety.

Mental Steps for Beating Test Anxiety

Working on the mental side of test anxiety can be more challenging, but as with the physical side, there are clear steps you can take to overcome it. As mentioned earlier, test anxiety often stems from lack of preparation, so the obvious solution is to prepare for the test. Effective studying may be the most important weapon you have for beating test anxiety, but you can and should employ several other mental tools to combat fear.

First, boost your confidence by reminding yourself of past success—tests or projects that you aced. If you're putting as much effort into preparing for this test as you did for those, there's no reason you should expect to fail here. Work hard to prepare; then trust your preparation.

Second, surround yourself with encouraging people. It can be helpful to find a study group, but be sure that the people you're around will encourage a positive attitude. If you spend time with others who are anxious or cynical, this will only contribute to your own anxiety. Look for others who are motivated to study hard from a desire to succeed, not from a fear of failure.

Third, reward yourself. A test is physically and mentally tiring, even without anxiety, and it can be helpful to have something to look forward to. Plan an activity following the test, regardless of the outcome, such as going to a movie or getting ice cream.

When you are taking the test, if you find yourself beginning to feel anxious, remind yourself that you know the material. Visualize successfully completing the test. Then take a few deep, relaxing breaths and return to it. Work through the questions carefully but with confidence, knowing that you are capable of succeeding.

Developing a healthy mental approach to test taking will also aid in other areas of life. Test anxiety affects more than just the actual test—it can be damaging to your mental health and even contribute to depression. It's important to beat test anxiety before it becomes a problem for more than testing.

Study Strategy

Being prepared for the test is necessary to combat anxiety, but what does being prepared look like? You may study for hours on end and still not feel prepared. What you need is a strategy for test prep. The next few pages outline our recommended steps to help you plan out and conquer the challenge of preparation.

Step 1: Scope Out the Test

Learn everything you can about the format (multiple choice, essay, etc.) and what will be on the test. Gather any study materials, course outlines, or sample exams that may be available. Not only will this help you to prepare, but knowing what to expect can help to alleviate test anxiety.

Step 2: Map Out the Material

Look through the textbook or study guide and make note of how many chapters or sections it has. Then divide these over the time you have. For example, if a book has 15 chapters and you have five days to study, you need to cover three chapters each day. Even better, if you have the time, leave an extra day at the end for overall review after you have gone through the material in depth.

If time is limited, you may need to prioritize the material. Look through it and make note of which sections you think you already have a good grasp on, and which need review. While you are studying, skim quickly through the familiar sections and take more time on the challenging parts.

Write out your plan so you don't get lost as you go. Having a written plan also helps you feel more in control of the study, so anxiety is less likely to arise from feeling overwhelmed at the amount to cover.

Step 3: Gather Your Tools

Decide what study method works best for you. Do you prefer to highlight in the book as you study and then go back over the highlighted portions? Or do you type out notes of the important information? Or is it helpful to make flashcards that you can carry with you? Assemble the pens, index cards, highlighters, post-it notes, and any other materials you may need so you won't be distracted by getting up to find things while you study.

If you're having a hard time retaining the information or organizing your notes, experiment with different methods. For example, try color-coding by subject with colored pens, highlighters, or post-it notes. If you learn better by hearing, try recording yourself reading your notes so you can listen while in the car, working out, or simply sitting at your desk. Ask a friend to quiz you from your flashcards, or try teaching someone the material to solidify it in your mind.

Step 4: Create Your Environment

It's important to avoid distractions while you study. This includes both the obvious distractions like visitors and the subtle distractions like an uncomfortable chair (or a too-comfortable couch that makes you want to fall asleep). Set up the best study environment possible: good lighting and a comfortable work area. If background music helps you focus, you may want to turn it on, but otherwise keep the room quiet. If you are using a computer to take notes, be sure you don't have any other windows open, especially applications like social media, games, or anything else that could distract you. Silence your phone and turn off notifications. Be sure to keep water close by so you stay hydrated while you study (but avoid unhealthy drinks and snacks).

Also, take into account the best time of day to study. Are you freshest first thing in the morning? Try to set aside some time then to work through the material. Is your mind clearer in the afternoon or evening? Schedule your study session then. Another method is to study at the same time of day that you will take the test, so that your brain gets used to working on the material at that time and will be ready to focus at test time.

Step 5: Study!

Once you have done all the study preparation, it's time to settle into the actual studying. Sit down, take a few moments to settle your mind so you can focus, and begin to follow your study plan. Don't give in to distractions or let yourself procrastinate. This is your time to prepare so you'll be ready to fearlessly approach the test. Make the most of the time and stay focused.

Of course, you don't want to burn out. If you study too long you may find that you're not retaining the information very well. Take regular study breaks. For example, taking five minutes out of every hour to walk briskly, breathing deeply and swinging your arms, can help your mind stay fresh.

As you get to the end of each chapter or section, it's a good idea to do a quick review. Remind yourself of what you learned and work on any difficult parts. When you feel that you've mastered the material, move on to the next part. At the end of your study session, briefly skim through your notes again.

But while review is helpful, cramming last minute is NOT. If at all possible, work ahead so that you won't need to fit all your study into the last day. Cramming overloads your brain with more information than it can process and retain, and your tired mind may struggle to recall even previously learned information when it is overwhelmed with last-minute study. Also, the urgent nature of cramming and the stress placed on your brain contribute to anxiety. You'll be more likely to go to the test feeling unprepared and having trouble thinking clearly.

So don't cram, and don't stay up late before the test, even just to review your notes at a leisurely pace. Your brain needs rest more than it needs to go over the information again. In fact, plan to finish your studies by noon or early afternoon the day before the test. Give your brain the rest of the day to relax or focus on other things, and get a good night's sleep. Then you will be fresh for the test and better able to recall what you've studied.

Step 6: Take a Practice Test

Many courses offer sample tests, either online or in the study materials. This is an excellent resource to check whether you have mastered the material, as well as to prepare for the test format and environment.

Check the test format ahead of time: the number of questions, the type (multiple choice, free response, etc.), and the time limit. Then create a plan for working through them. For example, if you have 30 minutes to take a 60-question test, your limit is 30 seconds per question. Spend less time on the questions you know well so that you can take more time on the difficult ones.

If you have time to take several practice tests, take the first one open book, with no time limit. Work through the questions at your own pace and make sure you fully understand them. Gradually work up to taking a test under test conditions: sit at a desk with all study materials put away and set a timer. Pace yourself to make sure you finish the test with time to spare and go back to check your answers if you have time.

After each test, check your answers. On the questions you missed, be sure you understand why you missed them. Did you misread the question (tests can use tricky wording)? Did you forget the information? Or was it something you hadn't learned? Go back and study any shaky areas that the practice tests reveal.

Taking these tests not only helps with your grade, but also aids in combating test anxiety. If you're already used to the test conditions, you're less likely to worry about it, and working through tests until you're scoring well gives you a confidence boost. Go through the practice tests until you feel comfortable, and then you can go into the test knowing that you're ready for it.

Test Tips

On test day, you should be confident, knowing that you've prepared well and are ready to answer the questions. But aside from preparation, there are several test day strategies you can employ to maximize your performance.

First, as stated before, get a good night's sleep the night before the test (and for several nights before that, if possible). Go into the test with a fresh, alert mind rather than staying up late to study.

Try not to change too much about your normal routine on the day of the test. It's important to eat a nutritious breakfast, but if you normally don't eat breakfast at all, consider eating just a protein bar. If you're a coffee drinker, go ahead and have your normal coffee. Just make sure you time it so that the caffeine doesn't wear off right in the middle of your test. Avoid sugary beverages, and drink enough water to stay hydrated but not so much that you need a restroom break 10 minutes into the test. If your test isn't first thing in the morning, consider going for a walk or doing a light workout before the test to get your blood flowing.

Allow yourself enough time to get ready, and leave for the test with plenty of time to spare so you won't have the anxiety of scrambling to arrive in time. Another reason to be early is to select a good seat. It's helpful to sit away from doors and windows, which can be distracting. Find a good seat, get out your supplies, and settle your mind before the test begins.

When the test begins, start by going over the instructions carefully, even if you already know what to expect. Make sure you avoid any careless mistakes by following the directions.

Then begin working through the questions, pacing yourself as you've practiced. If you're not sure on an answer, don't spend too much time on it, and don't let it shake your confidence. Either skip it and come back later, or eliminate as many wrong answers as possible and guess among the remaining ones. Don't dwell on these questions as you continue—put them out of your mind and focus on what lies ahead.

Be sure to read all of the answer choices, even if you're sure the first one is the right answer. Sometimes you'll find a better one if you keep reading. But don't second-guess yourself if you do immediately know the answer. Your gut instinct is usually right. Don't let test anxiety rob you of the information you know.

If you have time at the end of the test (and if the test format allows), go back and review your answers. Be cautious about changing any, since your first instinct tends to be correct, but make sure you didn't misread any of the questions or accidentally mark the wrong answer choice. Look over any you skipped and make an educated guess.

At the end, leave the test feeling confident. You've done your best, so don't waste time worrying about your performance or wishing you could change anything. Instead, celebrate the successful completion of this test. And finally, use this test to learn how to deal with anxiety even better next time.

Review Video: Test Anxiety
Visit mometrix.com/academy and enter code: 100340

Important Qualification

Not all anxiety is created equal. If your test anxiety is causing major issues in your life beyond the classroom or testing center, or if you are experiencing troubling physical symptoms related to your anxiety, it may be a sign of a serious physiological or psychological condition. If this sounds like your situation, we strongly encourage you to seek professional help.

Online Resources

Due to our efforts to try to keep this book to a manageable length, we've created a link that will give you access to all of your online resources:

mometrix.com/resources719/dssthumculgeog

It's Your Moment, Let's Celebrate It!

Share your story @mometrixtestpreparation